I, THE POET

I, THE POET

FIRST-PERSON FORM IN HORACE, CATULLUS, AND PROPERTIUS

KATHLEEN MCCARTHY

CORNELL UNIVERSITY PRESS

Ithaca and London

First published 2019 by Cornell University Press

Library of Congress Cataloging-in-Publication Data

Names: McCarthy, Kathleen, 1962– author.
Title: I, the poet : first-person form in Horace, Catullus, and Propertius / Kathleen McCarthy.
Description: Ithaca [New York] : Cornell University Press, 2019. | Includes bibliographical references and index.
Identifiers: LCCN 2019011316 (print) | LCCN 2019013345 (ebook) | ISBN 9781501739576 (epub/mobi) | ISBN 9781501739569 (pdf) | ISBN 9781501739552 | ISBN 9781501739552 (cloth)
Subjects: LCSH: Latin poetry—History and criticism—Theory, etc. | Horace—Criticism and interpretation. | Catullus, Gaius Valerius—Criticism and interpretation. | Propertius, Sextus—Criticism and interpretation. | First person narrative. | Point of view (Literature) | Self in literature.
Classification: LCC PA6063 (ebook) | LCC PA6063 .M33 2019 (print) | DDC 874/.010923—dc23
LC record available at https://lccn.loc.gov/2019011316

❧ CONTENTS

✿ ACKNOWLEDGMENTS

I have had the great good fortune to be surrounded for the last two decades by an extraordinary community of colleagues, students, staff members, and friends who have given me both the intellectual stimulation and the support necessary to write this book. (It may take a village to raise a child, but it seems to have taken the population of a fair-sized metropolis to get this book across the finish line.) Because this book was so long in the making, I am unable to record all the names that should be included here; I apologize for those omissions.

First and foremost (in every way) are two people who have been the bedrock of my intellectual and professional life for many years: Leslie Kurke and Nelly Oliensis. Even if I had never met them, the published work of these two brilliant scholars would have been immensely influential for my own thinking. But, in addition to that gift, as friends and colleagues they have supported me and urged me on throughout this project. I can truly say that this book would never have been written without them.

I would also like to take this opportunity to thank the people (in addition to Leslie and Nelly) who have read the book at various stages and helped me to see how I could improve it: Sue Schweik, Hertha Sweet Wong, Linda Rugg, Beth Piatote, Joe Farrell, Liz Young, Maurizio Bettini, Jane Raisch, Jocelyn Saidenberg, Morgan King, Tim Hampton, Mario Telò, John Shoptaw. The anonymous readers for the press generously gave me the benefit of their expertise and perspectives. I am very grateful for all the suggestions and advice I received; no one but myself is responsible for any errors that remain.

Beyond those who responded to the manuscript itself is a much wider circle of interlocutors who have shaped my thinking about these authors, about Latin literary culture, and about poetry more broadly, including all my colleagues (both in Classics and in Comparative Literature), the Townsend Fellows Group of 2017–18, and many undergraduate and graduate students over the years. Special thanks to Jim Phelan and the participants of the Summer NEH Institute on narrative theory for stimulating discussion that helped shape my argument in important ways. Morgan King provided important research assistance in the early phases, and Liz Harvey helped me enormously in the preparation of the final manuscript. Special thanks to Alex Press for his eagle eye. Deborah A. Oosterhouse did a wonderful job with the copy editing, and the whole team at Cornell University Press has been a pleasure to work with. I am also grateful for the support of the American Philosophical Society for a research fellowship.

I, THE POET

Introduction
Voices on the Page

Flavi, delicias tuas Catullo,
ni sint illepidae atque inelegantes,
velles dicere nec tacere posses.
verum nescioquid febriculosi
scorti diligis: hoc pudet fateri.

(Catullus 6.1–5)

Flavius, if your sweetheart were not the very opposite of charming and elegant, you would want to speak of her to Catullus and you wouldn't be able to shut up. But you're in love with some kind of feverish whore—you're ashamed to admit it.

These lines aptly demonstrate a gesture familiar to readers of Catullus: even as they mimic the feeling of offhand private conversation, they manage to present the poet's aesthetic program, by introducing the key terms *lepidus* and *elegans*. What is more, they include the poet's own name as a kind of wormhole that links the world represented in the poetry to the historical poet's own life. The mix of everyday and poetic—at the level of language as well as of the events represented—is one of the pleasures we go to Catullus for. As the poem continues, it sharpens these contrasts in a way that calls even more attention to the aesthetically powerful mismatch between ordinary objects and the poetry that describes them. For example, a high point of this poem is the virtuoso description of the squeaking bed that gives away Flavius's nighttime activities: "clamat . . . tremulique quassa lecti/argutatio inambulatioque" (lines 7, 10–11; the tottering bed shouts out, as it squeaks and walks across the floor). And, just in case we were in any doubt as to the ambitions at stake here, at the end of the poem the speaker promises to do what the poem has just done, by turning the inelegant beloved into elegant poetry:

> quare, quidquid habes boni malique,
> dic nobis. volo te ac tuos amores
> ad caelum lepido vocare versu.
>
> (6.15–17)

And so, whatever you have of good or ill, tell us. I want to exalt you and your lover to the skies with charming poetry.

Catullus claims to be able to elevate everyday life and everyday language into enduring art, but he does not dissolve the quotidian realm into the celestial. His poetry is designed to imply that it takes the brute facts of the real world as its raw material. He continually plays on our desire to be let in on the secrets of that everyday life by lacing the poetry with hints that the experiences represented are his own, as he does here by inserting his own name into the poem and, in a move that has broad consequences across the corpus, by representing the speaker as a poet. Although strictly speaking no one would believe this poem to be a transcription of a conversation Catullus actually had with Flavius (neatly translated into hendecasyllabic meter), the poem creates a powerful impression of the world these two characters inhabit and, by playing on the theme of secrets, reminds us of both our access to their world and the limits of that access.

Two effects are achieved here, in a way that tends to blur the distinction between them. On the one hand, the reader receives the impression that this world depicted in the poem preexists the text and stands independent of it; this need not be a naïve belief that this exact scene transpired one day, but just a sense of the three-dimensional solidity of these characters and their world. On the other hand, through a set of mise-en-abyme gestures (the first-person voice, further specified with Catullus's name and vocation), the poem asserts that although the speaker's language arises within the scene depicted, it also constitutes a work of art circulated under the name of Catullus. The combination of these two effects produces language that seems to exist both as speech between characters in the represented world and as a literary work intended to communicate with readers.

This double-sided use of language is completely familiar and causes us little trouble to understand, but I would suggest that this ease is not necessarily a good thing. I believe that we can gain clearer insight into what such poems do and how they do it by paying attention to this duality rather than reading past it. In order to grasp this duality, it will be useful to borrow a key distinction from narrative theory and refer to the dimension of the poem focused on the world of the characters as "story" and the dimension of the poem that consists of the words of the poem as they are received by readers as "discourse."[1] (More precisely, "story" designates no concrete element of the poem, but the impression created in the reader's mind of the world within which the characters live and speak.) By adopting this terminology I am not arguing that these poems actually are narratives but developing a critical vocabulary to acknowledge that in reading poems such as Catullus poem 6, the impression we receive of the characters in their own world influences our reading of the poem as a whole, even when we are focusing on thematic and stylistic features.

This two-track system depends on both the harmony between the two levels and the ways they clash. Catullus's poem yokes together the world of the characters and the world of the reader by means of the first-person speaker, who is positioned as both a character in the storyworld and the author of the text we are reading. The fit between the two roles is close but not exact, and one of the points where they diverge is in their motivations: the character in the storyworld wants to find out the identity of Flavius's lover, while the author of the text wants to use the representation of this scene to communicate with readers. I highlight the speaker/poet as a point of both coincidence and divergence, not only because it shows clearly the relation between the two dimensions, but also because this figure is the linchpin of the whole complex system. By implying that the speaker and the poet both are and are not unified, the poem asserts that social uses of language can be seamlessly unified with poetic expression but also that these two forms of expression are distinct. This slippery relation between the poetic speaker and the poet has been discussed previously by debating the potential autobiographical content of the poems, but I am reframing it here as a central element of

---

I refer throughout (except where noted) to Thomson (1997) for Catullus's text, to Goold (1999) for Propertius's text, to Klingner (2008; reprint of the 3rd edition from 1959) for Horace's text, and to Hall (1995) for Ovid's text. All translations are my own, with exceptions noted.

1. These fundamental terms of narrative theory have been used in various ways by various theorists; see Prince (2003, 21, 93) for multiple definitions with reference to specific theorists. For the purposes of this argument, I am using "story" in Prince's first definition: "The content plane of narrative as opposed to its expression plane or discourse; the 'what' of a narrative as opposed to its 'how'" (93). Because the word "story" has so many uses in English, when I use it in this technical sense, I will enclose it in scare quotes.

poetic infrastructure and one that has major implications for the ways this poetry relates to other, more everyday, forms of language.

In contrast to other conceptions that are formulated in terms of "persona" or "fiction," my argument is not aimed at disentangling the real (i.e., socially active) communication from literary communication, or subordinating one to the other. I am seeking to describe how first-person Latin poems produce their distinctive charisma by intertwining social and literary communication.[2] Central to the effects of such poems is the fact that we can see the poem's discourse as an artistic creation designed to communicate with readers who will have no other contact with the poet. Also central to their effects, however, is the fact that this orientation toward distant or future readers is almost never registered explicitly in the poem, which instead shows us an image of face-to-face communication in an intimate social world that readers can never access.

My approach is founded, in part, on the observation that the Roman poets themselves were in almost the same situation in relation to earlier Greek poetry that we twenty-first-century readers are in relation to their poetry: readers who perceive the poems as both "not-for-us" (written for their own social world and perhaps even for the specific people named) and "for-us" (powerfully expressive as well as aesthetically successful across great distance). One major difference, then, between my readings and those of many other critics is that I do not privilege the poets' immediate historical context as having more defining weight for interpretation. I am not positing that Latin poets would have been working with exactly the conceptions of literary communication that I describe here, but I do think it highly likely that they wrote

---

2. Oliensis (1998, 2–3) highlights what I am calling the intertwining of social and literary communication through the concept of "face"; this concept allows her to pinpoint the ethical stakes of neatly severing the persona from the author and also to stress the fact that poetic communication has consequences. "Horace's poetic 'face' is not identical to Horace, but it will be identified with him. . . . Critics . . . attempt to save Horace's face by attributing behavior they find offensive (for example, the misogynous obscenities of his epodes) to a conventional persona. . . . The author, in this view, is situated far above or behind the characters—including the first-person speaker—of his poetry, whom he views, perhaps, with the same critical eye as the modern critic. This may be a fair description of Horace's relation to certain of his personae. But the theatrical metaphor is misleading insofar as it obscures Horace's interest in the doings of his faces. . . . One premise of this study is that Horace's poems are not detached representations of society but consequential acts within society." The constructed nature of "face" and the complex role it plays in both the reception of the poetry and the social identity of the poet make it a perfect image to capture the way that first-person Latin poetry ambiguously associates and distances its speakers from their authors, as well as the ambiguous claims this poetry makes in regard to the key question of what it means to speak in and through poetry. What I hope to add to Oliensis's powerful formulation are the insights we can gain from analyzing the functioning of "story" and discourse in this body of poetry, since discourse is exactly the dimension of the poem in which the poet—as poet, not as persona or character—acts.

with the knowledge that their poems would encounter readers who would be as different from them as they were different from Alcaeus and Archilochus.[3]

One example of privileging the contemporary context is the reading practice Mario Citroni has developed, based on the claim that poems such as Catullus's polymetrics and Horace's odes are designed to be meaningful above all for their named addressees, secondly to others in the circle around the poet and addressee, and lastly to the general reader. "These poems [Horace's odes] present themselves more or less explicitly as interventions intended to have an impact (as consolation, congratulations, etc.) on the dedicatee" (2009, 76).[4] I agree with Citroni's contention that readers who know the poet and the addressee are likely to interpret poems in light of their understanding of the people and events named, but I do not believe with him that "the importance in these poems of the individual addressee's point of view does not usually conflict with the needs of address to a general reader: the two perspectives blend for the most part perfectly together" (78). This claim of harmonious blending significantly understates the difference between what it would mean for a poem to perform a real intervention in the life of the addressee and what it would mean for a general reader to read the poem assuming that such an intention exists and constructing a scenario in which that intention is meaningful for poetic effects.[5]

That difference is, in effect, the difference between reading without a "story" level (for the dedicatee himself,[6] the poem operates by making statements, asking questions, etc.) and reading with a "story" level (the general reader imagines a situation in which the poet voices these words to a companion and reads the result as a poem intended for circulation).[7] This distinction is clear

---

3. Edmunds (2001, 108–32) offers an analysis of the reading culture in Rome that supports this idea: "It was possible for Roman poets to conceive of their contemporaries reading them in the same way that these poets read earlier literature" (115).

4. I quote here from the English translation of Citroni (1983), published in Lowrie (2009b). This article was reworked and expanded as a chapter in Citroni (1995). Citroni (1995, 275–78) more fully takes account of the written form in which Latin poetry circulated (i.e., he is not assuming that the face-to-face encounter depicted in the poem literally replicates the communicative situation between poet and dedicatee), but he argues that the social institutions of patronage and *amicitia* within which the poems circulated make the communication with the "lettore privilegiato" dominant. For a useful overview and critique of Citroni (1995), see Edmunds (2001, chap. 5).

5. Cf. Quinn (1970, 160), who, in a headnote to Catullus 23, reconciles the (putative) original social impulse with the artistic polish of the poem by assuming two stages: "A poem . . . may be revised for publication, and thus acquire a second lease of life."

6. Citroni explicitly excludes female addressees from his analysis on the grounds that they are likely to be fictional (2009, 73). See below for further analysis of how the term "fictional" has operated in this debate.

7. Note also that Citroni thinks that the reading available to the dedicatee and those within the circle of poet and dedicatee is fuller and more satisfying: "a more complete understanding of the

in Citroni's formulation of how the general reader makes sense of Horace's *Epode* 11, which recounts the speaker's trials in love: the general reader "finds there a convincing piece of erotic lyric, and also feels he has access to psychological and sentimental conflicts and to the private network of friendships within which the book of epodes arose" (2009, 81). If Citroni is right that the dedicatee (Pettius, in the case of *Epode* 11) receives this poem as a communication structured by the friendship he shares with Horace,[8] then surely he is not reading it for "access" to a world from which he is otherwise excluded.

The cognitive action attributed to the general reader here, an act of reconstructing the scene and its participants from clues in the poem, is the act of perceiving "story." Depending on how we understand this cognition to affect the reading of the poem, we will generate different underlying theories of first-person poetry. For example, Gordon Williams titled the fourth chapter of his *Tradition and Originality in Roman Poetry* "Imagination and Interpretation: The Demand on the Reader." He foregrounds the need for readers to participate imaginatively in creating the scene and argues that this is an artistic strategy the poets use to avoid the explicitness of prose; what poets gain from this choice is "the creation of a sense of mystery" (1968, 171). In other words, while other scholars may assume that the information we receive about the scene is patchy because the "real" participants (poet, dedicatee) knew what was going on and did not need to have it spelled out,[9] Williams starts from the opposite assumption: that the external reader is a valued communicative partner for the poet and it is with the goal of creating a satisfying reading experience for that partner that the poet makes his or her artistic choices.

By sidelining the familiar terms of "persona" and "fiction," I am drawing attention to the fact that what distinguishes these two very different reading

---

significance of a Horatian poem depends on knowledge of facts the reader must reconstruct from elements external to the poem" (2009, 89).

8. For the sake of argument here, I am bracketing for the moment the problem of whether such an inference is valid. In the case of *Epode* 11, where the addressee is otherwise unknown (see Mankin 1995, ad 11.1 for speculation), the circularity of Citroni's reasoning is particularly striking. Lowrie (2009a, 99) has noted, in reference to Citroni's argument, "The danger lies in projecting onto Roman social history relations deriving from the poetry and then reprojecting these on the poems as if they had external explanatory value."

9. Or, in a related formulation most closely associated with Francis Cairns, the missing bits are missing because the ancient readers' knowledge of genre and other conventions made them unnecessary. "The reader, who shares Horace's knowledge of the commonplaces of the genre, will be rewarded by the recognition of commonplaces which are, on first reading, absent, and will supply mentally the missing connections of thought" (Cairns 2012, 442, referring to Horace *Odes* 3.13). This emphasis on literary conventions seems diametrically opposed to Citroni's emphasis on real social relations, but what they have in common is the assumption that the poem's "missing" information should be supplied from the reader's shared experience with the poet, and therefore both scholars emphasize a readership that is culturally (and probably chronologically) close to the poet.

practices has nothing to do with whether the events depicted really happened and instead is determined by which goal the interpreter deems to be primary: effective communication with the person addressed in the poem or with an unknown general reader. Each of these goals is characterized not just by a privileged recipient of the poem, but by assumptions about the relation between the poem's communicative burden and the forms of communication we use in ordinary social life. In Citroni's model, the poem is not-for-us and functions for the dedicatee in approximately the same way as ordinary social communication functions;[10] in Williams's model, the poem is for-us and designed to communicate between people whose only contact occurs through the poem itself.[11]

Thus what is at stake in these two interpretations is the difference not between fiction and nonfiction, but between a conception of poetry as like or unlike the communicative exchanges that occur in social life. While almost no one would claim that the stylistic elaboration that establishes a text as "literature" robs the poem of all substantive meaning, we see in this debate different fundamental assumptions about how literary texts can communicate.[12] In Citroni's model, stylistic elaboration presents no barrier to full effective meaning, as long as we conceive of the poem as anchored in a concrete historical context. But once we admit later and culturally alien readers as a genuine audience (not just late-coming gleaners) and once we accept that the text itself will be the meeting place for author and reader, how should we understand that moment of contact?

Latin literature is an unusually rich resource for studying this question, because the Romans (especially in the central period of about 200 BCE to 200 CE) were in the process of discovering how a thorough conversion to literacy changes cultural patterns. Their historical position is further accentuated by

---

10. In Citroni's (1995, 284–86) version of "literary communication" the poem is not merely a poeticized transcription of what the poet would have said to his friend in everyday life, but communicates to that friend through the stylization that poetic form offers.

11. Williams (1968, 202–6) considers the possible Greek background for this technique in Latin poetry and proposes that the Greek poets, performing for like-minded and socially undifferentiated audiences, could make clear in performance the difference between the poetic speaker and the performer's own identity (a key example here is Alcaeus fr. 10B L-P [P.Oxy. 1789], which uses the voice of a woman). On the other hand, "poets like Catullus and Horace made very different use of this example; and, with fine poetic instinct, adapted this technique of partial and gradual revelation to poetry which was intended for readers of all kinds and all times" (205).

12. Lowrie (2009a, 59–60) formulates the category of "the literary" as constituted by "a break from origins," specifically the act of disembedding poetry from ritual and making it available to audiences who do not share either the performative moment or the cultural assumptions that shaped it. In these ways, her analysis of Latin poetry's presentation of itself as performed or written shares key assumptions with my own investigation. In contrast to Lowrie (2009a), however, I intend to explain in greater detail the implications of communicating with unknowable future audiences through writing.

the fact that their most visible and most prestigious literary models are Greek texts that leverage the face-to-face practices inherent in *polis* life[13] to construct aesthetic practices that firmly embed literary communication within social, political, and religious institutions. As a result, the tension between social communication and literary communication in Latin literature has been perceived as lining up with the dichotomies of Greek vs. Roman and oral vs. literate, with connotations of full-bodied life on the one side and empty forms on the other. Since oral communication requires physical proximity and (to some extent) shared cultural institutions, it is easy to link it with social life. Writing, on the other hand, with its recognized ability to bridge distances of time and culture, easily lines up with the attributes of the literary (registered, of course, in the etymology of that term). Seeing Roman poets as both readers and writers, as both recipients of the Greek tradition and creators of their own, can help us to refine this broad-brush picture.

The shift from orality to writing will be central for my argument, though not in the ways this has usually been understood.[14] Writing does in fact change everything: as long as poems are conceived as songs that live in performance, the mechanisms that support their reperformance require a high degree of continuity between earlier and later cultural institutions (musical education, ritual practice, the function of poetry within social settings

---

13. That is, literature is adapted both to contexts within individual *poleis* (e.g., sympotic lyric and elegy, tragedy, comedy) and to Panhellenic contexts that support the network of *poleis* (e.g., rhapsodic performance of epic, choral performance of *epinicia* or hymns).

14. Dupont (1999) would seem to offer the sharpest possible contrast to the view of writing I am taking here, since her argument rests on defining axiomatically the "cold" reading of texts against the "hot" social interchange that happens in face-to-face communication (for these terms see 14). But evidence supporting my approach is actually embedded within hers. Although in general she claims that the kind of reading she calls "literary" (generated by the reader as a partner with the text, indeterminate, open to various branching possibilities) is alien to the ancient world, the exception is when authors rewrite older texts, as Virgil did Homer's (9). I would argue that oral communication is also conditioned by the indeterminacy inherent in language use, but Dupont's view of rewritings at least supports my claim that the Roman poets acted in response to earlier, especially Greek, texts in ways that reveal those earlier texts to be meaningful, even if not in the way the original authors might have intended or envisioned. I suggest that this experience alerted them to the possibility that their own texts would someday be read in this unpredictable way. Habinek (2005) also associates performance/orality with full social (and political) meaning, though he argues that this meaning is produced by the process of ritualization and therefore does not rely on face-to-face presence; in fact, a key point of Habinek's argument is that the ritualization of everyday language produced by song is extended in and through written texts (see esp. 16, 56–57). So while Habinek's view seems closer to mine than Dupont's (since it assumes that writing is not merely inert but socially active), it differs from mine in focusing on the meanings of written texts relevant for readers in the same society. For further analysis of how the shift to literacy shapes literary aesthetics, see Lowrie (1997, chap. 2; 2009a); in general, Lowrie's arguments differ from mine primarily because she assumes writing to be "decontextualized" (e.g., 2009a, 81) and "an atemporal possibility of iteration" (1997, 49).

such as the symposium, etc.).[15] Such a cultural continuity encourages poets to accentuate the potential for "reenactment" by people like themselves in essential ways.[16] Writing, on the other hand, because it makes texts (potentially) longer lasting and more stable,[17] allows texts to outlive their context of production and to encounter readers who share nothing with the author other than the text itself and the linguistic competence to read it. The literate elite of Rome was positioned to understand this phenomenon in a particularly acute way, a fact that is reflected in their intimate but ambivalent embrace of the Greek literary tradition.[18]

Writing (or, more precisely, the widespread assumption that poems will circulate in papyrus collections) introduces a hitch between the image of oral communication depicted in the poem and the poem's own medium for communicating with its audience. The assumption has generally been either that the Latin poets do not notice the gap between the storyworld speaker addressing a companion and a poet circulating a poem or that their admiration for performed archaic Greek first-person poetry is such that they seek to emulate it as far as possible despite the shift in medium.[19] I am not arguing that they perceived this gap in exactly the terms I outline here, as specifically setting up a tension between not-for-us and for-us. But, at a minimum, we have no evidence to support either of these two common assumptions that

---

15. More precisely, they require the *perception of* a high degree of continuity: these institutions of performance may change, but the culture of song and performance projects an image of stability.

16. "Reenactment" is Nagy's key term for describing reperformance not as imitation but as reinhabiting the moment of the original performance (see, e.g., 1994, 15). I will take up this question further below.

17. Both these effects are only relatively more valid for writing than for performance. Classicists, used to dealing with the loss of huge swathes of ancient literature and the tricky process of constituting critical editions, should be even less sanguine about the longevity and fixity of written documents than the general population.

18. See now Feeney (2016) on this central issue.

19. A few more recent attempts to resolve this impasse come closer to the conception of my own project, esp. Lowell Edmunds's *Intertextuality and the Reading of Roman Poetry* (2001) and Michèle Lowrie's *Writing, Performance, and Authority in Augustan Rome* (2009a). Both build on poststructuralist accounts of language and representation to create models that aim to account for the apparently awkward persistence in written collections of a poetic form that centers on an image of oral communication. The convergences and divergences between my approach and those of Edmunds and Lowrie will become clearer over the course of this introduction and later chapters. Breed (2006) pursues similar questions within the specific generic context of pastoral, with its fictional singers and layered quotation of a poetic tradition; while Breed mostly focuses on audiences contemporary with Virgil and on ways that writing is aligned with absence rather than presence, he also makes a case for the communicative power of writing to reach other audiences, e.g., "through the confrontation between orality and textuality readers of the *Eclogues* are encouraged to reflect on their role and on what the act of reading accomplishes" (152). Finally, let me note Don Fowler's influential contribution to this debate in his 1995 article "Martial and the Book."

downplay the importance of this gap. Further, the readings and analysis provided in this book will demonstrate that the gap between speaker and poet is functional—that is, allows the poems to do things they otherwise could not do.

In emphasizing the poems as written and circulated in collections, I am not just following recent arguments that have demonstrated that writing was central (not marginal) at Rome,[20] but extending the implications of those arguments to take account of the distinctively different kind of literary experience writing produces.[21] I argue that the Latin poets were conscious of future readers who would not be either simply replications of contemporary readers or a generalized "posterity." Much of the scholarship on these poems focuses on the poets' contemporary readers; the perspective I explore here has been comparatively understudied in proportion to its potential importance for understanding the poetry. Although I agree that a small number of readers—both socially close to the poets and, in many cases, highly influential—would have loomed large in the poets' desired reception of their work, again we should remember that their own experience as readers of earlier poetry might have balanced out this focus on their immediate reception more than is usually assumed.[22]

My argument starts from what Jonathan Culler famously called "the double logic of story": "One could argue that every narrative operates according to this double logic, presenting its plot as a sequence of events which is prior to and independent of the given perspective on these events, and, at the same time, suggesting by its implicit claims to significance that these events are justified by their appropriateness to a thematic structure" (2001, 194). This double logic could be rephrased to say that a narrative simultaneously

---

20. See, for example, from different angles Meyer (2004), Feeney (2005, 235–36), Parker (2009), Johnson (2010).

21. Miller (1994) theorizes the creation of the genre we know as lyric as closely linked to the shift to written collections. The feature of such collections that is important for his argument is that they juxtapose scenes or moments from the storyworld, without a determining temporal order, and thus allow such fragmentary glimpses to comment on each other. Miller's approach differs from mine both in privileging the storyworld (he treats the poetic collection as a narrative and its aim as the illumination of an individual psyche) and in assuming without argument that the storyworld speaker and the poet are unified.

22. Oliensis's concept of the "overreader" (1998, 6–7 et passim) acknowledges the dominating presence of powerful contemporary readers, but also contends that these readers are not the only ones with whom Horace concerns himself: "In the course of his career, Horace displays a growing awareness that his poetic faces will continue to circulate long after he himself has passed from view. It is this awareness that enables Horace to assert his authority even in (if not exactly to) the face of readers such as Maecenas and Augustus. It is the power of Horace's poems, finally, and not the power of Maecenas or Augustus, that will perpetuate Horace's name" (7).

asserts that the discourse exists for the purposes of the "story" (to describe and transmit the events of the storyworld) and that the "story" exists for the purposes of the discourse (the events of the storyworld are like props that allow the discourse to create its thematic and rhetorical effects). If we start from this formulation, we can see that it is not merely a question of choosing to privilege one level or the other, but of apprehending simultaneously the two levels and their competing claims of priority.

Although Culler's formulation is meant to apply to narrative texts, I believe that it can help us to understand the specific form of ancient first-person poetry. One might object that in applying this formulation to such poems, I am being too literal-minded or that I am ignoring the constitutive distinctions between lyric and narrative.[23] First, on the charge of literal-mindedness: unlike later poetic forms in Western literature, which veer away from realistic scenes of speech into apostrophe or self-contained meditation, the dominant form of first-person poetry for the Greco-Roman period was what I will call "addressive" poetry, poems that offer an image of social speech in context by presenting the voice of a speaker addressing a present, often named interlocutor.[24] Addressive poetry can hardly be said to be uninterested in dimensions beyond its representation of social life, but if we leap across its representational level in a single bound, assuming that this level exists merely to point beyond itself, then we are forcing ancient poetry into a Procrustean bed shaped by the norms of later poetry. Not all addressive poems are as

---

23. Culler's own theory of the lyric (presented most extensively in his 2015 book of that title) is squarely at odds with what I am proposing here. Central to (and axiomatic for) Culler's formulation of lyric is its nonmimetic nature (see esp. 2015, 109–25). I will engage with Culler's theory of lyric throughout my analyses. For now, it will be sufficient to suggest that his resistance to the notion that lyric might *sometimes* make use of mimesis is rooted in his commitment to lyric as a single transhistorical literary form; because a mimetic reading (one that situates the poetic speaker in a defined context) distorts the reading of much Romantic lyric, Culler believes it to be misguided for all lyric. (Note that here and elsewhere when I refer to transhistorical discussions of "lyric" I am using that term in its broad, postclassical sense, referring generally to short first-person poems, and not the classicists' meaning, which is defined by specific meters.) For an application of Culler's model of apostrophe to addressive Latin poetry, see Barber (2010). In my opinion, Barber overstates the apostrophic (unreal) qualities of address in Horace's odes, by assuming, e.g., thematic contradictions and other forms of disunity make the scene unreal. I do agree, however, that Horace's use of address and scenic context underplays their mimetic aspects (especially in comparison to Propertius and Catullus) and will explore this feature in later chapters.

24. Cf. Johnson's (1982) category of "I-You" poetry and especially the function a pseudo-dramatic setting performs for this category. Not only is the presence of an interlocutor important to his definition, but the speech takes place "at a highly dramatic moment in which the essence of their relationship, of their 'story,' reveals itself in the singer's lyrical discourse, in his praise or blame, in the metaphors he finds to recreate the emotions he seeks to describe" (3; Johnson's use of the terms "story" and discourse differs from mine). His description is a good example of how a reader finds rhetorical and thematic effects by constituting the poem as a scene of social interchange.

self-referential in this respect as Catullus 6, which builds around the theme of secrecy a proposition that the storyworld has its own solidity and will not make itself completely available for our inspection. Still, the choice to route the poet's communication to readers through a realistic scene of social life demands more rigorous explanation than it has yet received. To be precise, I am arguing not that we should grant more weight to the storyworld scene in our interpretations, but that we should acknowledge and theorize the weight we do regularly grant it and the ways that the apparent solidity of the storyworld shapes our experience of addressive poetry.[25]

The fundamental importance of address as a grounding element of this poetic form also offers an answer to the objection that my way of reading reduces the specifically lyric quality of such poems and assimilates them to narrative. The distinctiveness of addressive poetry *as poetry* resides in the very fact that it courts a narrative-like immersion in the storyworld without diminishing the intensity of its discursive dimension.[26] To say, however, that these poems create a storyworld in which the speaker addresses a companion and that this storyworld is an important element of the poem as a whole is not to say that the poems are narratives. They share this mimetic feature with narratives, but they use it to very different ends.[27] Further, addressive

---

25. Price (1983, 32) on novelistic narrative: "Narrative may be said to depress the metaphorical status of character and setting; it gives a coherence to all the elements on the level of action that deflects attention from their meaningfulness and from their position in the structure." This feature of narrative does not, of course, prevent those elements from having metaphorical status; it merely relegates that status to a less acknowledged component of the reading experience. Conversely, for the kind of poetry I am discussing, while we may organize our interpretations of the poems by focusing on the metaphorical and thematic effects of character and scene, these elements still retain "a coherence . . . on the level of action" that affects the reading, even if largely unacknowledged.

26. Recent decades have seen an increasing interest in the element of narrative within corpora of first-person poetry (e.g., for Catullus, Fitzgerald 1995, 28–29; for elegy, Liveley and Salzman-Mitchell 2008, and *Helios* 37.2 [2010]; the broadest claim of this type is to be found in Miller 1994, which assumes that constructing an image of the central lyric speaker is fundamental to the reading of these poems). While I find these investigations enlightening, they are generally focused on the question of how the reader's understanding of characters and events develops across a corpus and therefore have a different focus from mine. Lowrie (1997) seeks to theorize the narrative element in individual poems, and so is closer to my approach, but she starts by positing a constitutive opposition between lyric and narrative (associating narrative with linear and comprehensive sense-making and lyric with the nonlinear and fragmentary, see esp. chap. 1); although she is interested in the interaction between these two well-defined forces, the initial definition of them as opposites tends to limit the flexibility of her approach.

27. Compare this to Culler's formulation: "In narrative fiction the question of the relation between *story* and *discourse* or between what is enunciated and the enunciation is generally theorized as one of perspective—from what point of view are events reported (in fiction the priority of event to narration is presumed). How does lyric differ? In our examples, the present of discourse or articulation cannot be reduced to the narrating of past events; on the contrary, the narrated events seem to be subsumed by, trumped by, the present of lyric enunciation (narrating is no longer the

poems are usually lacking in two features thought by many to be constitutive of narrative: temporal sequence (addressive poems show us only a single moment in the storyworld) and implied causality of the events shown.[28] Although debating definitions of "lyric" and "narrative" is not my main goal, this study could contribute to a more subtle description of how these two literary practices relate to each other, a description that could refine the current, sometimes rigidly binary, definitions.

By distinguishing more carefully the various ways that "story" operates and varies from poem to poem, I hope to give readers sharper tools with which to identify and analyze the poem's deployment of its mimetic and nonmimetic aspects. Instead of proposing another rule to follow (e.g., "never confuse the poetic speaker with the author"), my argument is aimed at drawing out exactly how these poems use a storyworld for their effects. While my critical orientation shares with many others' an insistence (based in poststructuralist approaches) on registering the work done by representation,[29] I differ from these scholars in being less interested in the fundamental fact of representation and more interested in the creative effects that depend on readers' impulse to confound textual acts with facts in the world. This point becomes clearer if we contrast the habit of mind other interpreters are trying to correct with my own goal: rather than trying to get readers to acknowledge that the act of representation intervenes between them and the events related (and thereby fundamentally conditions the ontological status of those events), my goal is to focus attention on the ways that Latin first-person poetry both supports and thwarts this recognition, and uses the resulting bifurcated view as an engine of its artistic and communicative effects.

Beyond theorizing the impact the storyworld has on our reading practice, my argument at its broadest level is that the poetry we see in Catullus's polymetrics, in Horace's *Odes*, and in Propertius's first two books (my chosen test cases, for reasons I will discuss below) uses the duality inherent in first-person poetic structure to explore what kind of communication poetry

---

right word)" (2015, 36). Thus, although Culler differs from me as to the significance of a storyworld in lyric, his formulation of the principle echoes my claim that "story" and discourse do exist in lyric and compete for priority.

28. For a definition of narrative that emphasizes temporal sequence and causality, see Chatman (1990, 9). Purves (2014) entertains the possibility that Sappho 1 might contain elements of narrative, though ultimately labels it "anti-narrative" based on its iterative time scheme and refusal to specify exact identities (in keeping with the iterative and open-textured nature of performance). This is an example of how a consideration of the relation of lyric to narrative can show us something new about lyric, even if we end up maintaining the boundaries between the two forms.

29. Particularly illuminating discussions of this principle in relation to Latin poetry can be found in Wyke (2002, 11–45), Kennedy (1993), Sharrock (2000), Hardie (2002).

constitutes and what kind of agency this communication depends on. In this respect, my argument can be illuminated by Alessandro Barchiesi's claim that one of the distinctive practices of Augustan poets is what he calls "the 'folding' of genre" (2009, 418), that is, how genre moves from an external condition to an internal theme. For example, "Horace raises the construction and assertion of a lyric personality to the status of a significant recurring theme in his collection, and the problem of how to establish a personal voice that confronts the canonical voices of the Greek masters becomes not only a prerequisite but also a part of his poetic representation" (421). My argument takes this phenomenon one step further: not only is Horace (along with other first-person poets) exploring what it means to construct and assert a lyric personality, but exploring *through poetic form* the ways that such a personality is implicated in two distinct kinds of personal agency, the agency depicted in the poem's social setting and the agency implied by production and circulation of the poem itself.

Barchiesi's explication of Horace in relation to "the Greek masters" is highly relevant. The Greek poetic tradition matters here not just because it provided long-lasting and prestigious literary models, but also because of the manner in which it became available for the Romans. The Hellenistic collections of older poetry (especially of archaic lyric) embody the puzzle of what occasional poetry means once it is transmitted as a text, without its music and without the social contexts in which it was performed. This poetry was resonant and beautiful to Roman readers in ways that depended on their knowledge of its original contexts but also in ways that were irrelevant to those contexts, structured only by its reception in a foreign land.[30] I suggest that for Latin poets the experience of reading a temporally and culturally distant poetry that engaged powerfully with its later, unforeseen readers prompted new strategies for how addressive poetry might function as communication, strategies that pivoted on making insoluble the question of whether a poem's "context" is the social scene it represents or the book it appears in. These innovations, however, come disguised as evolutionary

---

30. My point is not that the authors try to write for future readers, but that they write with the knowledge that their poetry will be read by future readers in conditions they cannot imagine. The drastic change in conventions between the time of the poets of archaic Greek song culture and the literate cultures of Hellenistic and Roman times can be seen through the lens of Petrey's argument about illocutionary acts in writing in relation to illocutionary acts in speech (1990, 77–78). Petrey points to Austin's use of "I give and bequeath . . ." in a will as an example of a performative, but pushes this example further by specifying that the conventions that govern its meaning are the conventions active at the time of reception (the death of the testator, the opening of the will) not those at the time of composition and that those conventions might radically change the perlocutionary effects; for example if the state has since outlawed such legacies, the bequest becomes void.

survivals, and their effect is almost invisibly woven into the texture of the familiar Greek-inspired forms.[31]

Let me pause to underline one implication of this insoluble question, one that shows it to be parallel to the competing priority of "story" and discourse. If we accentuate the occasional nature of addressive poetry in its strict sense (i.e., that a given poem was composed precisely for its first performance), then the "speech" that the poem transmits functions as a heightened form of communication between the speaker and the addressee. On the other hand, if we see the poem as designed to appear in a book and the represented scene as engineered to serve the poem's thematic needs, then the relevant act of communication is no longer between the depicted speaker and addressee, but between the poet and reader. This is an obvious point but one that reveals itself to be surprisingly complex in its ramifications. As books increasingly become both an archive of older occasional poetry and the accepted format for circulating new poetry,[32] Latin addressive poetry develops its distinctive appeal by playing the depicted scene of communication off against its own communication with the reader, privileging neither the scene in which the communication is not-for-us nor the specific design of poetic discourse that is for-us.

In the next two sections of this introduction I will present in more detail the two key issues I have touched on briefly here: first, the structural relation between the poetic speaker and the historical poet, then the literary-historical context within which the first-century poets were composing. But before turning to those arguments, it will be helpful to go back to Catullus's poem 6 and see how my proposed method of reading works out in practice. As a first step, we can note that this poem creates a contrastive parallel between the social act of keeping/telling secrets and the literary act by which (in the world of the poem) the sordid affair will become elegant poetry. The friction produced by this contrast foregrounds the idea that the same act (telling about Flavius's affair) carries very different meaning and consequences depending on whether it is seen as a social act or as a literary act. This friction thus delineates two conduits of communication—the one depicted in the poem and the one that the poem itself constitutes.

---

31. Morgan notes that unlike the later Roman poets (especially Horace), the Hellenistic poets were not drawn to the stanzaic forms so central to archaic Greek poetry. "To mimic the metrical structures of archaic song to the degree that Horace did is thus a dramatic move, and one that is hard not to conclude was facilitated by the gulf that separated Rome and archaic Greece. . . . It perhaps required the truly radical cultural breach represented by a change of language for sung lyric to be reinvented as a written form" (2010, 185).

32. Key here is the argument of Krevans (1984).

So far, this interpretation can be derived just from considering the poem as the record of a speech that exists in the storyworld, the speech that the witty speaker addresses to his less elegant friend Flavius. But readers know that this is not a speech somehow smuggled out of the confines of the storyworld—it is an utterance orchestrated by the poet so that the poem as a whole will produce certain effects. Therefore, in addition to reading this poem as the speaker's words we also read it as invisibly framed by its status as a poem circulated for publication. Readers are always conscious on some level that our access to the poem is not really incidental (cf. "over-heard") but engineered. The mise-en-abyme structure of first-person poetry, however, allows us to entertain alongside that consciousness the possibility that the act of speaking in the storyworld is so fully unified with the act of poetic composition that the gap is negligible. I will be arguing throughout this book that Latin first-person poems experiment with a variety of struc-tural arrangements between the speaker and the historical poet, sometimes precisely differentiating the forms of agency they exert and at other times blending them into one.

How does this consciousness of the historical poet's agency play out in Catullus 6? We should note that within the storyworld, the ennobling poem is to come in the future and is implicitly made to depend on the speaker actually getting the name of Flavius's lover.[33] But even a casual reader of Catullus will see that this poem *is* the poem that exalts the lovers, and that the pleasurable effects of this poem do not depend on naming names. In other words, the social specificity of the storyworld—the exact identity of the lover, after all, is what generates curiosity at the storyworld level—is shown to be a springboard for poetic effects. We could say that the poem starts out by implying that the specificity of the social world matters, but the final effect is to discard these specifics in favor of aesthetic gratification.[34] But before we conclude from this example that the storyworld level of the poem functions merely as a set-up for the poem's real engagement with readers, we should consider that if Catullus had wanted to write a poem that sidelined specific identities, he certainly could have—in other words, he could have written the poem that is imagined at the end, rather than the poem we have. The poem he chose to write substitutes the back-and-forth of social intercourse for heaven-bound exaltation and accentuates the limits

---

33. Even this implicit link is left a little loose. It's probably important that the poem doesn't specifically say "If you tell me, I will exalt you," and instead says paratactically "Tell me. I want to exalt you."

34. As is argued by Fitzgerald (1995, 52).

of knowledge in social contexts, rather than inhabiting a transcendent realm in which such facts have no value. The overall effect, then, is not to point toward the indisputable fact that the poem is uninterested in finding out who Flavius's girlfriend is, but to show how Catullus's poetry relies on both the tantalizing obscured glimpse into the storyworld and the gesture by which the attractions of that storyworld are swept aside.

In addition to providing greater detail to our understanding of the poem's engagement with its own poetics, my reading of Catullus 6 differs from previous readings in granting more importance to the fact that aspects of the represented scene remain hidden from the reader. In other words, while I agree that Catullus here flaunts his ability to "produce elegance even out of the silence that betrays his friend" (Fitzgerald 1995, 52), I propose that silence (i.e., the withholding of knowledge about the storyworld) in this poem also confirms the impression that the speaker lives in a world that goes on around and behind the words on the page.

Speaker and Poet

In the example from Catullus considered above, we can see what happens when we perceive the speaker's words as framed by the poet's choice to offer these words as a poem. This complex effect allows the poem both to consist of the speaker's words and to be *about* those words, even though there is no comment expressed and we see no explicit framing device that concretely establishes the second-order nature of the speaker's words. This feature of the poetic discourse will come into focus more clearly when we compare that Catullan poem to another first-century poem that famously does make its framing explicit: Horace's second epode. This poem consists of a long praise of country life concluded by these lines:

> haec ubi locutus faenerator Alfius,
>   iam iam futurus rusticus,
> omnem redegit idibus pecuniam,
>   quaerit kalendis ponere.
>
>   (*Epode* 2.67–70)

When the moneylender Alfius, about to retire to the country any day now, said this, he called in all his money on the ides—but on the calends is looking to lend it out again.

Without these lines this poem would look like the vast majority of poems written by Horace, Catullus, and Propertius. The poem would present a voice that claims to occupy both the speaking position within the storyworld and the authorial position. But with these lines, the poem is instantaneously transformed into something more like a dramatic monologue. We may choose to follow Mankin (1995) and others in believing that the poem, even in its earlier stages, distances its speaker from Horace's authorial position by lacing his speech with mistakes in taste, judgment, and knowledge.[35] What is important here, however, is that the poem does not perform any such distancing *structurally* (by making clear that this speech is a quotation embedded within a poem rather than a poem in its own right) until the very end.[36] The distancing that is created through content, for example, by making the speaker seem unlike what we know of the historical author or by making him distasteful in ways that we assume the historical author would not want to have associated with himself, is fundamentally different from the structural distancing that framing creates.

Horace's second epode both participates in and comments on the usual practices of Latin first-person poetry. In fact, to my mind, the shocking aspect of this poem is not that the speaker turns out to be a low, contemptible character in the end, but how forcefully this poem comments on the duality that animates such poetry. The Alfius poem makes its framing explicit, but it also delays the revelation so that we can have the experience of reading this voice as the usual first-person voice, a voice that does not announce its difference from the historical poet's orchestrating agency but allows that difference to be expressed only implicitly. This poem ups the ante when it reveals the speaker to be not only a named third-person character but a self-deluding moneylender, in a move consistent with the design that makes explicit the framed quality of his speech. On both levels, the poem overemphasizes the gap between a ruminative monologue in the storyworld and the discursive action of the poem, drawing attention to this poem's comment on the usual practices of Latin first-person poems.

Notice that the only position this corrective authorial voice can take is the position of narrator ("when Alfius said this, he . . .").[37] A large majority of Latin first-person poems use the speaking position to yoke together the

---

35. "The speaker seems to envisage agriculture as free from toil (1n.), while his interest in just that (4n.) and in property suggests that he defines happiness in terms of wealth (1n.). And someone who rejects military and political concerns (5–8) can hardly be the H[orace] of the first Epode" (Mankin 1995, 64).

36. Some modern editions undermine the subtlety of this poem by enclosing the first sixty-six lines in quotation marks.

37. It is relatively common for scholars of Latin elegy (for example) to use the term "narrator" to refer to the poetic speaker (e.g., Wyke 2002). I find this practice obfuscates rather than clarifies the actual structures involved (since in fact the speaker in the storyworld is more like a character than

storyworld speaker and the authorial function, but in this poem the role of speaker has already been occupied by Alfius. There are some lyric poems that include more than one voice (e.g., dialogue poems such as Catullus 45 or Horace *Odes* 3.9), but in those cases, the two speakers occupy the story-world together and are addressing one another. In the case of *Epode* 2, what is required is a voice that stands outside the storyworld and describes or inter-prets it for us—in short, a narrator. This is corroborating evidence for my claim that the structure of addressive poetry shares important conceptual ground with narrative, with the proviso that in the former the mediating role is usually exercised invisibly rather than visibly.[38] We tend to think of the lyric speaker as occupying the entire horizon of the poem and in this respect dif-fering from the characters of novels, who are introduced, defined, described, etc. by a narrator.[39] But Horace's second epode shows that such first-person voices often depend on the kind of mediating action that narrators perform in narratives, an action that structures the experience of "overhearing" in a way that makes it meaningful rather than just random.[40] In the usual practice of Latin addressive poetry, that mediating action exists but remains invisible, established by the mere fact that these words have been offered as a poem.[41] By acting as narrator, the authorial voice in *Epode* 2 calls our attention to the

a narrator), but it does offer further implicit support for my contention that readers feel the need to register a presence in such poems that mediates between the storyworld and the reader's world.

38. Chatman (1978, 146–95) describes what he calls "nonnarrated narratives," i.e., "narratives purporting to be untouched transcripts of characters' behavior" (166). The clearest examples of this category are dramatic monologues (such as Browning and Tennyson excelled in; see Chatman 1978, 173–74), though he extends this category to include prose examples. In his later book *Coming to Terms*, he retracts this terminology (1990, 115–16), but for my purposes here his original impulse to distinguish this form from other narrative forms is helpful.

39. There are of course exceptions to this practice, such as narratives that consist wholly of quotations of character voices. In these cases, the character voices come much closer to what I am describing as the normal practice of addressive poetry, though given the different generic contexts that such texts inhabit there still is a wide gulf between minimally narrated narrative and addressive poetry.

40. Another way of understanding how "overhearing" becomes meaningful is to posit that the speaker himself is conscious of the eavesdroppers and engineers his speech to make sense to them as well as to his storyworld audience (see Fitzgerald 1995, 4–5, for a subtle formulation of this prin-ciple). The next two chapters will take up in detail the question of exactly how poems convey the speaker's degree of consciousness that his speech is a poem, but at a minimum we can say that this consciousness is not a universal characteristic of first-person poetry.

41. Edmunds's (2001) adaptation of possible worlds theory (following on the work of Levin 1976 and others) is an attempt parallel to my own to understand the relation between the depicted scene and the effect of the poem as a whole for a reader. One of the outcomes of Levin's theory is "a deeply implicit, external, and indeed a priori intentionality" (Edmunds 2001, 34), which I believe is parallel to the intention I attribute here to the historical poet, i.e., the intention of producing a poem and making it available for readers. Edmunds dismisses the usefulness for interpretation of acknowledg-ing such an intention, but this very basic, minimal intention is what produces the framing effect.

fact that some agency is required to mediate between storyworld speech and the poem as readers encounter it. This availability does not happen magically, and it is not created by any force within the storyworld but requires someone outside, someone who inhabits the same world as readers.

Part of my motivation for offering a more precise understanding of how such first-person poems work is to clarify the difference between content-based and structural methods for distinguishing between the speaker and the poet and thus to avoid the epistemologically (and even ethically) suspect move of using the personal characteristics of the speaker to argue that this figure cannot represent the poet.[42] The agency and actions of the speaker exist within the storyworld, while the agency and actions of the poet exist in the reader's own world and are responsible for making that storyworld speech available as a poem.[43] This distinction does not rely on any represented characteristics of the speaker and in fact is valid even in completely straight-faced autobiographical works where the speaker or narrator is designed to offer an accurate picture of the author.

As clear as this fundamental distinction is, the great bulk of Latin first-person poetry is designed to paper it over, to confound the actions that result in the creation of the poem with social actions in the depicted world. I will deal in the next section with the impact of earlier Greek poetry, which obviously is influential for this preference. Before going on to that familiar history, however, I would like to take a short detour through the debated concept of "the speaker." Although scholars of first-person Latin poetry long ago left behind documentary-style readings, I would argue that the field has not yet developed an accurate way of talking about how and why these poems both encourage and undermine the identification of the speaker with the historical poet.[44] More typical in recent decades than the naïve assimilation

---

42. For critiques of persona criticism that make clear the broader stakes, see, e.g., Wray (2001, 161–64) and Oliensis (1998, 2–3 et passim). On the other hand, Veyne offers an influential model of the difference between speaker and poet by relying on the concept of irony, and thus asserting the poet's ultimate control of all his effects; e.g., "his own words make us understand that he is amusing himself as well as his reader and is not really taking part in what he has brought on stage" (1988, 37).

43. Although I develop it in a somewhat different direction, I have found very helpful Krevans's formulation of the "poet-editor" figure, "the dual nature of the author of the poetic book. On the one hand, he is a poet composing individual poems; on the other hand, he is an editor arranging these compositions into book form" (1984, 26). By calling the voice internal to the poems "the poet," Krevans is seeking to link Hellenistic and Roman practice with the archaic practice of the poet who composes in and for performance; this notion is deeply implicated in the concept of occasionality, which I discuss in more detail below.

44. For example, Michèle Lowrie has offered a subtle reformulation of the term "fiction" (2009a, 63–92). She focuses, however, on the principle of indeterminacy, which is content to register the combination of proposing and denying the links between people / events depicted and

of speaker to poet is the peremptory claim that the speaker is a fictional character created by the poet, but without fully investigating the obvious ways that the poetry itself blurs the motivations and actions of these two figures. I hope to get further than just substituting "no" for "yes" to the question "is the speaker *really* the poet?" and reformulate the terms of the debate.

Because of the dominance of the addressive form in ancient first-person poetry, classicists tend to take for granted that such poems depict speakers. Theorists who are interested in nonaddressive forms or in the broad sweep of possible lyric forms, on the other hand, have taken more seriously the question of what it means to assume that poems have speakers.[45] An incisive essay on the dramatic monologue by Herbert Tucker can help to bring out the significance of this question for my argument. His conclusion is that "while texts do not absolutely lack speakers, they do not simply have them either; they invent them instead as they go" (2014, 153).[46] One central goal of my book is to identify and make available for analysis the process by which the poems of Catullus, Propertius, and Horace invent speakers as they go. The reasoning that persuades me that speakers are invented by texts also persuades me a fortiori that the speaker so invented is not any simple reflex of the historical poet. A second central goal of this book is to fully explore the implications of poetic structures, both when they assimilate the actions of speaker and poet and when they construct a gap between them.

The fuller context for Tucker's claim makes clear how it is related to a broader debate about the mimetic potential of lyric:

> To assume in advance that a poetic text proceeds from a dramatically situated speaker is to risk missing the play of verbal implication whereby character is engendered in the first place through colliding modes of signification; it is to read so belatedly as to arrive only when the party is over. At the same time, however, the guest the party convenes to honor, the ghost conjured by the textual machine, remains the articulate phenomenon we call character: a literary effect we neglect at our peril. For to insist that textuality is all and that the play of the signifier usurps the recreative illusion of character is to turn back at

---

the historical world, rather than developing a fine-grained analysis of how this alternation is constructed and how it functions.

45. Jackson and Prins (2014, 162–64) trace the history of the speaker as an invention of New Criticism, which uses the speaker as a way to preserve the notion of poetry as communication while sidelining the historical poet as a source of poetic meaning.

46. This essay was originally published in the influential 1985 collection *Lyric Poetry: Beyond New Criticism*, edited by C. Hošek and P. Parker. I give references here to the recent reprint in Jackson and Prins (2014).

the threshold of interpretation, stopping our ears to both lyric cries and historical imperatives, and from our studious cells overhearing nothing.

(2014, 153)

Tucker's larger point in this article is that dramatic monologue, although shunned by purists as not-quite-lyric because of its dabbling in character, scene, etc., can teach us something fundamental about the dynamic tension between language as "the play of verbal implication" and language's mimetic capacity, which carries in its train the gravest social, ethical, and historical implications.[47] Tucker is trying to unsettle the complacency with which readers of postclassical lyric either reflexively supply a human speaker (and thereby ignore the play of language) or cling to an antimimetic textuality, thereby resisting "the recreative illusion of character."[48]

Beyond the obvious encouragement to pay more attention to the ways that texts construct speakers, Tucker's essay offers an inspiration for my project on another level as well. Although it is important to note that the addressive poems I am concerned with are rarely dramatic monologues,[49] dramatic monologue provides a parallel, since it is a poetic form in which the poet communicates with readers in a second-order way through the totality of the poem—the speaker's words plus the frame provided by the poet's offering these words as a poem—rather than in a first-order way through the words themselves, understood to constitute a speech event.[50] The specific challenge presented by Latin first-person poetry is to understand poems that do not stabilize either the second-order or first-order strategy explicitly (or even implicitly) but constantly invoke both and allow them to coexist.

---

47. Tucker's understanding of dramatic monologue is that it quite pointedly challenges "pure" lyric exactly on the grounds of lyric's attempt to insulate itself from history. Responding to Olson's image of the poem as a balloon, he says "that the 'proper shape' of a poem, as of a balloon, arises not from sheer afflatus but as a compromise between 'internal' and 'external' forces is precisely my point about the framing of the dramatic monologue—as it is, I think, the dramatic monologue's (deflationary) point about the lyric" (Tucker 2014, 155, n. 16; cf. Olson 1969).

48. It is characteristic of Culler's resistance to mimesis in lyric that he quotes (2015, 116) only the first part of Tucker's passage I have quoted above (ending with "only when the party is over"). Barbara Herrnstein Smith (1968, 1979) offers a strong instance of the opposite impulse, theorizing lyric poems as "fictive utterances." My goal here is to avoid both these totalizing approaches.

49. I and most others reserve that label for a poem whose speaker is established as a specific character distinct from the author and in which a more specific plot is implied. Greco-Roman examples might include (besides *Epode* 2) Archilochus fr. 19 West (as explicated by Aristotle *Rhet* 3.17) and several of the poems in Propertius's last book.

50. "Speech event" is Culler's term for the central impulse of lyric "to be itself an event rather than the representation of an event" (2015, 35).

Tucker's demonstration of the ways that poems invent speakers helps us to see how the mimetic powers of language can be used for nonnarrative ends; his argument can have a bracing effect, forcing us to contemplate the fact that Latin addressive poems communicate with readers by offering a scene of communication. A major reason we have become inured to that artistic choice is that it replicates the form (though, I would argue, not the function) of earlier Greek first-person poetry. Thus I offer a reexamination of that history and its implications for first-century Latin poetry.

Performance and Text

> Technologically mediated voices have become so naturalized for us that we listen without the sense of estrangement that fascinated Victorian readers and writers, for whom literary and technological inventions of "voice" were a way to perform the dissociation and disembodiment of speech.
>
> *(Prins* 2004, 47)

> Our awareness of the true nature of art need not invalidate an emotional response.
>
> *(Fowler* 2000, 27)

Imagine the disorienting experience of hearing a recorded voice for the first time, the uncanny power of a voice that registers as both "natural" (human, social) and "artificial" (displaced, disembodied, produced by a machine). Although this particular experience was new in the nineteenth century and tends to be read as part of the history of engineering, it was part of a long tradition, and that tradition had as much to do with art as with science. Long before voices were produced and replicated by phonographic means, literature had offered technologically produced voices that straddled the boundary between human and artificial.

The Latin poets of the first century BCE experienced the confluence of two streams of literary technology: the traditional technologies of meter and form that they inherited from the archaic and classical Greeks, and the newer technology of the poetic "book," that is, a collection of individual poems designed by the author as a unified work, which was pioneered by the poets of Hellenistic Alexandria.[51] As Prins suggests for Victorian poetry,

---

51. Important work on Hellenistic literacy and book culture includes Krevans (1984 and 2007), Hutchinson (2008), Gutzwiller (1998), Bing (1988 and 2009).

I would argue that these technologies became artistically productive not primarily by masking their own action and fading from consciousness, but in their capacity to replicate images of the human voice in new and arresting ways. The implications of this view for the study of Latin poetry are profound and involve integrating into our analysis both the consciousness of poetic form as a technology and the realization that poets' creative imaginations might be stirred as much by opportunities to explore new possibilities as by the desire to use new technologies to re-create older forms.

Put simply, I want to question the assumption that Latin poets sought to replicate as faithfully as possible both the forms and effects of Greek poetry.[52] Because these Latin poets take up and respond to the durable Greek tradition of first-person poetry and because this tradition typically frames a poem as a moment of speech addressed to an interlocutor, we are in danger of taking these artistic choices as nonchoices, of seeing this as merely the normal or natural way to write poetry rather than as a very specific strategy with high stakes. I suggest that while the vivid and lifelike quality of poetic voices certainly plays an important role in Latin first-person poetry, so too do artifice, mediation, and displacement. Because the scene of oral communication depicted in the poem seems at odds with the poem's own written format, modern scholars have often assumed that when Hellenistic and Roman poets perceive this disjuncture, they see it as a loss, a gap that could never be closed despite their best efforts. But what if the later poets perceived this gap not as a problem to be solved but as a new opening within the contours of old forms? If we are seeking to analyze the techniques by which these poets produced captivating voices, we have to be on the lookout for ways that the twin forces of tradition and representational realism can obscure what is radical in this poetry.

As is well known, the poetic genres that the Greeks invented and the Romans inherited had their origin in performance—in ritual choruses and sympotic singing and a whole range of performance venues in public and private life. Equally well known is the fact that these performed songs/poems were transmitted through a combination of written text and various forms of reperformance. By the time of the scholar-poets of Alexandria (third century BCE), the basic principles of literary culture had changed enough that

---

52. Translation theory, with its increasingly skeptical approach to the concept of "faithfulness" provides a thought-provoking parallel, especially because translation (in both narrow and broad senses) was so central to the Roman literary sensibility and to the specific question of what Greek literature would mean for Roman. In classics, the study of translation has recently moved well beyond the simple consideration of turning a Greek text into a Roman text; see esp. McElduff and Sciarrino (2011), McElduff (2013), Young (2015), Feeney (2016).

the written text could be perceived not just as an aide-mémoire for future performances, but as the poem itself. None of this little historical sketch is controversial, but the conceptions that have been built on this framework have differed widely and have had enormous influence over the interpretation of Roman poetry.

The strongest barrier to a new conception of Latin addressive poetry is the "commonsense" assumption that because archaic Greek poetry was performed in venues that are themselves depicted in the poems (e.g., sympotic song, choral dance), such poems seamlessly integrate their function at their original occasion and their function when reperformed or read.[53] On this understanding, the performed poems possess a fundamental organic unity, as charismatic as it is impossible to replicate. This view not only holds out the hope of stepping into the same river twice (if later performances are deemed to reenact the original performance), but also transcends the potential divide between consequential social language and the artistic elaboration (and sensual pleasure) of song, since the ritual and social effects of the original performance are seen as woven into the texture of the poem.

What gets overlooked in the "commonsense" view is that the poem is never so fully integrated into its performance context as to be meaningful *only* there and then. Its functionality in that context always coexists with elements that exceed that functionality. Poetic diction, song, performance by a chorus can be explained as enabling the poem's ritual function,[54] but precisely because these elements distinguish the poem from other more ordinary utterances, they also allow for uses of the poem that go beyond its immediate utility in its original context.[55] What is almost magical about the effect of performed poetry is exactly the impression that these two aspects of the poem—its functionality in its setting and its highly embellished "artistic" form—are not at odds and are instead channeled into a single effect. This merging is not simply a feature of the poem or its performance, however, but an effect achieved (and even trumpeted) by the poem's rhetoric and its

---

53. This is the equivalent of Citroni's argument about literate poetry, discussed above.

54. On the ritual function of aesthetic elaboration, see e.g., Power (2011), Kurke (2012).

55. For an argument that strongly parallels mine, by recognizing the implications of this aesthetic component in hymns for Hellenistic poetics, see Depew (2000, 60–61): "I will examine how the presence of deictic language in hymns and in other kinds of Greek poetry, even in the Archaic period, marks an objectification of performances into texts, establishing a break between production and performance that some would deny for this period. As *agalmata* [ritual gifts for the gods], hymns are also *ktêmata* [possessions], negotiable commodities that potentially exist apart from the subjects who construct them and from the time and place in which they are performed." For a slightly different formulation, see Lowrie (2009a, 82): "Aesthetic form distances speaker and addressee, even when present—even in archaic Greece."

ritual context.⁵⁶ In other words, the commonsense view is ventriloquizing the poem's own claims as to its effects, rather than offering an independent analysis of the poem.

The continued tradition of performance does not really preserve the original moment for later audiences to reexperience, then, but sustains an aesthetic that valorizes the original performance and asserts the poem's engagement with a ritual and social context. Parallel to the way that aligning the present choral performance with that of earlier (even mythical) choruses acknowledges temporal distance in the very act of bridging it,⁵⁷ this very focus on the ephemeral moment of performance does not prevent later audiences from reusing the poem in new contexts, but provides a frame of interpretation in which the originating moment is deemed to be the source of meaning and worth. This is an aesthetic that highlights not-for-us and minimizes for-us.⁵⁸

My purpose here is not to enter the debate about the meaning of performed Greek poetry in its later circulation or to argue that this older poetry operated according to the same principles that I have suggested for first-century Latin addressive poetry. My purpose is merely to demonstrate that

---

56. Morrison (2007, chap. 2) offers an analysis of archaic narrators, especially in Pindar, that illuminates this rhetoric in detail. He shows how archaic poets construct their "pseudo-spontaneous" narrative effects and undermines the assumption that such apparent immediacy is merely the trace of real performance by contrasting Pindaric effects with Homeric, e.g., "Homer did not feel it necessary, unlike later Archaic poets, to construct an 'oral' setting for his poems" (73). Although Morrison's focus on narrators would seem to make his project quite different from mine, the Hellenistic narrators he is seeking to describe are actually quite similar to the first-person speakers in Latin poems (15; he quotes Hunter 1993, 111, on the distinctively Hellenistic "constant demand of poet-narrators to be recognized as the controlling voice behind the words of the text"; see also Morrison 2007, 16, "a prominent narrator . . . who is both like and unlike the author"). Morrison's argument stresses continuities between archaic and later poetry where I am more interested in the differences, but in large-scale ways, our arguments share fundamental principles.

57. See Henrichs's (1994–95) original notion of "choral projection," now widely and variously adapted by others.

58. This aesthetic may minimize the for-us dimension, but it does not drive it out altogether. Currie (2004, 53–54) downplays the significance of "informal reperformance scenarios" for Pindar's epinicians (especially sympotic performance), on the grounds that such performances were unlikely to be motivated by a desire to immortalize the *laudandus*, and therefore likely to lose the poem's specific wording and musical structure. Cf. Morgan (1993, 12, as quoted in Currie 2004, 54, n. 28): "In such surroundings, there is a danger that Pindar's song may sink into the undifferentiated mass of sympotic and informal poetry. That is, once it has lost its original occasion it may lose its specificity and uniqueness." Currie, however, does not quote Morgan's claim as to how that danger is hedged: "Pindar's strong personal presence. Each reperformance must contain his *sphragis*, so to speak; his song must appropriate the future occasion into its own present (the symposium, the revel), thus recreating the context of the original victory." This is an excellent example of how performed poetry meets the demands of highlighting not-for-us and, significantly, does so through the image of poet as both composer of the poem and speaker within the poem.

the prominence of the original occasion in performed poetry is the result of careful rhetorical and poetic work. The scholarship on performed Greek poetry has increasingly moved away from envisioning the two facets of the poem (in its original setting and as a disembedded text) as simply existentially unified and has recently offered various theorizations of how the two facets come to be perceived as unified. For example, while Gregory Nagy is a prominent proponent of "reenactment" as a concept that minimizes the gap between the poem's original and later performances, he also describes how the emphasis on the original moment (the not-for-us aspect of the poem) can coexist with the poem's immediacy for later audiences (for-us).[59] Other scholars have shed light on ways that the diction of the poems does not always foster the image of seamless unity and instead seems capable of drawing attention to competing moments of performance (including those that do not echo the venue or format of the original performance, e.g., choral lyrics reperformed monodically in the symposium), or to the division between composition and performance.[60] A final example of the shift in perspective in recent scholarship is the emergence of a more subtle notion of ritual itself, no longer seen as conservative by nature but as capable of marshaling the impression of unbroken tradition for its own purposes.[61]

I call attention to this recent work to show that the difference between the earlier and later poetic regimes is not between holistic immediacy and empty convention or even (just) between performance and writing, but between an aesthetic regime that seeks to encode its original performance as a key element of the poem and an aesthetic regime that allows the for-us dimension to exert more pressure against the attractions produced by the scene of

---

59. "Although the personification may remain anchored in a set time and place, realistically reenacted and represented as synchronically autonomous within a past far removed from the present [= not-for-us], the persona itself keeps coming alive in the here and now of performance [= for-us]" (Nagy 2004, 31). The difference between this position and my own is that in my formulation what comes alive and establishes contact with new audiences is not the persona but the poetic discourse itself, which finds its origin not in the storyworld but in the historical author.

60. See, e.g., the *Arethusa* volume of 2004, edited by Nancy Felson, especially the papers by Felson, Athanassaki, and D'Alessio.

61. E.g., Kowalzig (2007, 52): "ritual tradition is sanctioned by the widespread belief in its continuous practice. It derives its persuasive power precisely, and solely, through being believed to be transmitted through uninterrupted performance. While some one might think that they are enacting a religious tradition that already has a long history of transmission, it is often very clear that there is no such continuity—or, more importantly, not the same continuity. . . . A performative tradition is not a product of a direct linear descent through time but instead presents a creative handling of the past." Bell (1992) defined "ritualization" as crucially fueled by misrecognition; see Kurke (2005) for further analysis specifically in the context of choral lyric.

speech.[62] Although the scholarship of recent decades has shed more light on the mechanisms by which the scenario in the poem comes to be related to its (re)performance, the contrast with written poetry is still enormous. When poems that circulate in written collections depict scenes of oral communication, the link between the dimensions is *visibly* severed.[63] I would argue that literate poetry is not alone in its dual-track structure, but the difference between the represented scene and the written form of the poem itself lays bare the bifurcated form.

The major way my model differs from others is in the conception of what it means to write for "posterity." Although others see literate authors making use of the tension between performance and writing by playing the advantages of each off against the other, they tend to conceive of the advantages of writing primarily in negative form, especially the ability to evade the institutional or political pressures exerted by a contemporary audience.[64] This view of writing goes hand in hand with a view of "posterity" as an undefined mass, significant only in the sense that these readers are not contemporary readers

---

62. It is worth noting again that the effect I seek to illuminate here has often been approached by attempting to sort out fictional scenes of "original" performance from nonfictional. There is an inherent difficulty in this approach; as many scholars have shown, it is impossible in principle to separate so-called ocular deixis (referring to objects present to speaker and addressee) from so-called fictional deixis or *energeia* on the basis of the poem text itself without external evidence (e.g., Lowrie 2009a, 95–97 et passim, and Hardie 2002, 5–6 et passim; Calame 2004, while still arguing on the basis of pragmatic context that Hellenistic deixis is "fictional"). Even beyond this evidentiary issue, I believe that such an approach also fails to capture what is most important—not the question of whether the events depicted really happened, but the way such scenes function within the system of the poem.

63. And not only poems in book-roll collections; Furley (in a 2014 review of Day) casts doubt on the assumption that an inscribed epigram can be read as the trace of an original performance: "We know next to nothing about the rites accompanying the dedication of such statuary. For all we know there was no ceremony at all, let alone a religious service, with priest, prayer, libation, and so on, which D[ay] assumes. The artisan may simply have created the votive object and erected it for his client in the given sanctuary without further ado. In other words, the rationale of the votive may have been to *show to posterity* what a pious and successful person so-and-so had been" (2014, 85; emphasis in original).

64. "Hellenistic poets can deflect the problems associated with the position of the poet by placing a prominent narrator in the way, one who is both like and unlike the author" (Morrison 2007, 16). Lowrie persistently describes writing as "decontextualized," e.g., "Actual performance aligns notionally with performative discourse because both concern utterance in context. Decontextualization through writing blocks an utterance's potency, or at least alters it. Removed from its context, a prayer becomes a representation rather than the thing itself. Each has different sorts of cultural power" (2009a, 81). As her argument unfolds, the specific form of cultural power that writing possesses never gets worked out in a positive formulation, only the negative formulation of evasion, e.g., "Horace invariably sidesteps immediacy. This feature gives his poetry aesthetic independence and keeps it from embracing fully the occasional moment. The utterance of *Odes* 4.5 cannot be imagined in lived time and space. Rather, the distance involved in speaking to Augustus while absent accords with writing" (92). Also 215–17 et passim.

whom the authors would have known or who exerted political power. My model, by contrast, posits that although (in fact, *because*) the authors had no idea who these later readers would be or what their world would look like, they believe that the eventual reception of their work by such readers has real traction. Again, their own experience of being the readers unimagined by Greek authors gives this seemingly vague notion of unknowable future readers a very intimate aspect. In contrast to Michèle Lowrie's claim that writing is "decontextualized," I suggest that the communication that happens in writing does have a context, but it is a context the writer cannot predict. While archaic performed poetry may imagine immortality as an unending series of performances by a culturally uniform posterity, the Roman poets are spurred on by the tantalizing possibility that immortality could consist of having readers who transcend their imagination.[65]

The implications for reading Latin first-person poetry are substantial. First, let me be clear that I am not assuming that Latin poets (or other Roman readers) were availing themselves of any specific history/theory of performed Greek poetry; their own experience as readers would be enough to establish the powers that this poetry exerted, even when its Roman readers were distant from the specific events and personalities depicted. My argument is not that Latin poets had something like the perception of bifurcated functions that I have outlined here, but that they had the poems themselves that offered (seemingly without intending to do so) a glimpse into the inaccessible past and at the same time made meaningful contact with any and all readers.

The upshot is that we should reexamine our assumption that Roman poets are trying to work the same magic as their archaic Greek models, to re-create the aura of an original performance and to minimize later audiences' consciousness of the distance between their own cultural context and that of the poetic speaker before his own audience. Roman poets produced new poems not on the pattern of the original performed poems, but on the pattern of such poems as they themselves received them, poems that depict a speaker engaged with his/her own immediate world even while the poem as a whole reaches out to readers who have no foothold in that represented world.[66]

---

65. Among the many factors that might influence such a choice, it may also be relevant that Rome in the first century is a society in which cultural and political power is very much associated with writing (see, e.g., Meyer 2004; Habinek 1998, esp. chap. 4). Imperial power is sustained through writing, which activates authority over geographical, chronological, and cultural distance.

66. Cf. Barchiesi (2009, 421–22): "Horace develops a paradox that was already inherent in the tradition of lyric reperformance: by invoking Aphrodite with the words of, say, Alcman or Pindar, the speaker is both impersonating the author and distancing himself from the *origo* of the enunciation."

How might this recognition change the way we read Latin first-person poetry? It is not just a question of describing a poetic practice, but of reorienting assumptions and attitudes that have ossified around old conceptions. The comparison of oral to literate poetry has been guided by the assumption that to say that a poem represents a scene rather than reenacts a scene is to consign it to the status of an aesthetic also-ran. Words like "distant," "cold," and—in a certain code—"literary" are used to describe the representational nature of such a poem and to contrast it to the warm life assumed to be pulsing through poetry that reenacts an original communicative act.[67] (Those who can, do; those who can't, represent.) The mistake here, I think, is to imagine that in saying that a poem represents a scene, we are saying that it is merely autotelic and does not participate in any communication at all, while in fact this claim just acknowledges that the relevant communication is taking place between poet and reader *through* the poem rather than between the represented speaker and addressee *in* the poem. As my epigraph from Don Fowler reminds us, emotional engagement with art does not require aesthetic naïveté.

The fact that Roman poets read earlier Greek poetry in written collections has yet another consequence for their conception of poetic communication. The I-voice of the poems in a written collection may occupy center stage, but it coexists with another expressive agent: the editor, who leaves his fingerprints on the collection even though his voice is nowhere in evidence. Like the speaker, this agent too is aligned with the poet, but in this case the alignment is exact, since the historical poet is really the person responsible for the arrangement and publication of the poems. In contrast to the collections of earlier Greek poetry made by the Alexandrian editors, Latin poets are the editors of their own collections.[68] Further, the editorial motivation echoes the only authorial intention that we can reliably assume: the intention to offer these words as poems.

---

67. Dupont (1999) is a very visible spokesperson for this approach. Culler's (2015) insistence on lyric as epideixis rather than mimesis, although informed by a very different model of literary history and proposing that lyric acts rather than reenacts, could be lined up here as well. Good critiques of the romanticized contrast between Greek immediacy and Roman secondariness can be found in, e.g., Lowrie (2009a), Barchiesi (2009), Feeney (1998).

68. We will probably never have certainty as to which parts of the Catullan corpus were structured as collections by the author and circulated in that form. We can, however, have a high degree of confidence that he did organize and circulate some collection(s) in his own lifetime. For an overview that takes into account the intellectual history of the question, see Skinner (2011); for a view that is more skeptical about Catullus's own editorial control of the collection as we have it, see Kennedy (2014).

As other scholars have noted, poetic collections pivot between offering each poem as an autonomous work (i.e., its presence in the collection is merely a convenience) and offering each poem as an element of the collection, creating a tension between whether we see the individual poems or the collection as the "work of art."[69] In the Hellenistic collections of archaic poetry, the structure tends to preserve the autonomy of the separate poems, since in fact the poems predate the collection and had an independent life before they were collected. On the other hand, in Hellenistic and Roman single-authored collections the poems and the collection come into being together, and neither one holds either logical or temporal priority over the other. These later collections, then, allow for readings that accent the collection as a designed whole as well as readings that accent the individual poems.[70]

What is important for my argument is the fact that because of the prestigious example set by collections of archaic poetry, to accent the autonomy of the poems is tantamount to claiming that the poems predate the collection and even, to push the analogy further, that the poems arise within a world other than that in which the collection is made. (This impression is virtually equivalent to "story": the sense that the speaker's words existed and had meaning in their own world before they came into the assemblage of the text.) And yet, as those collections circulated and shaped later generations' understanding of Greek poetry, they fostered a new form of reception that was conditioned by the combination of the individual poems and the implied editorial impulse that brought them together. When Latin poets read archaic Greek lyric in such collections, they found poems that preserved their original addressive structure and single-minded focus on *hic et nunc*, but as readers they were also recipients of the editorial act, which issued from an agent other than the poem's speaker and which embodied the intention to offer these words as a form of contact with readers.[71] As a

---

69. See, e.g., Hinds (1996): "The collected poem is doubly framed, finding one set of contexts as a single bounded poem which may encode a time, a place, an addressee, and another set of contexts as its boundary dissolves into the larger unit of the book, calling the primacy of those points of reference into question and acknowledging larger worlds of reception which may always have been implied within the poem's occasionality." The 2001 publication of a papyrus containing part of a collection of Posidippus's epigrams has reinvigorated the debates about how such collections were organized. The essays of Gutzwiller (2005) provide an excellent entry point.

70. Again, a point well formulated and demonstrated in Krevans (1984).

71. It may be that this model was also operative for Hellenistic Greek poets, though, if so, it very likely would have taken a somewhat different form. As Krevans (1984, 105) points out, Rome "was a profoundly 'bookish' culture, more so even than Alexandria because books were accepted at Rome as the natural vehicle for literature, whereas Alexandria had a self-conscious fascination with the novelty of written literature."

result, these poets had a model for poetry that oriented itself toward future readers without representing either readerly reception or editorial agency visibly in the poem.

This, then, is what I mean by claiming that Latin first-person poems offer addressive scenes "framed" by their status as poems and, especially, as poems in a written collection. I am not suggesting that consciousness of the frame always dominates the reader's experience of the poem, but that understanding the frame can help us to articulate more precisely how the scene of oral communication operates in written poems and also the partial alignment we see between speaker and poet.

Overview of *I, the Poet*

A key principle that I will demonstrate in the following chapters is that both the degree of alignment between speaker and poet and, even more so, the basis on which that alignment is asserted have radical effects on the ultimate form, tone, and impact of various kinds of poems. (For example, creating this alignment by accenting the speaker's consciousness of poetic form is very different from doing so by referring to events contemporary with the historical author.) In the next two chapters I will focus on analyzing two particularly striking ways of positioning the agency of the poet in relation to the speech and events depicted in the storyworld. Each of these models represents an asymptote, which we can use to describe tendencies in individual poems; I am not proposing a taxonomy, in which each poem would be neatly slotted into one category or another.

The first pattern I will examine is one that quite strongly segregates the poet's artistic motivations from those of the speaker by heightening the sense that the speaker is reacting to his immediate context and minimizing his consciousness of the poetic status of his words. Poems structured on this model may or may not give a full picture of storyworld events, but the speaker's language tends to highlight features like questions and imperatives (which indicate a focus on engaging with his interlocutor) or shorter and simpler sentences (as if the speaker is trying to make his point before being interrupted or resisted). I call this model "conversational," not because its style is particularly colloquial, but because it situates the speaker's language as an attempt to meet needs in his social and emotional environment. Significantly, such poems exhibit a high degree of artistic polish and thus offer ample evidence of the poet's artistic agency and motivations, but these discursive features are not linked to the speaker's agency in the storyworld. The overall effect, then, makes clear the distance between the speaker's wholehearted focus on his own world and the poet's careful orchestration of the poetic discourse, thus expressing structurally the distinction between speaker and poet, in spite of the first-person form and in spite of the speaker's characterization as a poet. The poems I take as most forcefully demonstrating this model are those of Propertius's first book; I will also more briefly review Catullus's handling of address to show that while it is "conversational" in a loose sense, it does not have the same effects as Propertius's practice.

The second model I explore is one that hews more closely to the norms established by traditional performed poetry. In this case the speaker knows that his words have the special status of poetry, and his speech may be formulated with an eye to audiences other than the named interlocutor(s). In contrast to the speaker of conversational poems, who is focused on trying to exert his will through speech, the speaker in this performative model embodies the mastery of poetic form and the assurance granted to an authorized performer. In substance, his speech comes closer to what Culler calls lyric's "epideictic" function ("presentations of assertions or judgments that are not relativized to a particular speaker or fictional situation but offered as truths about the world," 2015, 35) than to the more conversational attempts to intervene in a specific situation. Poems built on this model are more likely to exhibit formal features that thematize the special status of address (such as extended vocative phrases) or that require suspension of thought (especially hyperbaton and hypotaxis) or that highlight the poem's overall structure (such as anaphora and parallelism). We can easily see how the agency of such a speaker echoes the agency of the poet crafting the text. The more detailed analysis in my second chapter will show, however, that these two figures are not completely aligned and that this partial alignment can play out in a variety of ways. The two main cases I study are Catullus's invective poems and Horace's hymns and dedicatory poems. In Catullus, the form of verbal performance invoked is one that is deemed to have social effect, with the folk ritual of *flagitatio* as its most extreme form. Horace, on the other hand, uses the image of hymnic performance to gesture toward poetry's ritual authority while simultaneously establishing that his own odes find their grounding in the context of reading.

After these two chapters have set the stage by surveying two different ways that "story" can be oriented to discourse, chapter 3 ("Poetry that Says 'Ego'") applies these findings to a particularly thorny problem: How should we interpret the fact that these authors invent first-person speakers who share their creators' names and vocations? From what I have said so far in this introduction, it will be clear that I don't think the answer to this question is to be found somewhere on the continuum of fictional to nonfictional. Instead, I use the previous chapters' discussions to illuminate how, in various ways, the speaking voice within the text can be separated from or aligned with the historical poet who crafts the text. Again, I analyze a subset of each author's work to allow for greater focus. For Propertius, I pin down more precisely the well-recognized shift in the characterization of the Ego from book 1 to book 2.[72] For Catullus, I analyze his ability to deploy both internal (i.e., centered on the speaker's experience) and external (i.e., centered on the poet's experience) perspectives in the poems that treat poetry and its reception, including famous examples such as poems 1 ("Cui dono"), 16 ("Pedicabo ego vos"), and 22 ("Suffenus iste"). For Horace, I explain how his representations of the symposium, the performance venue most woven into social life, take on special significance in defining the image of the historical poet within the poem and the corpus.

All three of the chapters described so far are focused on poetry that features the representation of speech (either conversational or performed) in the storyworld. The final chapter turns instead to poems that represent storyworld communication as written rather than spoken and thus raise a different set of questions about how this storyworld communication relates to the poetic discourse. A written collection of poetry was by no means radical and new in the days of Catullus, Propertius, and Horace, and yet it still was a phenomenon that starkly distanced these poets from some of the most important models in the literary tradition. In an ironic twist, the representation of their poetry as a written form of communication brings the Roman poets back closer to the situation of the archaic Greek lyrists, since in both cases the form in which the poem reaches its extended audience is echoed in the storyworld. In this chapter, I focus on Catullus's epistolary poems and the poems of Horace's first book of *Epistles*; each poet shines a spotlight on how the written form can be perceived as mediating between communicative partners.

In a brief epilogue, I sketch out a test case of how the principles I have delineated by focusing on Catullus, Propertius, and Horace might apply to a poet of the next generation. The exile poetry of Ovid uses the conventions earlier authors developed, by which the circuit of communication depicted in the poetry is framed by an implicit acknowledgment of the communication

---

72. E.g., Wyke (2002, 48): "the beloved's capacity to captivate begins the first book of Propertian elegies, but the next opens with a consideration of her role in the practice of writing. The elegiac man is now explicitly both lover and writer, the elegiac woman both beloved and narrative material."

between poet and reader, but in a body of poetry in which the stakes of both kinds of communication are almost impossibly high. The *Tristia* (from which I discuss only a few selections) present themselves as earnest attempts to use poetry to bring about the author's recall from exile (or at least to voice his complaints to allies), but are shaped just as strongly by the consciousness that they are, in effect, documenting his experience of political repression for readers of the future.

Finally, a few disclaimers as to the scope, aim, and design of this project. First, I am not arguing that the style of reading I advocate here provides a skeleton key for unlocking all first-person Latin poems, and not even all the poems in the collections I am focusing on. My goal in this book is, first, to show that there are valid reasons to consider the tension between "story" and discourse for poems of this type and, second, to offer examples of how such readings might proceed. This style of reading will add more to the understanding of some poems than of others, and even in the cases where it works best the resulting analyses are not meant to correct or substitute for other readings these poems have attracted, but to stand alongside them and enlarge the range of tactics we can use in approaching these poems. Further, my readings focus almost exclusively on formal and structural analyses rather than on the kind of thematic interpretation that is more familiar; again, I see my reading strategy not as an attempt to displace thematic readings but as a tool that can be used to produce and refine such readings.

With this aim in mind, it has seemed sensible to me to focus on only a few collections, and I have chosen three collections that offer an optimum balance of similarity (first-person poetry with central speakers prominently identified as poets) and difference (Horace, Propertius, and Catullus differ both in obvious features such as meter and style and in the more subjective aspect of "tone"). I realize that each reader will be able to think of several poets or collections (most obviously Ovid, Tibullus, Sulpicia, Statius, Martial, Virgil's *Eclogues*, Horace's other collections) whose exclusion from consideration here borders on the perverse. I understand that there would be benefits in organizing this book as a much more wide-ranging overview of how various poets make use of "story" and discourse.[73] I have opted instead for the benefits of multidimensional readings of a smaller set of poems: because

---

73. Roman (2014) exemplifies the benefits of a study organized around a broad chronological and generic sweep. Its analysis of the "autonomist rhetoric" in Latin poetry (i.e., a rhetoric that defines the value of poetry as disembedded from political/social life, not as it serves political, social, moral, etc. ends) overlaps to some degree with the questions I ask here, though from a thematic rather than formal perspective.

I am dipping back into the same collections (and sometimes even returning to the same poems) in different chapters, each poet and each collection is seen from several different angles.

And why these three authors? Beyond their obvious claims to centrality (all three were extremely influential in their own time and for later ages), Catullus, Horace, and Propertius offer distinctive and thought-provoking forays into the terrain of first-person poetry. Although they cannot stand in for the whole range of first-person poetry in Latin, these three authors and the specific parts of their corpora that I focus on here can give us illuminating examples of three different ways first-person poems make use of the relation between the depicted scene and the poem's overall communicative act. These three authors are broadly similar (writing short "personal" addressive poems), and their working lives collectively span a period of less than fifty years, but each one has a distinctive approach to the challenge of adapting traditional first-person forms to the new world of readers and writers.[74]

As my readings will show, there is significant variation even within the sets of poems I analyze from each author, but still we can see that Catullus's polymetrics, Horace's *Odes* (and the first book of *Epistles*), and Propertius's first two books develop distinctive approaches. Much more detail will emerge in the course of the book, but a rough outline can be constructed. Catullus and Horace each develop a way of bringing the speaker close to the position/agency of the historical poet. Catullus draws the figure of the historical poet into the storyworld, largely by making the storyworld reflect the contemporary realities of literary composition and reception. Horace, conversely, accentuates the discursive rather than "story"-based aspects of his representations and thus draws the speaker outward toward the historical poet. Propertius pursues a series of different strategies: in his first book, he emphatically splits the agency of the beleaguered speaker from that of the poet, but in his second book the speaker comes closer to the position of the poet, using the storyworld as a source of exempla rather than being

---

74. One familiar way of registering the broad similarities and specific differences among these corpora has been to invoke genre, as anchored by choice of meter, diction, etc. While genre studies offer great potential, too often this pursuit has proven somewhat circular, defining the genre by examining the characteristics of the poems and then using that definition as a framework in which to explain the poems. There is also a danger that this approach flattens out the poetic landscape by focusing on what is predictable or "normal" rather than on ways that individual poems or whole corpora may be departing from those norms. My investigation, which recognizes genre as a creative force but does not grant it explanatory power, is intended to complement genre studies, not replace them.

caught in its toils.[75] But, again, this very broad summary misses much of what is most interesting in the push-and-pull between various forces that we see play out in the poems themselves, and thus it will be that more fine-grained analysis that will be at the heart of this book.

---

75. The third book doubles down on the strategy of the second book. Obviously, Propertius's fourth book goes furthest in exploring new possibilities for the (non)alignment of speaker and poet; although the fourth book will not come in for analysis here, I believe that the argument I am making about Propertius's earlier books and about Latin first-person poetry more generally can shed light on that unusual collection.

 Chapter 1

Poetry as Conversation

Two adjoining poems at the end of Horace's first book of odes begin this way:

> Nunc est bibendum, nunc pede libero
> pulsanda tellus, nunc Saliaribus
>   ornare pulvinar deorum
>   tempus erat dapibus, sodales.
>   (*Horace* 1.37.1–4)

Now is the time to drink, to strike the earth with a free foot, now is the time to deck the couch of the gods with banquets fit for Salian priests, my friends.

> Persicos odi, puer, adparatus,
> displicent nexae philyra coronae,
> mitte sectari, rosa quo locorum
>   sera moretur.
>   (*Horace* 1.38.1–4)

I hate Persian ornaments, boy; garlands woven with lime bark don't appeal to me; stop seeking out the places where the late rose lingers.

Both poems are solidly lodged in the sympotic traditions of lyric, and both opening stanzas accentuate that tradition by giving instructions as to how one should properly celebrate such an event. Note that both openings also adhere to our expectations in explicitly invoking an addressee: fellow revelers ("sodales," line 4) in the first case and a single slave attendant in the latter. But most readers would not be tempted to say that these poems are very similar.[1] Poem 1.37 positions itself as a celebratory song and marshals all its lyric force to mark the specialness of the occasion: both the specialness of the historical occasion (Cleopatra's defeat at Actium) and the specialness of the sympotic moment in which this defeat will be registered with semiritualized drinking and singing and dancing. The insistent repetition of "nunc" in this opening stanza underlines the notion that the poem arises in an unrepeatable moment, the very pitch of historical significance and of personal significance. Poem 1.38, on the other hand, presents a situation in which the speaker seems unconscious of the momentousness of his words. This poem seeks to express the essence of a most ordinary pleasure, an afternoon drink in the shade. The moment it depicts is special only in the sense that it successfully embodies the tranquility and familiarity of all such moments. The second (and final) stanza of this poem will go on to tell us that common myrtle, a plant to be found in any garden but also sacred to Venus, is "not unfitting" ("neque . . . / dedecet," lines 6–7) for both the master and the slave in this solitary, stripped-down symposium. The role of the slave as addressee here further accentuates the poem's distance from the idealized symposium depicted in poem 1.37, where the sympotic term of art "sodales" properly stands in the vocative;[2] here, by positioning the slave as addressee, the poem calls attention to the basic implements on which functioning of the symposium depends, but which are deemed not worthy of notice in the more idealizing kind of sympotic poem.

The contrasts between these poems are surprising to no one with even a minimal familiarity with Horace's corpus, but the differences have usually been described as the contrast between public and private, between grand civic affairs on the one hand and the pleasures of drinking and love on the other.[3] This description is accurate, as is the consensus that the juxtaposition of these

---

1. The stark contrast of these two poems as a closural gesture for the first book has been often commented upon. See, e.g., Lyne (1995, 86–87).

2. See Habinek (2005, chap. 2) on "sodalis" as the technical term for a fellow symposiast, with implications for ritual effects.

3. Lyne (1995, 86–87); Murray (1993, 95) describes poem 1.38 as in keeping with the Anacreontic tradition, but acquiring Callimachean programmatic effects by means of its position in the book.

two poems at the end of the first book makes a programmatic point about the range of the collection and its author. But there is more to be explored here in the contrast between the songlike speech of poem 1.37 and the instructions of a master to a slave in poem 1.38. This difference is not primarily a difference of stylistic level, but a difference in the ways that the two poems position "story" in relation to discourse: in poem 1.37 the ritual aspects of the speaker's words make them function as poetry / song even in their storyworld instantiation, while in poem 1.38, the poem performs a kind of translation, rendering the master's offhand instructions for the slave as a poem for readers. Significantly, this translation from conversation to poetry also imbues the poem with metapoetic meaning and promotes a claim about aesthetics that operates at the level of poet and reader, not between the master and slave depicted.[4] The next chapter will explore more fully the performative model embodied in poem 1.37, while this chapter will focus on the conversational model seen in poem 1.38.

Part of the pleasure offered by ancient first-person poetry is the sense of being a "fly on the wall," as the poem allows us access to a moment of social interchange in the speaker's world. But it is less often acknowledged that this access covers a spectrum from the public performance of a song for listeners to the most private words imaginable, whispered to a lover or perhaps even to oneself. In distinguishing between the performative and the conversational, we should pay attention to features that imply the presence or absence of an audience in the storyworld and to features that mark the storyworld speech as special, as an authoritative performance rather than as conversational speech that must contend with the ebb and flow of social exchange.

I want to stress that the distinction in technique between the performative and the conversational rests wholly in the different relations they construct between "story" and discourse: this is not a distinction between stylistic registers (formal vs. informal), nor is the conversational technique an attempt to produce a convincing "realistic" illusion of everyday speech. In the performative mode, the speaker is positioned as the source of the poem's discourse, while the conversational mode implies that the words of the represented speaker are molded into poetry by an external agent, the poet. A quick look at the language of poem 1.38 will dispel any notion that this poem is meant to represent the way that masters ordinarily issue a command to their slaves. Only eight lines long, this poem amply demonstrates the artful hyperbaton and compression that prompted Nietzsche to describe Horace's odes as

---

4. This metapoetic reading has been especially well articulated in Fitzgerald (2000, 28–30).

"mosaics of words" (1889, 105). Further, the poem makes full use of its apparently mundane setting and content to generate a subtle metapoetic comment on style, summing up the value of simplicity and decorum, in short, of knowing when enough is enough.[5]

What I hope to show by emphasizing both the stylistic and thematic complexity of poem 1.38 is that poems that use the conversational technique are not necessarily more colloquial than poems that use the performative technique, nor are they more "narrative," that is, encouraging readers to pay attention to the storyworld for its own sake rather than for its thematic effects. The signal difference that the conversational technique introduces is that it constructs a speaker who is unaware of both the style of the discourse and the thematic freight of his words. The poet, not the speaker, is the agent to whom we owe the design of the discourse. While the songlike elaboration of performative poems aligns the storyworld speaker with the poet, the speaker in conversational poems is entirely focused on making something happen in his own world—in this case, to get the slave to bring him the right kind of garland. Like a character in a play, the speaker pronounces the words that his immediate situation prompts, not realizing that an audience will receive these words and interpret them as part of a larger artistic production.[6] For example, many of this poem's thematic effects depend on its position as last in the book,[7] a feature that clearly points to the designing hand of the poet-editor rather than to any bard-like skill on the part of the speaker.

Once we recognize that conversational poems attribute the discourse to the poet, separable from the speaker, other important implications become clear. In a performative poem the storyworld speech is "already" a poem (or song); its

---

5. This poem could also be read as an ironically deflated claim of poetic achievement, in answer to the spectacular image that ended the first poem in this book. Joe Farrell has pointed out to me (in conversation) this poem's ironic echo of the end of 1.1. There the speaker (emphatically identified as a poet) asks Maecenas to include him among the number of lyric bards, with which elevation he would strike his head on the stars; here the speaker (not identified as a poet) asks a slave boy for a garland of myrtle, as simple a crown as possible.

6. This analogy is not merely illustrative. It makes clear how the poems I am designating as "conversational" are similar to the subgenre of lyric that has been called "dramatic monologue." Dramatic monologue differs from what is usually called lyric both because the speaker is specified to be someone other than the poet and because the speech is given more storyworld context and motivation. Thus, this category can help us to clarify the form of first-person poetry I am describing here, but with the caveat that in the poems I am studying the speaker is not explicitly designated as different from the poet. See discussion of Horace *Epode* 2 in the previous chapter and, on dramatic monologue, esp. Tucker (2014).

7. See Lowrie (1997, 164–74) for a full analysis. Cf. Barchiesi (2009) on the effects of the opening position of *Ode* 4.1 in relation to Sappho 1.

presence in a poetic book mirrors the historical process by which real archaic lyric came to be collected and offered to readers. A conversational poem has no such alibi for its presence in a collection or even for its existence as a poem, since the speaker's speech to the addressee would be in prose and is aimed at practical and social goals in the storyworld. This fundamental difference between the two types implies that the speaker in performative poems is closely aligned with the poet of the collection, as a maker of special, authoritative speech intended for audiences, while in conversational poems we must mentally supply an intervening agent who has transformed the speaker's storyworld speech into a poem and offered it to an audience, and thus this form implies a gap between the speaker and the poet.[8]

The most important quality of conversational poems is the fact that they open a visible gap between the storyworld and the poem-as-discourse, and this gap has the potential to create a new position for readers, from which we can perceive the for-us aspects of the poem alongside the not-for-us aspects. In poems like the Cleopatra ode, the poetic speaker is performing before his fellow symposiasts. This is certainly a social occasion, but the symposium is a very special kind of social occasion, one that provides a home for performance within the interstices of everyday social intercourse. Perhaps this is why the symposium and the genre of lyric were so closely and so productively linked throughout ancient literary history, continuing long after the demise of the lyre as an accompaniment. The fact that the sympotic singer is performing for others makes it less strange that s/he is also performing for us, the readers; in effect, we are allowed a virtual presence on those couches, crowded around the flowing wine bowl. In conversational poems like poem 1.38, however, the situation is very different. This poem does everything in its power to emphasize that the master's command to the slave is not a self-conscious performance for an audience: it has a slave addressee (one before whom—according to slaveholding ideology—there is no need for performance or making an impression); it shapes its speech as a command, a form of speech that accentuates the instrumental function of language in getting things done rather than language's expressive or aesthetic effects; and, most significantly, it represents an apparently solitary symposiast, a figure that is a contradiction in terms since this cultural institution is precisely a form of gathering (as both the Greek *symposium*

---

8. My formulation of this principle is parallel to Krevans's (1984) notion of the "poet as editor," i.e., the poet not represented as speaker within the poem but operating on the poem from outside. It is significant that this role comes into being with the practice of composing poetic books, in which the book as a whole is an artistic product.

and the Latin *con*vivium mark with their prefixes).[9] In poem 1.37, we may be able to imagine ourselves as uninvited guests who can slip in unnoticed, but here our presence in the scene would be nothing other than intrusion. This tiny final poem of book 1, then, offers a good example of the way that the speaker in conversational poems is more fully enclosed in his/her own world—the storyworld—and not only unconscious of our presence as readers (as indeed the speaker of poem 1.37 also is unconscious of us), but also unconscious of him/herself as a performer. The convivial setting of the Cleopatra ode blurs the boundary between the storyworld performance (which is not-for-us) and the poem's engagement with readers (clearly for-us), while the slight conversational poem that follows sharpens the boundary between these two aspects of the poem.

Stylistically, what sets apart conversational poems is not colloquial diction or syntax, but the poem's ability to mimic language in the wild, as it confronts distractions, resistance, and even the agreement of interlocutors. The fact that these poems can gesture toward potential distractions and interruptions brings out clearly their position, teetering between special and ordinary: if they constituted a special performance, a space would be cleared for them and the speaker's right to continue would be unquestioned; if they were a fragment of ordinary speech, then they would not have all the attributes of poetic discourse (e.g., meter, hyperbaton). Although it has not been remarked upon as often as other aspects of the lyric mode (e.g., single voice, attention to the musical aspects of language), I think we should include the sense of assured continuity as a marker of lyric.[10] The conversational technique allows poems simultaneously to depict the matrix of social pressures into which the speech inserts itself and to resist the disintegrating force of those pressures.

I have begun this discussion with examples from Horace's *Odes*, both because these two adjacent poems so clearly demonstrate the contrast and to show that even though Horace does not foreground the conversational

---

9. Strictly speaking, the poem does not exclude the possibility of other guests, but it would be odd to make no mention of them and to state the propriety of the garland only for "me . . . bibentem" (lines 7–8). The contrast with Catullus 27 (another very short poem addressed to a slave attendant: "Minister vetuli puer Falerni") makes it clear that if Horace wanted to gesture toward the presence of other guests he could have done so even within the confines of two stanzas.

10. Lowrie (1997, 25–26) points to this possibility but does not pursue it fully. In giving evidence to support Culler's notion of the unnatural quality of apostrophe (as Lowrie paraphrases it, "we cannot invent a natural context into which to erase the fictitiousness of the utterance. . . . Lyric resists narrative and resists naturalization"), she takes as an example Horace's *Ode* 1.8 ("Lydia dic per omnis") and comments "can we imagine his saying the whole poem without interruption . . . ? I, for one, cannot."

mode as forcefully as Propertius and Catullus do, it still is a meaningful element in his poetic palette. There are certainly other Horatian odes that could usefully be analyzed in this chapter,[11] but in the interest of focus I will concentrate instead on Propertius's first book and end the chapter with a brief excursus on Catullus. Catullus's man-about-town persona might seem to be the most obvious example of how poetry models itself on conversation, but as I show in detail in the next chapter, many of his poems that center on address (and especially on aggressive address) are designed to show the speaker in control of the discourse, and so offer an example of the performative technique rather than the conversational.

Conversation in Propertius Book 1

How does Propertius establish this idea that the poems are thoroughly embedded in the social life of the storyworld and that they allow the reader to peek into moments of private life? The conversational technique that I want to explore here cannot be reduced to a set of concrete markers, but it will be helpful to examine some explanatory examples from poems that foreground this strategy more starkly than others. Rather than thinking of colloquialism or a low stylistic level as the marker of the conversational, it is more useful to think of conversational poems as highlighting the speaker's attempt to get and hold the attention of his interlocutor. For that reason, we often see what I will call *ego–tu* links, namely, a pattern of interwoven first- and second-person finite verbs and deictics (personal pronouns, possessive adjectives, and demonstratives such as "hic" and "iste"). Also striking are frequent questions, exclamations, and imperatives, that is, expressive forms that foreground the speaker's desire to affect the events and emotions of the storyworld. Sentences tend to be shorter and simpler, with less hypotaxis—a speaker who is worried about being interrupted will not launch into a three-couplet sequence of parallel clauses. In addition to these discursive features, such poems also often establish the conversational mode at the level of "story" by including a backward glance toward the history shared by speaker and addressee, by filling out the particular identities of the speaker and addressee, and in general by alluding more specifically to events.

Two adjacent poems in Propertius's first book illustrate how superficially similar poems can differ significantly in the degree to which they employ the

---

11. E.g. 2.17 ("Cur me querelis exanimas tuis?"), 1.11 ("Tu ne quaesieris"), 3.7 ("Quid fles, Asterie").

conversational technique. Poems 1.13 and 1.14 both begin emphatically with
"Tu," but as this opening is developed, the two poems diverge.

Tu, quod saepe soles, nostro laetabere casu,
    Galle, quod abrepto solus amore vacem.
at non ipse tuas imitabor, perfide, voces:
    fallere te numquam, Galle, puella velit.

(Propertius 1.13.1–4)

You, as usual, will take pleasure in my trouble, Gallus, because my love
has been stolen from me and I am left alone. But I won't imitate your
talk, faithless man: Gallus, may no girl ever wish to deceive you.

Tu licet abiectus Tiberina molliter unda
    Lesbia Mentoreo vina bibas opere,
et modo tam celeris mireris currere lintres
    et modo tam tardas funibus ire rates;
et nemus omne satas intendat vertice silvas,   5
    urgetur quantis Caucasus arboribus;
non tamen ista meo valeant contendere amori:
    nescit Amor magnis cedere divitiis.

(Propertius 1.14.1–8)

Though you lie stretched out comfortably by the Tiber stream and
drink fine Lesbian wine from Mentorean[12] cups; and though you marvel
sometimes at the little boats as they run so swiftly and sometimes at the
barges towed so slowly with ropes; and though the whole grove stretches
out its landscaped woods with trees as tall as those by which the Caucasus
is burdened—still, all that is not strong enough to compete against my
love: Amor knows nothing of giving way before great wealth.

The opening couplets of 1.13, addressed to Gallus, give a very strong sense
of the personalities of the speaker and interlocutor and also of the events
that have led up to this moment. These lines set the speaker and addressee
in close relation to each other—both are players in the game of love and
they might even echo one another ("imitabor," line 3), though the speaker
chooses to reject this possibility. The discourse underscores this mutuality
and mirroring by closely weaving together first- and second-person forms
(verb forms, possessive adjectives, pronouns, e.g., "tu . . . soles," "nostro

---

12. Refers to the famous fourth-century silversmith, Mentor.

laetabere," "ipse tuas imitabor").[13] Such *ego–tu* links not only heighten our consciousness of the two people involved, but also echo the pragmatic use of deixis in real conversation, where speakers often use themselves and their interlocutors as touchstones. In addition, Propertius uses vocative forms here three times in two couplets ("Galle" in lines 2 and 4, "perfide" in line 3), in this respect outdoing even other poems of the conversational type.[14] These opening couplets also quite emphatically use a "backward glance" to establish a temporal framework for this exchange, gesturing toward the past these two characters share ("quod saepe soles," line 1) as well as toward the future (the speaker's wish in line 4). Further, the sentences in these couplets are relatively short. Although the first sentence makes use of subordination, it does so in a loose, seemingly ad hoc way (e.g., the first and second "quod" have different grammatical functions). The second sentence avoids subordination in favor of parataxis. There are no obvious instances of parallelism, anaphora, or using the metrical structure to accentuate certain words or phrases. (Perhaps "perfide" occupying the fifth foot of line 3 would qualify as emphatic, but this is the only candidate.)

Turning to poem 1.14, we notice striking contrasts. Although the poem goes to great lengths to describe its addressee, it does so in a remarkably impersonal way. Beyond the important fact that the addressee is not named until line 20 of a twenty-four-line poem, we should note that the poem tells us nothing of the history between speaker and addressee, nor does it describe any events that might have led up to this speech or any specific outcome the speaker hopes to achieve. In fact, we get little sense in this poem of a scene or context within which it might be spoken.

The design of the discourse also differs conspicuously from that of poem 1.13. These eight lines form a single long sentence, defined not only by a high degree of hypotaxis, but even more obviously by careful parallelism and anaphora that bring the rhetorical and metrical structures into high relief. It begins with three clauses of subjunctive verbs dependent on "licet," with internal parallelism of two infinitive phrases dependent on "mireris" (3),

---

13. Such links may seem completely unremarkable in Propertius and in other first-person corpora, but closer examination shows that many individual poems and collections have a significantly lower frequency than we see here. Note that poem 1.14 also fronts its second-person address, and does include some second-person verb forms ("bibas," "mireris"), but it contains no possessive adjectives, adverbs of place or time, or first-person forms of any kind down to "meo . . . amori" in line 7, a line that is specifically designed to mark a contrast ("tamen") with what has come before. It is also striking that even within this second-person address, Propertius arranges the syntax to minimize the occurrence of second-person verb forms (and again in lines 7–8 similarly avoids first-person constructions: "non . . . ista . . . valeant . . . nescit Amor").

14. Gallus is addressed in the vocative yet again at line 16 for an unusually high frequency.

marked out by the emphatic anaphora of "et modo tam" (3–4); the third member expands and varies the pattern (as is common in tricolon structures) by shifting to a third-person verb ("intendat") and describes the scene itself rather than Tullus, thus increasing the universalizing impact of these opening lines. The fourth couplet finally resolves the syntactical suspension (hanging from the "licet" in line 1 to "tamen" in line 7) and completes the thought, rounding off this imagined scene with a personification of Amor (cf. the more concrete usage "abrepto . . . amore" at 1.13.2). The very suspension of thought produced by expanding the "licet" clause at great length before resolving the thought with "tamen" is linked to a nonconversational style, since it implies that the speaker believes himself to be granted the time and authority to develop this thought without interruption.[15]

While poem 1.13 illustrates the features that make a poem feel conversational, poem 1.14 can help us gain insight into the large number of first-person Latin poems that are not strongly marked as either conversational or performative. This poem aligns itself with traditional poetic practice inherited from the Greeks; it modifies that practice, but without rupturing the tradition. The speaker of poem 1.14 does not establish himself as a performer before an audience, as a sympotic singer addressing his companions would do, but the poem loosely instantiates that model, with its suspended syntax and its elaborate parallelism and anaphora. It also begins with an image of luxurious wine-drinking (lines 1–2), which it expands into something like a priamel (you prefer X, while I say Y is best), a rhetorical form that gestures toward the symposium. Poem 1.14 offers an instance of what poetry looks like when it preserves some of the key features associated with performed poetry but does not fully establish a scene of performance and the songlike texture of the performer's speech. This notion of a weak (or perhaps deracinated) version of performed poetry is important, because this is what readers have generally judged to be the result when Latin poets use the structural features of the poetry that had belonged to the face-to-face environment of the archaic Greek symposium. In juxtaposing poems 1.13 and 1.14, however, we can see that although this weak sympotic

---

15. Commentators have tended to note the kind of specific stylistic points I make here but have not articulated the implications of such differences. Richardson (1977) exemplifies a reading practice that registers the effects of these differences but does not theorize them in terms of poetic practice. He introduces poem 1.13 with a narrative placing it in the emotional ups and downs of the storyworld ("In a poem to Gallus, . . . P. announces the break up of his love affair," 180), while treating poem 1.14 as a disengaged meditation on love and wealth ("no mention is made of the breach with Cynthia. . . . Instead we find P. on top of the world . . . reading a lecture on love's superiority to wealth . . . he is speaking almost as much to himself as to Tullus," 184).

form is represented within Propertius's oeuvre, it coexists with another form, one that distinguishes itself more forcefully from that traditional model and stakes out new poetic territory.

What happens in these poems after the opening couplets I have quoted is different but equally important: the two poems look more alike or, more accurately, poem 1.13 sheds some of its most emphatically conversational features and begins to look more like poem 1.14.[16] This pattern is not unusual, with the opening couplets being the most strongly marked as conversational. Obviously, the opening couplets set readers' expectations and thus can establish the notional scene of conversation even if the rest of the poem veers toward a style less focused on the interlocutor and the storyworld context. But more important than the negative conclusion (i.e., that the conversational techniques need not be sustained throughout the poem in order to effectively produce the sense of a social scene) is the fact that this typical swerve explains how such poems can be both radical and familiar. The opening couplets create the counterintuitive effect that we are somehow spying on a moment from private life, but the overall tone and style of the poem support our general expectations for the elevated, refined use of language that defines poetry as special. Perhaps one reason why readers have not generally identified what I am calling the conversational technique as a specific undercurrent in Latin poetry is that it comfortably shares a boundary with the more public, more self-consciously performed mode that the Romans inherited from Greek (performed) poetry.

By blending the conversational into more traditional forms—both within poems and across the book—Propertius creates a distinctive new way of delivering on lyric's promise to meld social speech with song. Many poems in his first book make little or no use of this technique, but where it is used it forcefully marks the difference between the speaker and historical poet and alluringly elevates ordinary speech into artful poetry. This effect, even in a subset of the poems, is enough to jar us out of our expectations for how poetic discourse relates to the storyworld, and it is supported by the overall treatment of the Ego in this book.[17]

---

16. For example, poem 1.13 incorporates parallelism marked by anaphora ("haec . . . haec," lines 9, 11; "vidi ego" at lines 14–15, the latter an unusual instance of anaphora begun in a pentameter and carried forward into the hexameter) and brings in mythological exempla (similar in effect to the geographical names in poem 1.14), again in parallel clauses marked by anaphora (lines 21–24).

17. It has become conventional, especially since Veyne's (1988) influential example, to refer to the first-person speaker of Latin love elegy as "the Ego," in order to designate the distance between this figure and the poet. The speakers in Horace and Catullus, although they also differ from the historical poets, seem more aligned with their creators (as will be explored fully in the course of this book) and thus have generally not attracted the same terminology.

The Ego as Poet?

The conversational technique outlined above supports a general consensus about the elegiac genre and particularly about Propertius's first book, namely, that it depicts poetry as integrated into the back-and-forth of ordinary life. I think we can refine this basic concept; I would argue that this collection does not exactly integrate these two realms but explores on several levels the relationship between poetry and the speech of real social life. In addition to the conversational technique I've just described, the collection makes use of the Ego (the first-person speaker of the poems) as the spokesperson for a specific kind of poetry that makes very strong claims for social effects. Since it has long been assumed that the Ego's poetic ambitions are central to the metapoetics of this book, it will be worth demonstrating in some detail that these ambitions apply strictly to the Ego as a character in the storyworld and do not account for Propertius's own poetic goals.[18]

No poems better illustrate this book's complex view of poetry than 1.7 and 1.8. These poems have, of course, long stood at the center of any discussion as to the nature of this collection, since poem 1.7 so explicitly sets out a justification of elegy's distinctive subject matter ("nostros agitamus amores," line 5) and style ("mollem . . . versum," line 19) in contrast to the more dignified genre of epic, and poem 1.8 so conveniently provides an example of exactly how the lover might use poetry to sway the beloved.

Poem 1.7 begins with these lines:

Dum tibi Cadmeae dicuntur, Pontice, Thebae
    armaque fraternae tristia militiae,
atque, ita sim felix, primo contendis Homero
    (sint modo fata tuis mollia carminibus),
nos, ut consuemus, nostros agitamus amores,   5
    atque aliquid duram quaerimus in dominam;
nec tantum ingenio quantum servire dolori
    cogor et aetatis tempora dura queri.

---

18. Claims about the aims and strategy of poetry are also clearly represented in this book by a metapoetic vocabulary that operates through metaphor or metonymy (e.g., "mollis," "tenuis," mentions of Coan silk, etc.). While I acknowledge the importance of this practice, too often these metaphorical claims have been treated without acknowledging that they operate on a different level than the claim that the Ego is a poet. Since the Ego is a character in the storyworld and the metapoetic vocabulary exists at the level of discourse, we can see that the choice to foreground these two features as key to the book's own claims about its poetics already confirms my claim that both "story" and discourse are important in this book.

While you, Ponticus, are singing of Cadmean Thebes and the grim armament of brotherly warfare, and—bless me—you vie with Homer, first and best (if only the fates are gentle to your poems), I am as always pursuing my love affair/love poetry, and seeking something that will work against a hard-hearted mistress. I am compelled to serve not my talent but my pain and to lament the hard times of my youth.

In these lines the Ego posits a view of elegy that makes it parallel to social language, both as the expression of personal affect ("dolori," line 7) and as the instrument through which he might persuade his beloved ("aliquid duram quaerimus in dominam," line 6), and he differentiates it from epic on these grounds.[19] This vision of what makes elegy special has found its strongest statement in Wilfried Stroh's 1971 book *Die römische Liebeselegie als werbende Dichtung*.[20] And yet even Stroh, who made this notion of social "usefulness" (*Nützlichkeit*) central to elegy's aims, implicitly acknowledges that this quasi-rhetorical conception of the genre coexists with another conception, which comes closer to recognizing poetry as an aesthetic achievement, designed not to persuade the addressee but to circulate among readers. Stroh labels these two forms as "direct" and "indirect" forms of wooing (*Werbung*): direct wooing (most obvious in poems 1.7, 1.8, and 1.9) implies that the poem wins over the beloved by persuasively presenting the Ego's devotion; indirect wooing (present in book 1, but taking on increasing importance in book 2) wins over the beloved through the promise of immortality that the poetry will bring (1971, 54–78).[21] To paraphrase Stroh's argument within the terms of my own: Propertius foregrounds questions of poetry's effects and offers two complementary answers: one (the direct form of wooing) that envisions the words of the poem operating as a parallel to social speech in the storyworld, and one (the indirect form) that sees the poem achieving its effects by making contact with unknowable future readers and recognizes that this effect depends centrally on the artistic quality of the poetry, not just its merit in expressing the Ego's devotion. Stroh downplays the difference between these

---

19. See Stroh's (1971, 21) influential formulation of this notion: "Properz klagt und wirbt um seine Geliebte und wird dabei ein großer Dichter, er klagt und wirbt nicht *um* ein großer Dichter zu werden. . . . Der eigentliche Zweck dieser Dichtung bleibt der Nutzen in der Liebe" (emphasis in original).

20. James (2003) offers an updated version of Stroh's basic premise but deploys the concept of "usefulness" to draw out from the genre an image of the "learned girl" who is the object of the poet's persuasion. This approach offers a precise reading of storyworld dynamics but fails to account for the divergence between the Ego's goals and those of Propertius.

21. Wyke (2002, 57–58) critiques the direct/indirect distinction as an attempt to account for the divergences between Propertius's first and second books. In chapter 3 I will focus more fully on the question of how to characterize this shift.

two conceptions of poetry's effects, highlighting instead their common utility for winning over the girl. Once we are attuned to the ways that the conversational technique draws attention to the operation of "story" and discourse, though, we can see that this two-track form of persuasion acknowledges that poetry functions differently for the Ego and for the historical poet. In fact, it becomes clear that the indirect form of persuasion comes close to treating the girl like any other reader, one who will read the poetry not as a message to herself but as poetry that is intended for an audience.[22]

In effect, Stroh's formulation of the direct and indirect forms of wooing shows that the Ego's view of poetry (focused on making things happen in the storyworld) comes embedded within another view of poetry, one that more closely captures the real situation of Propertius's work, as an artistic product that will gauge its success by its effect on readers, not on the recalcitrant girlfriend. This essential principle becomes even clearer once we focus on the form of the poems in this book, not just their content, as Stroh tends to do. In the case of poem 1.7, Stroh reads its claims about poetry as if it were a preface or some other paratext, implicitly addressed to the reader and meant to explain the poet's goals. He does not take account of the poem's addressive format, nor does he acknowledge that this poem violates the Ego's own dictates—it is, after all, not a heartfelt plea intended to soften the girl's resistance, but a statement of poetic principles addressed to a fellow male poet. If we take into account the structure of poem 1.7 and not just its content, it becomes clear that the poetic manifesto described here belongs to the Ego in the storyworld and is not the pattern on which Propertius has constructed his collection.

In fact, remarkably few poems in the first book could be described as "aliquid duram . . . in dominam": poems 1.2, 1.8A, 1.11, 1.15, and 1.19 are the only poems in book 1 addressed to the girl (not always named as Cynthia).[23] Even within this small set, complaint and rebuke (e.g., about the girl's heartlessness or greed) feature as prominently as blandishments and claims of devotion. In other words, even these poems do not seem wholly guided by what is most likely to win over the girl; rather, they are offered as emblematic instances of the Ego's verbal engagement with his difficult girlfriend. These poems do not all strongly exhibit the features of the conversational technique I identified above, but they do participate in the logic of that poetic

---

22. See for example Stroh on poem 1.18 (1971, 11–12, n. 12) where he explains that this apostrophic poem (clearly *not* addressed to Cynthia in the usual way) implies a separation between the Ego's roles as lover and poet and Cynthia's position as a reader.

23. I will treat in greater detail below two poems (1.17 and 1.18) that address Cynthia apostrophically, i.e., in a way that makes clear she is not present to the speaker.

mode, by relaying in highly wrought poetry a moment from the Ego's social life. The point I want to make here is not (just) that many poems fail to line up with the Ego's proffered manifesto, but that a key conception of Propertius's first book—the notion that poems can take the mimesis of social life as a central goal—is at odds with that manifesto, which treats poetry almost as a branch of rhetoric.

Poem 1.8 brings into more precise focus the question of why and how this book of poems accounts for itself. This poem is usually printed by modern editors as two poems (1.8A and B), because lines 1–26 are addressed to Cynthia, while lines 27–46 narrate the aftermath of that conversational scene and describe Cynthia in the third person (there is no address in 1.8B). The first part of this poem (1.8A) is the clearest example of poetry as erotic persuasion in book 1, as the speaker tries to prevent Cynthia from following another lover to the icy realm of Illyria.[24] The second section (1.8B) not only departs from this persuasive goal, but explicitly comments in its closing lines on the logic of "elegy as courtship poetry":

> hanc ego non auro, non Indis flectere conchis,
> > sed potui blandi carminis obsequio.   40
> sunt igitur Musae, neque amanti tardus Apollo,
> > quis ego fretus amo: Cynthia rara meast!
> nunc mihi summa licet contingere sidera plantis:
> > sive dies seu nox venerit, illa meast!
> nec mihi rivalis certos subducet amores: 45
> > ista meam norit gloria canitiem.
>
> > > > (1.8B. 39–46)

I was able to change her mind not with gold or Indian pearls, but with the homage of endearing verse. So the Muses do exist and Apollo is not slow to help a lover—these are the ones on whom I rely in my love affair: the incomparable Cynthia belongs to me! Now I can walk on the highest stars: come day, come night, she is mine! And no rival will steal away this established love from me: this is a glory that will live to my old age.[25]

---

24. The opening couplets of this poem make great use of conversational elements (cf. Wyke 2002, 14). It begins with a brief question, marked by vocative address and *ego–tu* links ("nec te mea cura moratur?"); most emphatically, "igitur" (in line 1) positions this line as part of an ongoing conversation, the elegiac version of in medias res. But this strongly conversational opening quickly gives way, first to an expansive description of the addressee (lines 5–8 with anaphora of "tu"), then into wishes/prayers, before turning to a fantasized scene of Cynthia sailing away and then to a second fantasized scene of his ongoing devotion.

25. This translation borrows from Goold (1999), especially for lines 40–41.

This poem offers strong evidence for Stroh's model, which claims that elegy itself sees its purpose as erotic persuasion. What that model leaves out, however, is the fact that the poem's second half produces this exalting comment through unaddressed third-person narration, a form suited for engagement with the reader rather than among the inhabitants of the storyworld. Through this formal shift from address to narration, the poem acknowledges that courting poetry itself is not the overall aim of this book, because the kind of poetry that comments on the origins and purpose of poetry has no place in courting poetry.

This is exactly my contention: that although the endearments that win over reluctant lovers are represented in this book, they do not account very fully for Propertius's poems and rather are depicted as the poetry produced by the Ego.[26] The two poems on which Stroh's argument most centrally rests (1.7 and 1.8) are perfect examples of my thesis: poem 1.7 is addressed to a fellow male poet and discusses poetic genre, while poem 1.8 starts out as an attempt to persuade the beloved but partway through shifts in an emphatic way to comment on poetry's persuasive powers rather than enact them.[27] This kind of theorizing about poetry, not in the expository manner of an *ars poetica*, but framed as a conversation between poets (1.7) or as an "explanation" of an event in the storyworld (1.8B) is the distinctive core of Propertius's first book.

I have highlighted Stroh's argument because it successfully captures both the fact that elegy is a highly self-conscious genre, constantly commenting on its own premises,[28] and the fact that elegy's own origin myth makes the instrumental use of language in everyday life central to the genre, especially

---

26. When we track down the instances in this book where the Ego is explicitly represented as a poet (not by implication and not by a metapoetic reading), they are remarkably few and cluster, again, in poem 1.7 and the closing lines of poem 1.8B. At 1.11.8 the Ego worries that a rival has stolen Cynthia "e nostris . . . carminibus," though in the rest of this poem only the use of "libelli" in line 19 promotes the identification of the Ego as poet. We can add to this small number of explicit instances a few more that are only slightly less explicit: poem 1.9 (a bookend with 1.7) continues the argument for the practical effects of elegy (as compared to Ponticus's chosen genre of epic), but it nowhere characterizes the Ego as a poet or describes his poetic activity as poem 1.7 did. Poem 1.20 is quite striking in this respect, since the whole logic of the poem implies that the speaker is a poet, but in place of the expected vocabulary of poetry, literary tradition, books, etc., the opening and closing couplets frame the speaker's action as a "warning" ("monemus," line 1 and "monitus," line 51), thus accentuating the social function of this mythological tale.

27. Poem 1.9 should be considered in this context too. Like poem 1.7, it is addressed to Ponticus (though the vocative is delayed until line 26); it begins by repeating the governing ideas of the earlier poem—namely, that genre is linked to the poet's life and that elegy is preferable to epic, because it benefits the lover in his aims—but here the accent is on the epic poet's lack of resources in love. After line 16, however, the literary polemics fade to be replaced by a more general warning about the trials of love.

28. Cf. Conte (1994) on elegy's hermetic self-absorption.

the attempt to use language to gain control. But as long as we align the Ego's poetic goals with Propertius's poetic goals, we will miss the fact that this collection places that elegiac origin myth within a broader perspective. Just as the conversational technique puts a scene of social life front and center while acknowledging the poet's artistic agency more obliquely, so too the vision of poetry as parallel to social speech is framed by indications that poetry is operating in a mode incommensurable with such use.

I am proposing a new way of reading Propertius's first book, not only by calling attention to the conversational technique and its implications but by radically decentering the Ego. Whatever scholars and readers have claimed that this book is engaged in—and the suggestions have been wide-ranging—they have generally taken for granted that the Ego is the primary means to that end. I will argue instead that the Ego is just one element of the book's attempt to explore what it means to communicate with readers through poetry.[29]

The contrast with Catullus and Horace will bring this feature into focus. Poem 1 of Catullus's collection ("Cui dono") works strenuously to align the speaking first-person voice with the artistic agency that has produced the book that the reader holds in her hands. Although such explicit alignment does not occur very frequently in Catullus's corpus, this early and prominent example conditions our response to the numerous poems that identify the speaker as a poet and that engage in debates about reading and writing poetry, encouraging us not only to see the speaker as a poet, but to attribute to the speaker the production of the very poems we are reading. Horace, especially in the *Odes*, is even more emphatic in depicting the poetic speaker as responsible for the poems as they come into the hands/ears of readers. The identification of the speaker as a poet is very frequent, but even more tellingly Horace's emphatic use of the performative technique often makes the poems comment on their own status as poetry coming into existence (e.g., "quid prius dicam solitis parentis / laudibus," 1.12.13–14; What should I speak of before the customary praises of the [divine] father?). We can assess the distinctiveness of Propertius's first book even more clearly by

---

29. I agree with the well-demonstrated claim that a major preoccupation in this book is discussing poetics through metaphor (Zetzel 1996 and Sharrock 1990 are just two examples), but I want to call attention to the very fact that these arguments about poetry are expressed through metaphor and thus differ from the pronouncements that the Ego makes in his own voice. While I find Zetzel (1996) generally persuasive in its analysis of Propertius's aesthetics and the generic attributes of elegy, I believe he accepts as axiomatic the unity of poet and lover ("to speak of Roman elegy as being in some sense 'about poetry' is automatically redundant: the persona of the elegist is a poet/lover seeking a subject that is both text and mistress; there is no distance at all from bed to verse," 82) in a way that underestimates the potential to play these two elements off against each other.

noting that the same author in his second and third books will employ the kind of alignment we see in Catullus and Horace. The opening couplet of his second book is

Quaeritis, unde mihi totiens scribantur amores,
    unde meus veniat mollis in ora liber.

You ask me why I write so often of my love affairs, why my book is soft upon the lips.

In a later chapter, I will explore this turn in Propertius's artistic goals, but for now this little survey of other collections shows that he has made choices in his first book that specifically downplay an impulse to see the Ego as the author of these poems.

Narration in Poem 1.3

If ideas about poetry are established only partially through depicting the Ego's poetic career, how does this book present its broader, more capacious view? I will focus here on two distinctive patterns through which this book depicts the relation between poetic expression and social experience. The first is the use of the verb "queror" (and related words) to delineate a form of speech that is poised between the back-and-forth of social life and an autotelic form of self-expression. The second is this book's handling of characterization. Drawing on Phelan's (2005) terminology, which defines the mimetic, thematic, and synthetic functions of character,[30] I will argue that Propertius's first book specifically draws attention to these competing aspects of character. Since the mimetic function of character is that which sustains the storyworld, while the other two functions operate within the discourse, the tension between these functions in turn draws attention to the dynamic relation between "story" and discourse. My argument is not that Propertius wrote these poems with the specific goal of airing propositions about "story" and discourse, but that in the course of experimenting with the forms of addressive poetry he inherited, he pushed and pulled on the

---

30. Phelan (2005, 20): "Responses to the mimetic component involve an audience's interest in the characters as possible people and in the narrative world as like our own. Responses to the thematic component involve an interest in the ideational function of characters and in the cultural, ideological, philosophical, or ethical issues being addressed by the narrative. Responses to the synthetic component involve an audience's interest in and attention to the characters and to the larger narrative as artificial constructs." See McCarthy (2010, 165–79) for a fuller discussion and application of Phelan's model.

links between the first-person voice and the implied scene of speech in ways that gave rise to new forms.

Poem 1.3 shows both these patterns at work. As a narrative of a late, drunken homecoming, this poem demonstrates how deeply "story" and discourse are intertwined in this book's overall aims. Most obviously, it deepens the reader's knowledge of the storyworld in a way that makes us feel we are gaining access to the Ego and Cynthia in the context of their ordinary lives. And yet this poem also parades its departure from the discursive regime that governs the rest of the book: it constructs the storyworld not through the speech of the Ego to an interlocutor, but through unaddressed past-tense narration, a form that comes close to acknowledging the need to explain the fictional world for readers. I argued above that the conversational technique in many poems in Propertius's first book creates a gap between the motivations of the speaker and those of the historical poet; in poem 1.3, we see that principle pushed much further through the poem's narrative structure, which implicitly takes readers as its audience.

This distancing effect, however, coexists with the fact that the narrator (like all first-person narrators) both lives the events of the storyworld and is in control of the discourse (telling his own story). The key to Propertius's distinctive handling of "story" and discourse is that he develops a first-person position that implies unity between the speaker and the poet in a large-scale view, but within the details of the language he suggests a greater distance. The main first-person speaker in poem 1.3 not only directs his voice outward toward readers but, significantly, gives himself no lines to speak in the story-world scene.[31] Cynthia, on the other hand, is put into the position most often occupied by the Ego in other poems, as the storyworld speaker whose speech is richly resonant for readers but who remains ignorant of the fact that this speech constitutes poetry for the external audience.

> Qualis Thesea iacuit cedente carina
>   languida desertis Cnosia litoribus;
> qualis et accubuit primo Cepheia somno
>   libera iam duris cotibus Andromede;
> nec minus assiduis Edonis fessa choreis   5
>   qualis in herboso concidit Apidano:
> talis visa mihi mollem spirare quietem
>   Cynthia consertis nixa caput manibus,
> ebria cum multo traherem vestigia Baccho,

---

31. I.e., he never quotes himself speaking in the storyworld or even uses a speech report (e.g., "I argued with her . . .").

et quaterent sera nocte facem pueri.   10
hanc ego, nondum etiam sensus deperditus omnis,
    molliter impresso conor adire toro;
et quamvis duplici correptum ardore iuberent
    hac Amor hac Liber, durus uterque deus,
subiecto leviter positam temptare lacerto   15
    osculaque admota sumere tarda manu,
non tamen ausus eram dominae turbare quietem,
    expertae metuens iurgia saevitiae;
sed sic intentis haerebam fixus ocellis,
    Argus ut ignotis cornibus Inachidos.   20
et modo solvebam nostra de fronte corollas
    ponebamque tuis, Cynthia, temporibus;
et modo gaudebam lapsos formare capillos;
    nunc furtiva cavis poma dabam manibus:
omnia quae ingrato largibar munera somno,   25
    munera de prono saepe voluta sinu;
et quotiens raro duxti suspiria motu,
    obstupui vano credulus auspicio,
ne qua tibi insolitos portarent visa timores,
    neve quis invitam cogeret esse suam: 30
donec diversas praecurrens luna fenestras,
    luna moraturis sedula luminibus,
compositos levibus radiis patefecit ocellos.
    sic ait in molli fixa toro cubitum:
"tandem te nostro referens iniuria lecto   35
    alterius clausis expulit e foribus?
namque ubi longa meae consumpsti tempora noctis,
    languidus exactis, ei mihi, sideribus?
o utinam talis perducas, improbe, noctes,
    me miseram qualis semper habere iubes!   40
nam modo purpureo fallebam stamine somnum,
    rursus et Orpheae carmine, fessa, lyrae;
interdum leviter mecum deserta querebar
    externo longas saepe in amore moras:
dum me iucundis lassam Sopor impulit alis.   45
    illa fuit lacrimis ultima cura meis."

Picture how the Cretan princess [Ariadne] looked, as she lay exhausted
on the deserted shore while Theseus sailed away; picture how Andromeda, the daughter of Cepheus, looked, as she lay in her first sleep after

being freed from the hard cliffs; picture, as well, a worshiper of Bacchus tired from her constant dancing, who has dropped down on the grassy bank of the river Apidanus; that's how Cynthia looked to me, breathing softly and peacefully with her head propped up on her folded hands, when I dragged home my drunken steps and the slaves were shaking the torches late at night. [10] I had not yet completely lost my senses, and I tried to approach her, softly pressing the couch; and although those two demanding gods, Love and Wine, were ordering me (already overcome by the effects of both passions) to make an attempt on her by lightly slipping my arm underneath her and, with my hand in place, to steal late kisses, still I did not dare to disturb my mistress's sleep, fearing rebukes born of that anger I knew so well; but instead I gazed fixedly at her, just as Argus gazed at the strange new horns on Io's head. [20] And now I was taking the garlands off my own head and putting them on yours, Cynthia, and now I was taking pleasure in arranging your scattered hair, now I was giving you apples as a secret gift with my cupped hands; all these gifts I was lavishing on ungrateful sleep, gifts that often rolled out of your lap; and whenever you sighed with an occasional movement, I stood stock still believing in an empty omen, afraid that your dreams were bringing you unaccustomed terrors, that some man was possessing you against your will; [30] until the moon hurrying past the parted shutters, that vigilant moon with its lingering light, opened with its gentle rays her eyes that had been closed in sleep. She propped herself up on her elbow on the soft couch and said, "So at last has an insult brought you back to our bed by shutting you out of another woman's house? For where have you spent the long hours of a night promised to me, you who come tired out now, ah me, when the stars have faded? Oh, you wicked man, if only you could experience the kind of nights you always force poor me to have! [40] For I was fending off sleep now with spinning a crimson thread and, at other times, though I was tired, with a song on the Orphean lyre. From time to time I quietly complained to myself in my loneliness that I frequently am kept waiting while you indulge in other affairs:[32] until Sleep gave me, already drooping, a push with his pleasant wings. That was the final cure[33] for my tears."

---

32. Goold (1999) understands "externo . . . amore" as referring to the idea that the relationship between Cynthia and the Ego is itself irregular and renders this line "in unmarried love waiting is often long."

33. Here I follow Heyworth's (2007b, 20) interpretation.

The poem begins with a famous sequence of three mythological heroines in distress (Ariadne, Andromeda, and a bacchant), to whom Cynthia is compared in her sleep. This opening sequence (lines 1–6) deploys in force all the features that run counter to the conversational mode (most obviously, mythological content, syntactic parallelism,[34] and anaphora), thus strengthening the impression that these lines unify the speaker's expressive intent and poetic intent. These lines also delay the introduction of the storyworld scene: only in line 7 do we come to understand that a scene from the life of the storyworld (rather than from the mythological storehouse) will be narrated and that the speaker is positioning himself as a first-person witness ("talis visa mihi," line 7) and narrator. Thus, before we get the (partial) alignment of the narrator in the discourse with the character (the Ego) in the storyworld, we get a chance to experience something closer to the poet's voice speaking to us directly through the discourse, a voice not lodged in any storyworld scene at all.

As the poem proceeds it comments obliquely on the relation between "story" and discourse, in part by making us very conscious of the narrator's own discursive act in relaying the events.[35] The scene described in lines 21–30 succeeds in making the storyworld come alive for the reader, but that effect is starkly contrasted with the Ego's failure to engage with Cynthia. Strikingly, in line 22, the narrator introduces second-person address ("pone-bamque **tuis, Cynthia**, temporibus"), an effect carried through line 30 by two other instances of second-person forms ("duxti" in line 27 and "tibi" in line 29). This is an odd instance of a principle I will address in more detail below, that of poetic apostrophe, that is, an address that is marked as incapable of real effect, since it is directed at an inanimate object or abstract idea or absent/dead person.[36] This instance of apostrophe is handled in a way that accentuates the formal structure of the narration and especially the distance between the plane of discourse and the plane of "story": just as narrators

---

34. Especially as it creates a long sentence that suspends its thought over several couplets: "qualis" is not answered by "talis" until line 7.

35. For example, lines 11–20 narrate a storyworld action (the Ego wavering as to whether to approach and seize Cynthia), but that action is largely overshadowed by the two competing lenses through which it is described: as a very abstract pseudo-mythological struggle in which the Ego is assailed by Liber (the god of wine) and Amor (lines 13–14; cf. the similar use of Argus in line 20) and contextualized through the history between Ego and Cynthia ("expertae metuens iurgia saevitiae," line 18), as one moment in their ongoing relationship. The narrator describes this moment in ways that call attention to his narratorial position through metaphor and figurative language, even as he also deepens the reader's sense of the storyworld in all its concreteness.

36. That is, apostrophe as has come to be understood in the scholarship on poetry, especially lyric poetry, not its (mostly ancient) meaning in rhetoric. (See Waters 2012.) I will discuss this principle more fully below, with citations to relevant bibliography.

cannot speak to characters, the speaker can address but cannot effectively engage with Cynthia. Her deep sleep offers a storyworld explanation for why she does not respond, but the poem's overall third-person narrative form makes it clear that the words "addressed" to her belong to the poem's discourse (aimed at readers), not to the speaker's attempt to wake her in the scene described.[37]

The poem ends by describing Cynthia waking up and offers a quotation of her speech. After rebuking him for his absence in language that sounds very much like the Ego's usual complaints about her, Cynthia closes with a description of her solitary vigil. These lines clearly depart from the formal strategy the poem has used up until this point, by handing off the position of speaker to a character; they also bring to a culmination this poem's exploration of "story" and discourse. In substance and even (largely) in form, Cynthia's speech echoes the Ego's claims of devotion and accusations of injustice that we see in poems throughout the corpus. (See especially lines 43–44, which except for the feminine ending of "deserta" would be at home in almost any other poem in the book.) So these lines not only produce a formal shift (with the discourse quoting a character voice rather than constituting the first-person lyric voice), but they also suggest a certain interchangeable relation between characters who are otherwise positioned as complementary opposites. This fact has been interpreted in storyworld terms, for example, by saying that this poem "reveals" that the Ego is not as faithful as he pretends elsewhere or that this poem gives us Cynthia's side of the story. It has also been interpreted as pointing to the poet's control of the discourse, a position closer to my own view:[38] Cynthia's adoption of the voice of the abandoned one foregrounds the process by which character voices come to be produced through the poet's discourse; usually this character voice is that of the Ego, but here it is that of Cynthia.

In place of the more usual format, in which the Ego's voice yokes the storyworld together with the discourse's orientation toward readers, this poem presents us with the combination of a narrator's voice (clearly in the discourse) and a character's voice (clearly in the storyworld). This unusual structure serves as a comment on Propertius's more normal procedure in this book. In other words, it shows that the usual procedure is not merely a replication of older forms—in which the speaker invisibly stitches together

---

37. The consistent use of imperfect and perfect tense verbs throughout this section underscores its narrative character.

38. For different variations on this approach, see Breed (2003), Robinson (2013). Also, while the conclusions in Kaufhold (1997) stress storyworld implications, the argument operates along the lines of the more recent interest in the poet's control of discourse.

for-us and not-for-us—but a development of that tradition into a new form, in which "story" can play a different role.

Specifically, I want to suggest that this poem sheds light on a new kind of voice produced in this collection, a voice that claims emotional and social experience as its matrix and yet floats free of any instrumental use by a specific character in a specific situation. This voice, which seems generated both by social need and by poetic aims, is defined in Propertius's first book as the voice of elegy itself and frequently marked, as here, by the verb "queror." This elegiac voice is most often depicted as issuing from the Ego; what I hope to demonstrate, however, is that this collection as a whole makes clear that the association with the Ego is not essential and is rather the product of artistic design. Central to the conception of the elegiac voice is that it unifies (or at least blurs together) a conception of language as issuing from well-defined speakers (with specific social and emotional attributes) and a conception of language as noninstrumental and defined primarily by sound and other abstract patterning rather than by its content. The lines quoted above from Cynthia's speech perfectly sum up the attributes that cluster around the verb "queror" in elegy: solitude, the slide between "complaining" and "lamenting" (i.e., voicing one's dissatisfaction whether or not there is any hope of change), and an iterative quality (repetition does not diminish the power of this kind of speech).[39] In this case, although the poem frames Cynthia's speech as a rebuke to the Ego, it is also brought into an almost explicit alignment with song. The poem does distinguish between singing with the lyre and voicing complaints softly to oneself, but the line of demarcation is very faint. Cynthia here plays the lyre for herself without any audience and also complains softly to herself of her lover's lapses.[40]

The organizing principle of Propertius's first book, as established most visibly in this poem, is that the voice of elegy is capable of speaking through characters, not just being spoken by characters. This principle fits with what

---

39. Strictly speaking "querebar" in line 43 refers to the self-addressed speech she indulged in before the Ego dragged himself home, but the content attributed to this action (complaining of being left alone while he indulges other loves) fits almost exactly with the content of lines 35–40, so I think we can consider this verb as describing the speech of Cynthia as quoted in the poem. This underscores my main point here, that "queror" constructs a concept of speech that encompasses both solitary lament and ends-oriented complaint voiced to another.

40. The speech divides neatly into two sets of three couplets (35–40, 41–46). The content of the first section focuses exclusively on her relationship to the Ego and his bad behavior; this section uses the conversational technique noticeably, though not as emphatically as some other instances. Although the second section continues the relatively simple sentence structure, it shifts into declarative sentences (into narration, in fact) and contains no second-person forms. This shift away from the conversational technique underscores the in-between status of the elegiac voice, a voice that takes on the aesthetic and resonant qualities of song and yet remains anchored in the matrix of social life.

I described in my introduction as "the competing priority of 'story' and discourse." To imagine that the "speech" of the Ego and of other characters is generated by individual psyches or prompted by specific events is to assign priority to "story" and to assume that the discourse serves the purposes of "story" by giving readers access to the lives of the characters. On the other hand, to imagine the characters as vessels that give the elegiac voice certain tones and properties is to assign priority to discourse and to assume that discourse makes use of "story" for its own purposes. The design of Propertius's first book, on full display here in the third poem, maximizes the tension between these two elements and avoids resolving their competing claims to priority.

The elegiac voice elides the social and the poetic in yet another way: this is a voice defined both by its poetic beauty and by its association with social powerlessness. Not only does the elegiac voice express longing and lament, but in every case (as I will show below) the elegiac voice expresses yearning for an effectiveness that is utterly out of reach. The design of this book underscores the nonteleological nature of the elegiac voice by distinguishing it from the language that specific characters in specific situations use to achieve their aims and goals. Instead, the elegiac voice is associated with characters or situations that are a priori defined as hopeless—it is speech that is spoken in spite of the knowledge that it can change nothing.

Apostrophe and the Elegiac Voice

The verb "queror" and the noun "querela" have long been recognized as terminology for elegy's mournful content and form, but the full implications have not been explored.[41] My contention is that the verb "queror" comes to be emblematic of elegy because it precisely combines the elements of ends-oriented social speech (i.e., complaining in order to make someone else change his/her behavior) and a lamentation (often solitary) that provides solace not because of its social effects but just in the act of lamentation itself. Its usage in book 1 shows these two potential meanings to be distinguished

---

41. Occurrences in Horace especially support the notion that this term is closely linked to elegy (e.g., *Ode* 2.9.18) and he makes this explicit at *AP* 75–76. The Catullan poem in which this term and its derivatives appear most often is 64 (to describe the fruitless complaints/laments of Ariadne and Aegeus), but it also is used by Attis in 63 (describing his own lamentation) and by the lock of hair in 66 (that of the queen mourning the departure of her husband). Saylor (1967) gathers the evidence. James (2003, 108–21) gives a sustained analysis of the "querela" as a building block of elegy. She notes, as I do, that it refers to self-addressed lament and argues that the more ends-oriented aspect of complaint is not exactly "querela" itself, but the diffusion of that extraliterary practice into elegy's persuasive toolkit.

quite sharply.[42] When the domineering woman is the subject (with the obvious exception of Cynthia's speech quoted above), this word connotes success in changing the behavior of others, most strikingly in poem 1.6.[43] When the Ego, or even other men, are the subject (1.7.8, 1.8.22), the verb accentuates the act of self-expression with no expectation that it will have effect, or the possibility of a complaint with real traction is simply dismissed (1.4.28). Poem 1.5 illustrates the associations of "queror" for men particularly neatly, as the Ego describes for Gallus what troubles await him in love:

> et quaecumque voles fugient tibi verba **querenti**,
> nec poteris, qui sis aut ubi, nosse miser!
>
> (1.5.17–18)

And whatever words you want to say will escape you as you try to complain, and—poor you!—you won't be able to figure out who you are or where.

If we take seriously the ways that "querelae" differ from the ends-oriented poetic manifesto advocated by the Ego, we can begin to envision a poetry that is rooted in emotional and social experience but does not limit itself to echoing the aims of social speech; it offers instead a form of expression that transcends social speech and succeeds both because of its emotional resonance and because of its autotelic beauty. This more transcendent form of poetry tracks closely with Jonathan Culler's formulation of the key poetic trope, apostrophe, a trope that gains its transcendent power exactly by transposing the social act of address ("O wild west wind . . .") into the plane of discursive action.[44]

Propertius's poem 1.18 most emphatically works out the idea that "queror" designates something like apostrophe,[45] a voicing that loosely takes

---

42. "Queror"/"querela" appear fourteen times over the 706 lines of book 1 (1.3.43; 1.4.28; 1.5.17; 1.6.8, 11; 1.7.8; 1.8.22; 1.16.6, 13, 39; 1.17.9; 1.18.1, 26, 29). The frequency in later books is noticeably lower: six times over the 1,339 lines of book 2, seven times over the 970 lines of book 3, and seven times over the 952 lines of book 4. (The number of lines in each book is based on Goold's text.)

43. In the context of explaining to Tullus why he cannot travel with him the Ego describes Cynthia's angry reaction to the suggestion ("queritur nullos esse relicta deos," line 8; she complains that if I leave her behind there are no gods) and then sums up his powerlessness in the face of her resistance ("his ego non horam possum durare querelis," line 11; I cannot last a single hour in the face of such complaints). See also 1.17.9.

44. Culler (2001, 144–63) is the classic statement. See now also Culler (2015, 211–43) and, specifically for classical poetry, Hutchinson (2010).

45. But see also poem 1.17, which likewise establishes the absence of the addressee early on—"desertas alloquor alcyonas" (1.17.2; I address the lonely gulls), "absenti . . . tibi" (1.17.5; for you, though you are not here)—but is thematically less focused on apostrophe.

the form of a communicative exchange but uses language for what it *is* rather than what it *does*.[46]

> Haec certe deserta loca et taciturna **querenti**,
>   et vacuum Zephyri possidet aura nemus.
> hic licet occultos proferre impune dolores,
>   si modo sola queant saxa tenere fidem.
>
>   (1.18.1–4)

This is indeed a lonely and silent place for me as I lament; only the breeze of Zephyr inhabits the empty grove. Here I can bring forth my hidden grief without fear of reprisal, if only the deserted rocks can keep faith.

These lines seem expressly designed to establish the notion that "querela" is a counterintuitive phenomenon: an act of social language that can take place in solitude and without social effect ("impune," line 3). Importantly, like apostrophe, this kind of complaint gains its meaning from using a form that sets up the expectation of social traction and yet is deployed in a way that renders that effect void. In other words, although I am claiming that this conception of "querela" involves the use of language as an end in itself rather than aimed at social effects, this is not merely ornamental language, which provides satisfactions through its materialities of sound and rhythm; it is language that parallels the workings of communication in social life but transposes these to another realm, in which the communication is transcendent rather than instrumental.[47]

Later in this same poem (lines 25–32), we see two further instances:

> omnia consuevi timidus perferre superbae   25
>   iussa neque arguto facta dolore **queri**.
> pro quo continui montes et frigida rupes
>   et datur inculto tramite dura quies;
> et quodcumque meae possunt narrare **querelae**,
>   cogor ad argutas dicere solus aves.   30

---

46. This poem has recently become a prime case for metapoetic arguments; most relevant to my argument are Pincus (2004) and Phillips (2011).

47. Culler's (2001, 160–63) formulation of apostrophe suggests the notion of a "discursive temporality," a temporal regime that is nonlinear, reversible, etc.—in other words a regime that is able to make the notion of "time" meaningful in the poem, while using it in a way that undercuts all the usual properties of time. I am suggesting here a parallel use of social language, one that grounds itself in the notion that language is used to accomplish things in the world (especially, for elegy, to bring to fruition the desires of individuals) and yet sets up a situation in which that very property is rendered void.

sed qualiscumque's, resonent mihi "Cynthia" silvae,
    nec deserta tuo nomine saxa vacent.

In my fear, I have learned to bear all the demands of that haughty
woman and not to complain with shrill grief of the things she's done.
In return for this, I am given the endless hills, cold rocks, and comfort-
less repose in the trails of the wilderness.[48] And whatever my complaints can tell of I am forced to speak in solitude to the clear-voiced
birds. But no matter what you are, let the trees echo "Cynthia" and let
the deserted rocks never be empty of your name.

These two instances neatly contrast the two sides of the verb "queror." The
first (line 26) denotes an instrumental complaint to the beloved, speech with
which the lover tries to describe his experience to her in order to convince
her to see things his way and/or to change her behavior; significantly, this
form of speech is negated—it is something he can imagine but cannot bring
himself to perform. The second (line 29) preserves the notion that "querelae" are important for their content, as they express a story of suffering, but
shifts the meaning of such a tale by taking only birds as its audience.[49] So the
complaint/lament that cannot be voiced to the beloved is instead brought
forth for the birds and rocks.

The elegiac voice, which posits its identity as (counterintuitively) both
social and poetic, supports the principles I have argued are generated by the
conversational technique. Pincus's (2004) interpretation of the lines above
pinpoints the fact that they contrast the speaker's social silence (he speaks, but
in a way that renders his speech void) with the abounding sound of his surroundings; further the idea of repetition in the last two lines (as the trees and
rocks preserve and replicate the name "Cynthia") points to the replication of
this voice and this moment through the mechanisms of literary circulation.[50]
Pincus further connects this dynamic to the notion of *fides*, highlighted in
the poem's opening (line 4) and to this book's more general theme of testi-
mony, that is, calling attention to the ways that an observer might speak out

---

48. Translation of lines 27–28 draws from Goold (1999).

49. Note that the speaker is designated as "solus" and the birds as "argutas," i.e., having the
kind of vocal qualities (clear, sharp, shrill) that the speaker denied himself in line 26. Throughout
this poem, in keeping with the pastoral conceit of the pathetic fallacy, animals and the landscape are
envisioned as sympathetic and almost endowed with human emotions and even human voice (see
esp. lines 19–22 and 31–32). See further Pincus (2004).

50. Pincus (2004, 179–84). The link to literary circulation depends not only on the imagery of
echoing, but on the specific materiality of ancient books ("liber," the word for book, is derived from
the putative use of tree bark for early books) and on this poem's emphatic allusions to Virgil's tenth
eclogue, and thus yet another form of repetition.

or make available facts that otherwise would be kept silent by the primary participants. The most compelling example of this in Pincus's argument is the voyeuristic structure of poem 1.10, in which the speaker as "testis" (line 1)—both witness and testicle—describes an erotic scene between Gallus and an unnamed girl. As Pincus notes, both in poem 1.18 and in 1.10, Propertius is in effect calling attention to the bizarre and yet little-noticed fact that love poetry makes public what logically should be private; he calls attention not just to the fact of such unaccountable publicity, but to the mechanism of it—*how* private whispers between lovers become publicly circulated poetry.[51] Pincus's explication of this poem makes it line up clearly with the effects I have noted for the conversational technique—a technique that overemphasizes the appearance of private, offhand conversation, thereby implicitly (and paradoxically) calling attention to the literary act through which this moment becomes poetry and is available for readers.

My analysis of poem 1.18 shows that in Propertius's first book apostrophe turns out to be less different from "realistic" address than we would have expected—not because he renders apostrophe in a realistic way, but because the addressive architecture of his other poems only partially grounds them in a social exchange. I have so far pursued this argument by demonstrating how the elements of book 1 that seem most socially grounded (the Ego's poetics of social utility, the settings of poems that specify the speaker's motivation, etc.) are themselves framed by elements that implicitly acknowledge the agency and aims of the historical poet. By focusing on the elegiac voice, I have argued that characters—like the other elements of this book—are also governed by the distinctive amalgam of "the social" and "the poetic" that defines this book. The final set of poems I will examine here experiment even more radically with throwing voices.

Character and Voice

Up to this point, I have attached no importance to the serial organization of this book, but it does seem significant that the poems divide into

---

51. Pincus (2004, 184) on poem 1.18: "it seems from reading the poem in its entirety that to proclaim faith is to break faith, to reveal those things that ought to be kept silent. All of the apostrophic questions in this poem have been produced in the hope that nature can keep silent and thereby preserve *fides* (*tenere fidem*, 4). That this ambivalence towards revelation is inscribed in a scene of textual production seems not at all accidental, especially in elegy, which so often interrogates its status as simultaneously public and private." In n. 28, Pincus goes on to explain the link between this public/private dynamic and elegy's claim that it is addressed to a specific girl even while orienting itself to a broader audience: "This paradoxical dynamic—the splitting of the audience between real and imagined—forms, I believe, a significant attribute of poetic representations of the essential character of elegy as a genre."

three fairly clear groupings. After an opening run of three programmatic poems, poems 4–15 employ the addressive mode (and often the conversational technique) quite emphatically, setting each poem as a speech in a specific social context; the book then closes with a final group of poems (16–22) that (mostly) cohere thematically with the rest of the book, but experiment with various odd instantiations of voice.[52] In addition to the two apostrophic poems (1.17, 18), we find two poems with unreal speakers: poem 1.16 spoken in part by a house door, and poem 1.21 spoken by a dead (or dying) man on the battlefield. I will focus on these two poems, but also take into consideration the book's final sign-off in poem 1.22.

These two unusual poems (1.16, 21) participate in this book's development of an elegiac voice and even come surprisingly close to the presentation of such a voice that we have already seen in poems 1.3 and 1.18. The most significant similarity that binds these four poems together is that they each feature a voice that successfully engages with the reader, seemingly from within the experience of the storyworld, while also distinguishing that successful contact with readers from the characters' inability to communicate effectively in the storyworld. In poem 1.3 the narrator obviously communicates with readers rather than with his lover; Cynthia's lament, although it is not explicitly aimed at readers, in its last three couplets takes on the qualities of the elegiac voice in transcending the storyworld communicative circuit.[53] In poem 1.16, again we have two speakers, the door, which addresses readers, and the lover who speaks within the storyworld, unconscious of an audience beyond; these two speakers parallel, respectively, the positions poem 1.3 assigns to the narrator and to Cynthia, whose songlike speech slips free of any implied interchange in the storyworld. In poem 1.18 the Ego's speech is unconstrained but also markedly without effect in the storyworld since, like the lover of 1.16, he addresses inanimate objects; this poem comes closest (in its closing lines) to

---

52. The exception in this group is 1.19; although it does not strongly depict a specific scene or motivation for this meditation on death addressed to Cynthia, it does basically fit the norms of the addressive mode. The other poem in the book that it most strongly resembles is 1.2, which uses the addressive mode but does not make the presence of the interlocutor or the immediate social or physical surroundings matter much for the poem. I do think poem 1.19 is a genuine exception to the pattern I see in the latter part of the book, though I also think that since it is preceded by two poems that address Cynthia apostrophically, its difference is downplayed (perhaps like the resurgence of the live Cynthia in poem 4.8 after we have been treated to the performance by her ghost in poem 4.7). I would also note that poem 1.20 has neither an unreal speaker nor an unreal addressee, but it does strikingly change the structure we saw earlier in the book by relating an extensive mythological narrative, framed by an address to Gallus spelling out the parallels with his own situation. Unlike the earlier poems, in which the storyworld was used to provide context for the speaker and his speech, here we have an uncontextualized speaker creating a mythological storyworld.

53. It is also significant that the poem ends without acknowledging or exploring the effect of her speech in the storyworld (for example, by having the Ego reply).

acknowledging concretely the ways that such speech, while void in the story-world, constitutes a powerful form of contact with readers. Finally, poem 1.21 draws on the traditions of funerary epigram to naturalize (partially) the effect of speaking from beyond the grave, but modifies the usual pattern of epigrams to produce something closer to an addressive poem, by specifying the speech situation and motivation quite concretely. The resulting poem is hard to make sense of, still more to categorize, but it produces almost the nth degree of elegiac voice.

These four poems feature, respectively, two human speakers (1.3), one inanimate and one human speaker (1.16), a solitary human speaker and inanimate addressees (1.18), and a dead/dying human speaker (1.21). Both the similarity of the underlying patterns and the very visible differences are important. Some of the unreal speech situations (apostrophe to birds and trees, a door introducing the lover's serenade, etc.) obviously parallel the forms of circulation by which poems become public property. Rather than taking this fact as simply the operation of a metapoetic agenda through figurative language, I suggest that such figuration is part of this book's wider exploration of the relation between speech and poetry, between life and art, and between private and public. So the fact that apostrophic and addressive poems end up being quite similar does not mean that the choice to remove the speaker from a realistic speech situation is trivial.

In poem 1.16 we can see how specific stylistic choices thematize the tension between separate but coexisting circuits of communication. First, it may seem too obvious to mention, but I hope in light of the argument so far we can see new significance in the fact that the door does not address anyone in the storyworld or really anyone at all; like the narrator's action in poem 1.3, the door makes clear (especially in lines 1–16) that it is, in fact, explaining the storyworld for readers and thus has to introduce itself and explain its history.[54]

Quae fueram magnis olim patefacta triumphis,
   ianua Patriciae vota Pudicitiae,
cuius inaurati celebrarunt limina currus,
   captorum lacrimis umida supplicibus,
nunc ego, nocturnis potorum saucia rixis,   5
   pulsata indignis saepe queror manibus,

---

54. The narrator of 1.3 does not have to fill in any of these blanks because in the absence of specific characterization of the first-person voice in this book, we take it to be the Ego.

et mihi non desunt turpes pendere corollae
    semper et exclusi signa iacere faces.
nec possum infamis dominae defendere voces,
    nobilis obscenis tradita carminibus;   10
nec tamen illa suae revocatur parcere famae,
    turpior et saecli vivere luxuria.
has inter gravius cogor deflere querelas,
    supplicis a longis tristior excubiis.
ille meos numquam patitur requiescere postes,   15
    arguta referens carmina blanditia.

I, a door vowed to the cult of patrician chastity, in days gone by was opened for great triumphs, my threshold was crowded with gilded chariots and sprinkled with the tears of captives, but now, wounded in drunkards' nighttime battles, I often complain when struck by unworthy hands and I am never without shameful garlands hanging on me nor without torches lying before me, the traces of a locked-out lover. [8] I am unable to fend off slanderous talk from my mistress, I who was once noble but now am subject to obscene incantations/poems, and still she is not called back to have regard for her good name and from a life more shameful than the license of the times.[55] [12] Amid these complaints, I am forced to lament even more deeply, made sadder by the long-lasting vigil of a suppliant. He never allows my doorposts any peace, pronouncing his songs with artful allurement.

When we take account of what the door tells us about itself, we can see even more strongly how it is aligned with the elegiac voice. The door starts (as the Ego did in poem 1.1) by contrasting its present humiliating existence to the respect of self and others that it used to enjoy. The door's "domina" (line 9) and her disregard for common decency have changed everything.[56] In this context, we will not be surprised to see that the verb the door uses to describe its pointless attempts to alter this bad situation is "queror" (line 6; see also "querelas" in line 13). Thus the door's act of speaking fulfills the expectations

---

55. Using Goold's (1999) translation for lines 11–12.
56. Morgan King (work in progress) emphasizes that their common humiliation by the "domina" is just one element that makes the door and the lover into mirror images of each other. Her argument also draws out the implications of the fact that the door can hear the lover's song but the lover cannot hear the door's lamentation, while the reader is positioned to receive both voices, a point that has been key for my own understanding of this poem.

I have argued are set in motion by the word "queror": recounting one's griefs is a solace in itself even though it cannot change the situation.[57]

Although the self-righteous door immediately seizes the reader's attention, this turns out to be only the opening gambit in this poem's attempt to rearrange the basic building blocks of elegy. Again, it is useful to compare this poem to poem 1.3, where the main voice takes the role of narrator to explain the situation to readers before introducing a second voice; in poem 1.16, however, the quoted speech stretches over almost thirty lines and far outweighs the door's speech, thus creating a different relation between the two speakers. The door introduces the serenading lover's speech by referring to it as "arguta . . . carmina blanditia" (line 16), picking up on key terms that encourage the reader to associate this speaker with the blend between useful and artful that characterized the Ego's poetics in poem 1.7. We could see this poem, then, as a microcosm of the book as a whole: the Ego's understanding of poetry is granted the spotlight but is surrounded by a frame that shows it to be just one element in the book's communication with readers.

It is important that the door functions here as something like a narrator, as the voice that explains the situation to readers and introduces the lover and his serenade. This poem can help us to describe further the elegiac voice, especially the ways it cuts across the storyworld grid of characters and events. The unreal speaker in poem 1.16 and Cynthia in poem 1.3 are converse outcomes of the same impulse, that is, the impulse to show the elegiac voice as anchored in emotion and social experience but also transcending any mimetic context. Cynthia looks superficially like realist characters, but the handling of her actions, voice, motivations, etc. undermines the sense that she has the solidity of a person in the world and shows her to be an amalgam of character and allegory. The door in poem 1.16 is clearly different from realist characters, but then its voice, history, and attitudes end up being surprisingly coherent and familiar. Poem 1.16 shows what it looks like to push both strategies as far as possible: it takes to the extreme the notion that voice is associated with physical body and with a specific outlook/history, as if the only way to use language expressively is to be a character with a voice; but the unreal character thus produced (a door) also reveals the arbitrariness of assuming that voices have to be associated with a real body and a real consciousness.

---

57. This poem also reveals that the stance of the speaker (abandoned, ignored, unable to make his/her voice heard) establishes the elegiac voice, even when the content of the speaker's views is against the "free love" attitude so characteristic of elegy. Here the door is almost parodically conservative in its championing of martial triumphs and its condemnation of luxury.

Poem 1.21 is a particularly enigmatic example of a poem that uses voice, scene, and character in unexpected ways. This short poem and its equally short successor (1.22) are the only poems in the book that make no reference to amatory travails and instead place themselves in the chaotic contemporary world of the civil war and its aftermath. This fact in itself—together with the placement of these two poems at the end of the book—implies that these poems claim for themselves a somewhat different status in relation to the historical poet and to the world he lives in.[58]

Tu, qui consortem properas evadere casum,
    miles ab Etruscis saucius aggeribus,
quid nostro gemitu turgentia lumina torques?
    pars ego sum vestrae proxima militiae.
sic te servato possint gaudere parentes,   5
    haec soror acta tuis sentiat e lacrimis:
Gallum per medios ereptum Caesaris enses
    effugere ignotas non potuisse manus;
et quaecumque super dispersa invenerit ossa
    montibus Etruscis, haec sciat esse mea.[59]   10

(1.21)

You, a wounded soldier from the Etruscan fortifications, who hasten to avoid a like fate, why do you turn your bulging eyes at my groaning? I am the nearest of your comrades. On these terms may your parents be able to rejoice over your safe deliverance, let your sister find out from your tears what has happened: that Gallus, though rescued from the midst of Caesar's forces, was not able to evade unknown hands;

---

58. Nicholson (1999) does a good job of laying out the ways that poems 1.21 and 1.22 undermine any claim that the characters are simply representing people in the world (cf. Phelan 2005 on the mimetic-thematic-synthetic triad of character function). Nicholson shows that the thematic and synthetic functions of these characters threaten to eclipse their mimetic function, but also "encourage the reader not to view mimetic and semiotic readings as mutually exclusive" (1999, 145). Perhaps because he is arguing against a tradition of wanting to find the truth behind Gallus, however, in practice his readings tend to overstate the degree to which the thematic and synthetic effects he traces in the characters of 1.21 and 1.22 overshadow their mimetic functions.

59. It is certainly reasonable to believe that some of the obstacles to interpreting this poem are the result of its garbled transmission, but that seems unlikely to account for all of its oddities. Heyworth's preferred reading in line 6 (he begins the line "me soror Acca") accentuates the storyworld dynamic, by including the first-person pronoun and by giving the sister a specific name. I note in particular that it is the circuitous way this speaker expresses himself that makes it so hard to sort out the proper text in the latter part of the poem. Even with Heyworth's emendation, the poem only minimally makes clear who the "soror" is and how we are supposed to understand her to be connected to the speaker and/or addressee.

and whatever bones she finds scattered over the Etruscan hills, let her know that these are mine.

Poem 1.21 combines in an almost unimaginable way the immediacy that Propertius constructs through the conversational technique with the plangent song that resonates for a broader audience. To put this more concretely, the speaker in this poem is clearly placed in the position usually defined by the conversational technique—that is, he is focused on influencing those in his immediate surroundings and unconscious of the potential effect of his words as a poem—and yet the style of this poem is closer to the ordered, polished speech associated with an authorized performer, whose audience listens with rapt attention. The opening vocative ("Tu") might excite expectations of the conversational technique, but it is followed first by a relative clause and then by a noun phrase in apposition, both expanding on the identity of the person addressed. As I will show below and discuss more fully in the next chapter, these elaborated vocative phrases are a key marker of the performative technique, as can be seen in their prominent use in prayers and other ritual addresses. Further, except for the simple single-line sentence in line 4 ("pars ego sum vestrae proxima militiae"),[60] the sentence structure of this poem makes full use of hypotaxis and expresses the wish for burial in roundabout and elliptical terms.

Perhaps this poem's most striking departure from the conversational technique is the lack of *ego–tu* links. The entire force of this poem is focused on invoking the bond between speaker and addressee and proclaiming the addressee's duty to aid in a proper burial, and yet, with the exception of "pars ego sum vestrae proxima militiae" (line 4), the wording avoids linking the speaker and addressee together. This effect is particularly noticeable in the latter part of the poem, where the introduction of the sister shifts the poem into a predominantly third-person mode of expression. The poem also phrases its key "information"—the death of the speaker—in indirect discourse (7–8), thus further deepening the odd sense that the most affective elements of this poem are rendered in language that does not mark the pragmatic involvement of speaker and addressee.

The reason for this oddly impersonal rendering is fairly obvious: the poem's clear invocation of funerary epitaph as a model. And yet, recognizing this model does not resolve the puzzling aspects of this poem. This poem seeks to combine the voice from beyond the grave (well established in the

---

60. Perhaps not coincidentally, this line is also the only line in the poem that contains a significant *ego–tu* link and a "backward glance."

tradition of funerary epigram) with the conversational technique, in which readers are allowed to witness the unfolding of a scene. Thus, in place of the universal passerby (*viator*) who would normally be addressed in a funerary epigram, and in place of the timeless present in which the voice of the dead usually speaks, this poem displaces the stately style of epigram into a very specific time and place, a moment of chaos and tragedy.[61]

Like poem 1.21, the final poem in the book also unambiguously invokes a clear literary precedent, the *sphragis* or seal-poem that establishes the author's identity and (in theory) the authenticity of the poems circulated under his name. Similar to funerary epigram, the *sphragis* is also a literary form that pivots between a claim that language functions neutrally to offer a reliable account of facts in the world and the implicit acknowledgment that the words of a *sphragis* are capable of bringing "facts" into existence rather than merely retailing them.[62] Another parallel with the previous poem is the fact that this final poem situates itself in reference to the public events of the civil war, rather than solely in reference to the private, unverifiable, and repeated events of the Ego's amatory adventures.

> Qualis et unde genus, qui sint mihi, Tulle, Penates,
>   quaeris pro nostra semper amicitia.
> si Perusina tibi patriae sunt nota sepulcra,
>   Italiae duris funera temporibus,
> cum Romana suos egit discordia cives—   5
>   sic mihi praecipue, pulvis Etrusca, dolor,
> tu proiecta mei perpessa's membra propinqui,
>   tu nullo miseri contegis ossa solo—
> proxima suppositos contingens Umbria campos
>   me genuit terris fertilis uberibus.   10
>
>   (1.22)

What kind of a man I am, where my family comes from, what household gods I have—you ask these things, Tullus, in view of our constant friendship. If you know the graves of Perusia, graves of our homeland, the deaths Italy suffered in terrible times, when Roman discord harried

---

61. Gutzwiller (1998, 11): "The authorial disengagement later associated with epigrammatic style is . . . an inheritance from the traditional objectivity of earlier inscribed verse."

62. In the case of funerary epigram, the recognition of language's generative potential is evidenced by the disembedded circulation of such poems. See, for example, Gutzwiller (1998, 89–102) on Leonidas of Tarentum's (presumably fictitious) epitaphs for the working poor and the long tradition of epitaphs for famous poets that circulated as poems, rather than being inscribed on tombs.

her own citizens—ah, you, dust of Etruria, are a cause of grief especially for me, since you allowed my kinsman's body to lie exposed and do not cover the poor man's bones with any earth—the closest part of Umbria, bordering on the low-lying plains, a fertile place of rich fields, gave me birth.

In style, this final poem abruptly juxtaposes two strategies that have been key to Propertius's first book and are perhaps nowhere else in the book brought into such close contiguity: the conversational technique (not strongly marked in the opening lines here, but relevant),[63] and an apostrophe, which unexpectedly takes over the poem in lines 6–8, where the speaker turns to address the dust of Etruria, which refused burial to his kinsman. Not only does the apostrophe abruptly shift the stylistic level of the poem, it intervenes at exactly the point when the logic of the if-clause ("if you know of Perusia's history in the civil war . . .") is about to define the speaker specifically in terms of the side-taking in civil discord.[64]

So this turns out to be a very odd *sphragis*, as if designed to display the conflicting pressures of private social speech and public proclamation of identity. The poem starts off as if conditioned by the social bond between speaker and addressee, but in doing so raises the question of why a close friend should need the kind of information allegedly requested.[65] In effect, the opening couplet points to the mismatch between addressive poetry and the public reception it courts: it is the reader, not Tullus, who will want this background information. If we then assume that the poem is engineered to meet the needs of the reading public and the address to Tullus is

---

63. The early vocative, string of questions (indirect questions repeated as if echoing Tullus's inquiries), moderately strong *ego–tu* links ("mihi, Tulle," line 1) and the clear backward glance ("pro nostra semper amicitia," line 2) tell in favor of the conversational technique here but are at least partially balanced out by the anaphora of qu- sounds at the beginning of clauses (at line beginnings and at the caesura of the first line) and, as the poem continues, the long hypotactic sentence that begins in line 3.

64. The abruptness of this shift is accentuated by the fact that it happens in a pentameter, which we would expect to cohere closely with the thought of the preceding hexameter rather than to go in a new direction. Heyworth (2007b, 98) comments on the unusual practice of starting a new line of thought in a pentameter in defense of his reading of 1.21.6. "The grouping of unusual cases in I xxi–xxii suggests that Propertius may have been laxer in his style in these apparently early and certainly untypical compositions." I make no claim about dating, but it does seem significant that this unusual practice would (potentially) crop up twice in two short poems, so strongly linked in other ways. Even more intriguing, the third example Heyworth cites from book 1 is the narrator's introduction of Cynthia's speech at 1.3.34. I propose here no specific interpretation of this pattern, but it seems plausible that these three poems that stretch the somewhat rigid norms of elegy in other ways might also have encouraged experimentation with metrical practice.

65. Heyworth (2007a, 100).

mere window dressing, the poem confounds us by withholding the author's name,[66] thus thwarting the prime function a *sphragis* is supposed to fulfill.[67] The next few couplets repeat this bait and switch in a new key. They start off as if about to proclaim the speaker's identity as a partisan in the civil wars before "turning away" to address the Etruscan dust—in terms that are (again, as in poem 1.21) reminiscent of funerary epigram—so the point about civil war allegiances gets partially obscured by the universalizing language of mourning.

The irruption of the real contemporary world into the poetic scene in these last two poems is an important shift, and yet these poems still in many ways continue according to the patterns I have been describing for this collection. In particular, these poems express in new forms the same ambivalence as to whether they should be understood as arising within the scene they depict or are independent of that scene, which has been invented as a kind of conduit for this discourse. These final two poems demonstrate a poetic practice that Propertius will pursue more energetically in books 2 and 3, by downplaying the gap between speaker and poet and representing instead something closer to the poet's own agency in creating the discourse.

One final observation on poem 1.22 will suggest that here in book 1 Propertius is capable of depicting the contemporary world and his own place in it, but not (yet) interested in knitting that context together with the actual production of poetry. Another way that this poem is at odds with the tradition of the *sphragis* is that it contains no indication that the speaker is a poet, still less that he is the composer of the poems we have been reading. This poem, and in a different way poem 1.21, breaches the boundary between the private elegiac world that accounts for most of the rest of the book and the world Propertius inhabited. In this way, these poems function as his signature in his real role as historical poet, the role that has been expressed only obliquely throughout the book and usually obscured by the more visible Ego. It is significant, however, that in this gesture he defines himself by the experience of the civil war and not by his poetic output.

By drawing attention to the conversational technique, I have endeavored to show that there are reasons to perceive a split between the Ego and the historical poet in Propertius's first book, reasons that are not just generated

---

66. Heyworth (2007a, 100–101) notes the genitive of the author's name embedded in the syllables of the second line: "PRO nostra semPER amiciTIa." (In a strange twist on life following art, Heyworth confesses himself unable to recover the name of the person who drew his attention to this playful gesture.) This verbal trick fits with the overall pattern I have described, by which the discourse not the "story" is where Propertius appears in this book.

67. Compare, e.g., *Georgics* 4.563, "Virgilium me."

by resistance to autobiographical readings. This book is structured to put storyworld speech—the speech of the Ego in his own life and for concrete purposes, as he speaks unconscious of any external audience or any artistic value in his words—at its center and yet simultaneously to register and even celebrate the specifically poetic status attained by the poem as a whole. The result is that the agency of the historical poet in this book is systematically acknowledged, and not just through metapoetic allegory or the figure of the Ego. This acknowledgment resides in the very fact of these words being offered as poems; the consciousness that these will be received by readers is key to the difference between the Ego's effusions and Propertius's poetic production. We could rephrase this to say that while the Ego perceives the poetic elaboration of language to heighten its desired social effects (e.g., to persuade the girl or to make her beauty famous), Propertius uses poetic elaboration to mark the difference between poetry and social speech, and one of those differences is that poetry has a legitimate claim on the attention of people outside the immediate social setting.

Thus, by putting the relation between the Ego and Propertius on a new footing I am also rephrasing questions that have always been central to elegy, including even in its own self-description. Latin elegy, especially in its amatory variety, poses the question of whether its value lies primarily in the depth of emotion it expresses or in the distanced perspective it provides, as it universalizes and elevates ordinary events onto a mythological scale (sometimes literally transforming ordinary events and people into mythology). Many readers will probably recognize this as a restatement of the old subjective vs. objective debate. For much of the twentieth century, that debate was phrased in terms of literary history, especially the widely shared view that Latin poets were interesting primarily for what they could tell us about their Greek sources. But I think we can see within the contours of this question a more basic conundrum about a poetic genre that seems to define itself both as a variant of and in opposition to ordinary social speech and that uses the names of its authors to project the impression that giving voice to real experience is its very foundation.

Excursus: Conversation in Catullus

I have analyzed above the conversational technique in Propertius in order to make clear that it rests on a specific set of formal features (involving syntax, diction, word order, etc.) and not just a loose impression of casualness or colloquialism. When we compare Catullus to Propertius we can see that although Catullus is much more likely to use colloquial language and although many of his poems are often loosely described as "conversational," his polymetric poems are actually significantly less influenced by the specific conversational technique I have described. My overall argument about Catullus's polymetrics is that these poems seem conversational (in the looser sense) but are largely built on the model of performance not conversation. They seem conversational because they are almost always addressed to present human interlocutors and because they very strongly highlight the emotional and social impulses of the speaker. As I demonstrated above, the sense that the speaker's words are engaged with his fellow inhabitants of the storyworld and that they are aimed at producing certain specific effects in that world is a key effect of the conversational technique. Catullus's poems differ from those of Propertius's first book, however, in suggesting that the speaker (unlike Propertius's Ego) is in control of the poem's discourse and thereby minimizing the gap between speaker and historical poet. There are two major ways that Catullus brings together the speaker and the poet. First, he draws on models of verbal performance to imply that the speaker's speech is expressed in its specific discursive form already in the storyworld. Second, he constructs a storyworld in which poetry operates not as the magically seductive power Propertius's Ego believes it to be, but basically in the ways it would have operated within Catullus's own environment (in books, as an object of judgment, circulated among elite men, etc.). These aspects of Catullus's practice in the polymetrics will be analyzed more fully in the chapters to come (chapter 2 for the performative models and chapter 3 for the representation of poetry in Catullus's storyworld). I will briefly examine here Catullus's use of the vocative, since that practice offers a concrete instance of how he typically treats the addressive form and reveals implications for how his speaker is positioned in relation to the storyworld and to the poet. In addition to clarifying a key principle for Catullus, this brief analysis also helps to sharpen the argument I have made about Propertius by providing a contrasting example.

The elaborated vocative phrase (especially in the opening lines) points to the distinctive way that Catullus orients his speakers toward the storyworld and renders this address performative. In fact, we could go further and say that the qualities that define Catullus by consensus—a sense of immediacy and even urgency, a distinctive blend of the common (even obscene) with the elevated, a sense of the speaker present before us in all his messy individuality—all these qualities are part of a broader pattern that builds performative poems on a conversational foundation. The vocative has a special role to play in both performative and conversational techniques, and therefore it is illuminating for Catullus's style to see how he deploys it.

Of the fifty-seven poems in the polymetric section of the corpus,[68] only a handful of poems (10, 45, 53, 57, 59, 60) are completely lacking in vocative address,[69] and the great majority (forty-one out of fifty-seven) have vocatives in their first or second lines, often as the first word of the poem.[70] This is a striking pattern, though it obviously fits with the emphasis on address in ancient first-person poetry. The high frequency of poems that contain (and especially begin with) vocatives offers some evidence in itself that the scene of a speaker addressing an interlocutor is a key building block for Catullus's poems.[71] When we look in more detail, however, at exactly how these vocatives are handled, we can see that they call more attention to the act of speaking than to the scene of speech. Catullus very often elaborates these vocatives by filling them out with, for example, relative clauses, participial or adjectival phrases, or nouns in apposition: all these forms can be used to add weight and sometimes (mock) solemnity to the vocative.[72] This elaborated vocative phrase could justifiably be considered a true signature of Catullus's style. Just a few examples:

> Passer, deliciae meae puellae,
> quicum ludere, quem in sinu tenere,
> cui primum digitum dare appetenti
> et acris solet incitare morsus.
>
> (*Catullus* 2.1–4)

Sparrow, my girl's darling pet, with whom she plays, whom she holds in her lap, to whose avidity she offers the tip of her finger and stirs up harsh biting.

> Aureli, pater esuritionum,
> non harum modo, sed quot aut fuerunt
> aut sunt aut aliis erunt in annis.
>
> (*Catullus* 21.1–3)

---

68. The numbers run 1–60, but we have no poems for the numbers 18, 19, and 20. The fragments 2b, 14b, and 58b have varying claims to be counted as separate poems (58b most obviously); for the sake of simplicity I am not counting any of them as separate here.

69. Several of these poems are narrative; poems 10 and 45 quote characters using vocative forms.

70. I am including in this count apostrophic vocatives, such as "O colonia" (17) and "Adeste, hendecasyllabi" (42), and also self-address, as in poems 8, 46, 52.

71. Fain (2008) places Catullus's practice in the context of the stylistic development of epigram from its early origins to Martial. His detailed analysis establishes that among the features that distinguish Catullus's style in the polymetrics from that in the elegiac epigrams, is that the polymetrics almost invariably (in over 75 percent of the poems) use a vocative in the first few lines, while for the epigrams this figure is 61 percent.

72. Williams (1968, 143 et passim) calls this the "circumlocutory address" and associates it with formal hymnic style.

Aurelius, father of hungers, not only of the present hungers but of as many hungers as have been or are or will be in the future.

Salve, nec minimo puella naso
nec bello pede nec nigris ocellis
nec longis digitis nec ore sicco
nec sane nimis elegante lingua.

(*Catullus* 43.1–4)

Hello, girl with a not-so-little nose and not-so-pretty feet and not-so-dark eyes and not-so-long fingers and not-so-dry mouth and certainly with a really not-so-elegant tongue.

These examples are just a sampling, but they show how stylistically varied and inventive Catullus's vocative phrases can be. Although the poems of Propertius's first book use vocatives at about the same frequency as Catullus does, where Catullus tends to introduce descriptions of the addressee in these extended vocative phrases, Propertius uses more declarative syntax to achieve the same end. Compare to the previous excerpts these lines from Propertius.

Quid mihi tam multas laudando, Basse, puellas
    mutatum domina cogis abire mea?

(*Propertius* 1.4.1–2)

Bassus, why do you compel me to change and leave my mistress by praising so many girls to me?

Non ego nunc Hadriae vereor mare noscere tecum,
    Tulle, neque Aegaeo ducere vela salo.

(*Propertius* 1.6.1–2)

Now I do not fear to explore the Adriatic sea with you, Tullus, nor to spread sail on the Aegean.

tu pedibus teneris positas fulcire pruinas,
    tu potes insolitas, Cynthia, ferre nives?

(*Propertius* 1.8A.7–8)

Can you really press the frosty ground with your tender feet, can you bear the unaccustomed snows, Cynthia?

Unlike Catullus, who more often tarries over the vocative and expands it with one or more phrases (and even clauses), Propertius tends to characterize the addressee and situation through the statements and questions put into the mouth of the speaker. At first glance, this may seem to be a trivial stylistic difference since the overall effect—highlighting the relation between speaker and addressee and (often) showing the scene in which they meet—is very similar. I would argue, however, that Catullus's choice to foreground his vocatives and develop them in so signal a fashion offers a window into his overall practice. Through their discursive elaboration, these vocative phrases underscore the very act of address, and it is no accident that such extended vocatives are at home in the language of hymn, where the very act of invocation has religious significance. In this respect, such phrases can be seen as markers of the performative technique, which implies (in contrast to the conversational technique) that the speaker's utterance in the storyworld has the discursive features of performed song and is set in a moment that is recognized as special.

CHAPTER 2

Poetry as Performance

Dianae sumus in fide
puellae et pueri integri:
Dianam pueri integri
  puellaeque canamus.

o Latonia, maximi   5
magna progenies Iovis,
quam mater prope Deliam
  deposivit olivam,

montium domina ut fores
silvarumque virentium   10
saltuumque reconditorum
  amniumque sonantum.
            (*Catullus* 34.1–12)

We are held in the safe-keeping of Diana, we unmarried girls and boys:
let us, unmarried boys and girls, sing of Diana. O daughter of Leto,
great offspring of greatest Jupiter, you whom your mother bore near
the Delian olive tree, to be mistress of the mountains and of the verdant woods and of remote glades and of resounding streams.

Poem 34 is unusual in Catullus's corpus; closer to the long wedding hymns preserved as poems 61 and 62 than to the other poems in the polymetric section, it presents itself as having a grounded, historically specific origin in performance, as if it were only later brought into this written collection along with sundry other poems. Such an implied origin story has important implications for my argument. It positions the storyworld speakers (here, the chorus) as fully conscious of the specifically poetic qualities of their words (because hymns are efficacious through their very words and rhythms) and of the fact that they are performing before an audience in a ritual setting. These features of the poem very clearly distinguish between the not-for-us dimension of the poem (the original performance with its original audience and original ritual aims) and the for-us dimension (the poem's afterlife in a collection for readers, in which it can be read both as a record of that original performance and as a self-standing work of art). Further, the Aeolic stanzas, the repetitions (of single words, but also of phrasal structures such as the multiple genitive plurals in the third stanza), and other features establish the language here as highly ordered and finely wrought, that is, as language that has been elaborated with specifically poetic form.

Catullus's poem 34 is a perfect example of what I mean by the "performative technique" in Latin first-person poetry.[1] But I also want to include under this term poems like the following:[2]

O furum optime balneariorum
Vibenni pater et cinaede fili
(nam dextra pater inquinatiore,
culo filius est voraciore),
cur non exilium malasque in oras   5
itis? quandoquidem patris rapinae
notae sunt populo, et natis pilosas,
fili, non potes asse venditare.

(Catullus 33)

O most excellent of bathhouse thieves, Vibennius Sr., and you, too, his whorish son (for the father has the filthier right hand while the son has the greedier ass), why don't you two go into exile, to some awful hellhole, since in fact the father's thievery is well known to the public and, Vibennius Jr., you can't sell your hairy buttocks for a penny.

---

1. Whether this poem was written for performance and / or actually performed in a ritual for Diana is not relevant for the argument I'm making here, which concerns how these poems represent their own origin stories. On the question of ritual performance of Latin hymns, see, e.g., Feeney (1998).

2. These two poems stand side by side in the collection, but I am not putting any interpretive weight on that fact.

This poem does not announce its own performance (as poem 34 does with "canamus," line 4), but it does position its speaker as making a pronouncement, condemning these two lowlifes on behalf of the community. The people have passed judgment, and the speaker is here to deliver the news. Although the speaker's language falls short of the imperative we might expect of a real legal judgment, its sarcastic question in lines 5–6 comes very close to that. This sense of a judgment being delivered is prepared for in the opening lines with the elaborate vocative, here marked by the formal "O." While we may choose to see this poem as a tongue-in-cheek parody of real performance or as a more casual statement jocularly clothed in momentous language, what is important here is the fact that—unlike the speakers we saw in Propertius's most conversational poems—the speaker here positions himself as making some kind of public pronouncement and making it for an audience. The Vibenni (father and son) are the addressees, and clearly the speaker aims to have an effect on them, but the poem's structure and its explicit mention of the public judgment imply that the speaker also presumes that he is speaking before and on behalf of other members of the community as well.[3] While the "ritual" into which we might imagine this poem to insert itself is less clearly delineated than a festival in honor of Diana, it still evokes the sense that the speaker is pronouncing exactly these words in exactly this form before an audience in order to produce certain effects.[4] I am not trying to convince anyone that poem 33 is actually a hymn or even a parody of a hymn, but just drawing attention to the fact that Catullus's invectives very often operate on a logic that reveals them to be "performative" in the sense we are more used to accepting for hymns, that is, presenting the speaker as conscious of the artful, elaborated arrangement of his words, as well as of the fact that he is performing before an audience and that these words are meant to be efficacious in the world.

These three elements—special diction, the special status of the occasion, and the special effect of the utterance itself—are the basis of the technique I will be describing as performative. The study of performance and performativity in all their various forms has had a profound effect on the study of Latin poetry (as well as many other fields in the humanities) over the last few

---

3. The poem is one long sentence with a vocative phrase taking up the first half of the poem, implying both that the speaker has been granted the time and attention to make this pronouncement and that he marks out its special status by making the language point to its own addressive action.

4. The presence of an audience is not made explicit in either poem. In the case of the hymn our knowledge of festivals automatically supplies the audience. In the case of invective, the very fact that the performance context is less formalized means that we feel less certain about whether an audience would necessarily be present. I will demonstrate below that the influence of *flagitatio* (a performance form that clearly assumes an audience) in Catullus's corpus makes his invective poems reflect the impression of an audience.

decades. My use of the terms here is not identical with their use by other scholars, though it draws on some of the most prominent threads of the "performative turn." Let me specify that while there is good reason to believe that the poems of Catullus and Horace were recited and/or read aloud,[5] that type of performance is not what my argument is aimed at illuminating. In place of this most literal meaning of the word "performance," my argument draws instead on the scholarship that has formulated performance as an act that takes place within the bounds of social and political life. Two particular strands of this discussion will most influence my own.

First, what we might call the philosophical approach, associated especially with Austin, Searle, and Butler. Beginning with J. L. Austin's paradigm-shifting lectures *How to Do Things with Words*,[6] this approach focuses on the capacity of language to produce effects in the world (its performative capacity), as distinguished from language's capacity to reflect or describe phenomena (its constative capacity). While originally proposed as an advance in the philosophy of language, this orientation toward language's productive function and the more general theoretical orientation of "speech act theory" came to have wide applicability in many fields and was especially influential in literary studies.[7] Judith Butler produced the second paradigm shift in this debate with *Gender Trouble* (originally published in 1990), in which she applies the notion of performativity to explain how the seemingly immutable "fact" of male and female bodies is constructed and sustained through the constant performance of acts that produce sexed and gendered bodies.[8]

Butler's development of the philosophical strand can actually be seen as a bridge to the second important strand of research into the meaning of performance, one we might call the "anthropological" or "sociological."[9]

---

5. Skinner explores the pedagogical consequences of thinking of Catullus's poems as performed; she does not assume Catullus replicated the performance dynamics of the archaic symposium but picks up on aspects of the poems that "virtually cry out for oral delivery" (1993, 63). For a more skeptical view of the importance of recitation, see Parker (2009).

6. Delivered as lectures in 1955, first published in 1962.

7. For developments of this theory specific to literary criticism, see esp. Petrey (1990) and Pratt (1977).

8. Butler (1993, 1–2): "'sex' not only functions as a norm, but it is part of a regulatory practice that produces the bodies it governs, that is, whose regulatory force is made clear as a kind of productive power, the power to produce—demarcate, circulate, differentiate—the bodies it controls. . . . 'sex' is an ideal construct which is forcibly materialized through time. It is not a simple fact or static condition of a body, but a process whereby regulatory norms materialize 'sex' and achieve this materialization through a forcible reiteration of those norms." I quote here from the introduction to *Bodies that Matter* (1993).

9. There is no single foundation text for this line of thought, though Walter Benjamin (and to some extent Émile Durkheim) is sometimes cited as a key early figure (see, e.g., Habinek 2005, 3–4),

This theoretical approach is related to the philosophical in the fundamental premise that language is capable of producing the effects it may seem only to describe, but its focus is broader in that it includes various forms of communication (such as ritual actions or even all instances of mimesis) and bodily behavior, as well as the social and political frameworks within which those actions take on their meanings. Various versions of this anthropological approach have become central to Roman studies in the last few decades. Some of the most central and most characteristic institutions of Roman life—such as the triumph, declamation, religious ritual—have offered fertile territory for this approach and have led some to suggest that Roman culture is peculiarly "theatrical."[10] This understanding of performance has been conceived as operating both in circumstances that are structured and marked as special (the amphitheater, the rostra, etc.) and almost invisibly within the contours of everyday life, where neither the performer nor the audience are conscious of the performative element (similar to the performativity that constitutes gender in Butler's formulation).

Individual studies of performance and performativity take the central ideas in different directions and operate under the signs of different methodologies. Just a few examples from the works most relevant for my project: Selden's famous essay *"Ceveat lector*: Catullus and the Rhetoric of Performance"* (originally published in 1992) most strenuously applies the essential insights of speech act theory, though its final section begins to develop the more sociological analysis of Roman public culture that would become central to scholarly debate within a few years. Brian Krostenko's *Cicero, Catullus, and the Language of Social Performance* (2001) uses the techniques of sociolinguistics to delineate how the elite culture of the republic defined itself in part through deploying a vocabulary of aesthetic judgment. David Wray's *Catullus and the Poetics of Roman Manhood* (2001) explicitly models its analysis of social performance on the anthropological work of Michael Herzfeld, who did fieldwork in the villages of the modern Aegean, documenting the concrete practices through which men compete to establish their (individual and collective) masculinity. Sarah Culpepper Stroup's *Catullus, Cicero, and a Society of Patrons* (2010) explicates late republican social and intellectual life

---

and structuralist anthropology (under the aegis of such scholars as Claude Lévi-Strauss), especially in its work on ritual, has been an inspiration.

10. Some key examples of "first wave" publications that demonstrate the wide methodological range within which the concepts of performance, performativity, and theatricality have been applied in Roman studies: Gleason (1995), Gunderson (2000), Flower (1996), Bartsch (1994), Dupont (1985), Coleman (1990). See now the overview of several different aspects of performance provided by Lowrie (2010).

by putting under a microscope the transition between the earlier tradition of "liberal performance" (esp. oratory) and the rise of textuality.[11] Finally, Michèle Lowrie's large-scale analysis in *Writing, Performance, and Authority in Augustan Rome* (2009a) takes up the social and political effects generated when literate texts self-consciously appropriate the logic of performance alongside acknowledging their own written form.

This brief overview can help to put into perspective my own use of the term "performative." Most fundamentally, the aspect of performance that will matter most for my argument is the specially activated (and generative) quality of certain utterances and the fact that this activation depends both on linguistic markers and on the social/ideological context of the utterance. Linguistic markers include the use of specific vocabulary (e.g., dedicatory formulas or performative verbs such as "spondeo") or formal properties, such as the various kinds of redundancy that characterize *carmina* in Latin.[12] The aspect of social and ideological context that will concern me most here is the fact that the speaker must be socially recognized as the right kind of person to make this utterance in order for it to have effect, so the speaker's authoritative positioning is central to the notion of performance; far from being a precondition, however, creating this authoritative position is often the point of the performance.[13] The examples with which this chapter began—the choral ode in honor of Diana and the verbal lashing of an undesirable citizen—both ground themselves in assumptions about the power of the right words, said in the right circumstances by the right speaker(s).

I will focus here on a subset of performative action that overlaps to some degree with the notion of "ritual," itself a highly contested and variously defined concept.[14] Like performance, ritual has been studied both as a special, set-apart activity (which draws its authority and effects from the ways it differentiates itself from ordinary action) and as patterns of actions in ordinary social life. For the most part, I will be employing the first sense, in which ritual is recognized by the participants as special and as specially effective. In this chapter I will analyze the performative technique in two specific subsets of first-person poetry with visible links to ritual: Horace's religious

---

11. Some other key interventions in the scholarship on Catullus could also be seen as implicitly leveraging the notion of performance, though it is less explicitly foregrounded, e.g., Richlin (1992), Fitzgerald (1995).

12. Meyer (2004, 44–72) offers a stylistic account of the *carmen* style as it appears in various legal, political, and religious documents.

13. Well established in Richlin (1992) on the logic of invective.

14. I find useful the formulation of Bell (1997, 74): "the peculiar efficacy of ritual activities, which distinguishes them from literal communication, on the one hand, or pure entertainment on the other. . . . most performance theorists [of ritual] imply that a successful or effective ritual performance is one in which a type of transformation is achieved."

odes and Catullan invective. These poems make use of performative utterances that are set apart as special and presumed to have consequences that inhere in the very language and the very act of voicing (i.e., not just by being persuasive or monitory). Equally important, these performative utterances embody a communal sense of what makes an utterance special—either a near-mystical power that lies in certain authorized combinations of words or the power that lies in an authorized person speaking the proper words in an authorized context. These two kinds of power—the power of special words and the power of special speakers/situations—are in fact tightly interwoven, each representing merely a slightly different weighting of the same elements. I am calling attention, however, to the possibility of these different weightings because in what follows I will show that the first, the power of special words, can help us account for the performative element in Horace and the second, the power of special speakers and special contexts, can do the same for Catullus.

Poems such as these define the relation between the storyworld and the discourse differently from the pattern we saw in the previous chapter. In poems that accentuate the conversational technique, the speaker is focused on what is happening in the storyworld and seems oblivious to the fact that his words constitute a poem. Such poems, then, point obliquely to the agency and activity of the real historical poet who has crafted these words as a way of communicating with readers. In poems that accentuate the performative technique, on the other hand, the speaker is still very much focused on storyworld events and still desires to make something happen in his world, but because the storyworld context (e.g., a religious ritual) requires a very special form of speech, it naturalizes the crafting of poetic effects. Poems built on this model thus develop to the highest degree the attractions of not-for-us: they position the speaker's words as a communicative act at a specific moment in time, with specific participants for a specific purpose. On this understanding, we readers are getting access not to a poem designed to communicate with us, but to a poem that just happens to outlive its original context.

The fact that such poems play up their not-for-us identity, by appearing to be remnants of an earlier, socially embedded performance, makes it tempting to think that the driving force behind these poems is a longing for that social matrix and communal reception (to say nothing of the union of ritual effectiveness with poetic form). Viewed this way, it is the Latin poet's lack—of the venue for a captivating performance, of a relatively small and culturally cohesive community as audience—rather than any sense of opportunity or innovation that generates these poems. I think it is more accurate, however, to see these poems as inventing a way (distinctive from the conversational technique) to combine the elements of not-for-us and for-us. In conversational poems the figure of the historical poet is nowhere to be seen but leaves a discernible trace as the one who turns offhand conversation into poetry. Although this trace is subtle, it is significant and it underscores the poetry's overall orientation toward readers. Performative poems, because they situate the poetic agency in the storyworld, associate the historical poet with the inaccessible world of not-for-us and therefore seem less interested in the reader as a partner in communication. In performative poems we really do have to work our way through not-for-us in order to get to for-us, but, as I aim to show in the readings that follow, Horace and Catullus each develop very specific strategies for positioning the poem as a communication with readers too.

The two poems quoted above can help orient us to Catullus's strategy. Most readers would agree that poem 33 ("O furum optime") is closer to Catullus's usual practice in the polymetrics, in which instances of performance belong not to high (religious) ritual but to folk ritual (such as *flagitatio*) or to categories such as invective. Catullus's chosen forms of performance tend to highlight the way that the relation between performer and audience expresses social authority and creates social effect. While the formal patterning of language plays a role in marking this utterance as special, equally important is the way that the poem establishes itself in relation to the community and establishes its speaker as one who has the power to utter effective pronouncements. This specifically Catullan form of performance, then, makes use of language's special powers to produce effects, but also highlights the social world within which those conventions have meaning.

Horace's odes, on the other hand, more often highlight the underlying principle of performative language itself, that is, that certain exact forms of language have their own almost magical power, and that these powers transform the moment in which the poem unfolds (including the moment of reading) into something set apart and even sacred. This emphasis on the specialness of form is less bound to the image of social context; its applicability even to a corpus of written poems makes possible the kind of powerful but disembedded lyric performance that is central to Horace's poetics.

This difference in the way that the two poets make use of performative forms also explains the difference in how their authorial personas operate within the poetry. Horace's emphasis on poetic form as the carrier of special meaning allows him to bring the poetic speaker closer to the real position of the historical author, since the power of the discourse depends not on its depicted social setting but on the words themselves (authored by the real man). I realize that this sounds counterintuitive, since we are used to accentuating the fact that in the first three books of the *Odes* (and for most of the fourth book) Horace avoids any reference to his own poetry as written and instead maintains the fiction of song. This insistence on song as medium is

very important to Horace's aesthetic positioning and especially in establishing his relation to tradition, but I would argue that it is important exactly
because it underlines the notion that form itself rather than context is what
makes words powerful.[15] In Catullus, on the other hand, the real historical poet is pulled into the storyworld, with the motivations for his poems
assimilated to storyworld events (e.g., to answer an insult, to establish his
slighted authority). The special quality of poetry performed before an audience inheres, for Catullus, in the notion that these words are driven by social
impulses and have social effects, so they are more thoroughly integrated with
their storyworld context.

I argued in the previous chapter that Propertius establishes the for-us aspect
of his poetry by making clear his role in producing poetic discourse from the
"raw material" of conversation,[16] which he then plays off against the not-
for-us aspect of a random scene from private life. Horace establishes the for-us
aspect by accentuating the fact that the poetic discourse—equally available to
any reader—is where the communication really resides. It is fair to say that both
Propertius and Horace developed ways of writing poetry that acknowledge the
role of readers, including readers beyond the social circle and historical moment
of the authors, even though this outward-reaching aesthetic is partially counter-
vailed in each case by a not-for-us element. Catullus, on the other hand, more
radically balances the two elements of for-us and not-for-us, yielding poems that
engage powerfully with readers while also seeming almost entirely absorbed
with the social world they depict. The arresting result is a corpus of poems that
allow readers to feel unusually intimate with the poet, but that also make readers acutely aware of their ignorance as to the people and events of this world.[17]
Broadly speaking, Propertius's way of using the storyworld is more novelistic
(the storyworld does have great weight, but that weight is assumed to be granted
to it by the poet's design), Horace's is more lyrical (the power is in the discourse,
not in the "story"), and Catullus makes it ambiguous whether the power of the
storyworld is constructed or a representation of the real forces he is up against,
thus avoiding a univocal orientation toward the storyworld or toward readers.

---

15. Lowrie (1997 and 2009a) has been most energetic in calling attention to the meaning of
Horace's choice to represent his written poetry as song.

16. At least in book 1—see the next chapter for a discussion of how this changes in book 2.

17. Quinn (1982) exemplifies a way of reading that emphasizes our intimate connection with the
poet, melding the lyrical/poetic refinement with a puzzle-like reading strategy that reconstructs the
events within which this poem would make sense as speech. Also consider that while there has been
a considerable industry devoted to working out the prosopography of Horace's addressees, often
these findings are used to pin down the thematic resonances of the poem rather than to build up a
picture of Horace's social life.

Horace's Hymns and Dedications

Hymns and other religious poems are among most prominent cases where Horace uses the tradition of performed Greek poetry as a catalyst for his own compositions. (In the next chapter I will take up his other central obsession with performance, the tradition of sympotic song.) I will examine here several different ways that poems of this type make use of the frame provided by ritual performance, especially by varying the impact of "story." This is not a question of how much "story" a poem contains, but how that "story" is oriented in relation to the discursive act the poem itself constitutes. At one end of the spectrum, we see two ways of tightly aligning "story" and discourse: one is the "performative" alignment implied in phrases like "I praise," in which the "story" consists simply of the performer producing the discourse; the second is what I will call, following Culler (2015, 35), the "epideictic" alignment, in which the poem simply consists of the discourse itself and gives no image of its own production or performance; in this case the "story" it produces is not the scene of utterance but whatever descriptive or narrative material the speaker introduces. At the other end of the spectrum, we see poems that use "story" in a way that reveals the speaker not just as the performer of these words, but as a character with specific attitudes or motivations or as enmeshed in certain social settings, coming close at times to the use of "story" I described in the previous chapter as the conversational technique.[18]

Hymns are poems designed for ritual performance: they not only depend on the performative efficacy of language (in the philosophical sense of language that produces the action it names, e.g., praise of the divinity) but conceive of the poem itself as the offering to the god.[19] These two self-reflexive properties mean that hymns focus on their own discourse to a very high degree: they usually contain performative utterances that refer only to the song itself (e.g., "canamus," Catullus 34.4) and their "story" consists of the performance itself (the "story" of Catullus 34 is simply the chorus singing and dancing). On the other hand, dedicatory utterances are conceived as accompanying ritual offerings, not as themselves constituting such offerings and thus include an important role for physical actions in the storyworld.[20] Poems built on this logic do not necessarily subordinate discourse to "story,"

---

18. It is a bit misleading to talk about this as a spectrum, because in fact what changes between these forms is not the proportion of discourse to "story," but the manner in which "story" is deployed. Still, the image of a spectrum can be helpful in conveying the idea that some examples give the impression of an extreme privileging of discourse and others of an extreme privileging of "story."

19. Discussed above in the introduction, in the section "Performance and Text."

20. Cf. Pulleyn (1997, 55): "the most significant functional difference between a hymn and a prayer is that the former is a sort of negotiable *agalma* which generates *charis* whereas the latter is not."

but they open the possibility for "story" to operate in a variety of ways beyond just focusing on the performance itself.

Of course, in Horace's *Odes* 1–3 both these forms of religious performance get filtered through the medium of written poems circulated in a collection. Lowrie (2009a) has already offered compelling arguments against the simplistic assumption that the written form leaves only two options: believing in a "virtual" performance that happens in books just as in sanctuaries or, on the other hand, believing that writing strips these poems of everything but a distant echo of "real" meaning.[21] She elaborates fully the ways that these poems generate indecision about their status and effectiveness. What I hope to do here is to build on that foundation by looking more closely at very specific formal properties of Horace's hymns and dedications, with the insight provided by the "story"/discourse distinction, to see how these poems grapple with questions of meaning and efficacy.

If we recall the paradox of deixis as it has been discussed in relation to performed poems—namely, that while deixis might seem to secure the speaker's physical and temporal context and thereby reliably guarantee the poem's relation to its (original) performance, this property can be used fictionally to create the impression of such a context[22]—we should realize that Horace could have written poems that exactly replicated the relation between speaking voice and context that he found in his Greek models. In that case, the literate identity of such poems would have been clear from their circulation in (author-designed) collections and because we know from other sources that the Romans' performance culture was quite different from that of the Greeks. And there are in fact poems in *Odes* 1–3 that fit this pattern. For example, poem 1.10 ("Mercuri facunde") lacks the final prayer its mythic narrative might have seemed in service of, but otherwise does not declare itself distinct from performed hymns. Similarly, while the precise content of poem 1.12 ("Quem virum") distances the poem from Greek models, with its litany of Roman historical figures culminating in Augustus, the form and structure of this poem do nothing to rule out performance.[23]

Instead of simply importing these qualities of performed poems into literate poems, Horace developed these performative genres guided by specific formal properties he saw in those earlier poems and by his knowledge of the difference between that distant world of song and his own. Contrary to expectation,

---

21. See also Feeney (1998), Barchiesi (2009).

22. Discussed above in the introduction, in the section "Performance and Text"; see the index, s.v. "deixis."

23. For both the examples mentioned here we have at least fragments of specific Greek poems on which they were modeled: for poem 1.10 Alcaeus's hymn to Hermes (308 Lobel-Page) and for poem 1.12, Pindar's Second Olympian Ode (see most recently Athanassaki 2014).

however, he uses these formal properties not to re-create a performance context or to airbrush the difference between that context and his own literate poems, but to create a new kind of discursive force that is native to writing. As we will see in the examples below, Horace typically either disrupts the image of a coherent hymnic performance or introduces hymnic elements into poems designed on a different plan, thus resisting the totalizing logic inherent in a performed hymn.[24] The first of these patterns has already been well described in the scholarship, especially by Lowrie (2009a, 75–81), who pinpoints the effect in poem 1.21, "The second-person-plural address . . . has the strange effect of removing the speaking voice from the speech acts denoted" (75–76), and concludes: "I think Horace consciously uses formal devices—addressing the chorus instead of the gods . . .—to generate indecision" (79).[25] We can use this observation as a starting point for examining this poem's relation to performed hymns.

> Dianam tenerae dicite virgines,
> intonsum pueri dicite Cynthium,
>   Latonamque supremo
>   dilectam penitus Iovi.
>
> vos laetam fluviis et nemorum coma,   5
> quaecumque aut gelido prominet Algido
>   nigris aut Erymanthi
>   silvis aut viridis Gragi,

---

24. Cairns (2012, 442) notes "Horace's characteristic technique in anathematika [dedicatory poems], as in other genres, of introducing some topoi explicitly and others in an highly allusive way" but explains this by supposing that "the reader, who shares Horace's knowledge of the commonplaces of the genre, will be rewarded by his recognition of commonplaces which are, on first reading, absent, and will supply mentally the missing connections of thought." Rather than assuming that these blanks or glitches are meant to be filled in by the reader's knowledge of generic traditions (and thereby producing always basically the same poem), we can consider the possibility that the gaps are real gaps.

25. Most readers agree that this poem fails to offer the expected alignment between a choral song of praise and the speaking voice in the poem (for which we conveniently have an example in Catullus poem 34; surely it is relevant that Horace chose to invoke this predecessor so unambiguously and yet does not follow its lead in this major respect), but disagree as to the meaning of this phenomenon. E.g., Williams (1968, 155–56) posits that Horace reconfigures the relation between speaker and chorus in order to make his own authoritative presence as poet more visible: "The political motive which drove Horace to [this choice] is characteristic of the new relationship between poet and community. . . . The traditional form is used to give depth and solemnity to the political statement." Feeney (1998, 43): "Horace's elaborate instructions to the non-existent choruses of boys and girls foreground the poet's own power as not just the stage-manager but the literal creator of the entire 'event.'" La Bua (1999, 175–78) gives full weight to Horace's innovations on the hymnic model (and, like Williams, highlights the political motivations) but still stresses how closely this hymn inserts itself into the tradition. Cairns (2012, 196–99) is an outlier, arguing that this poem's "built-in stage directions" are consistent with the tradition, though the only examples he cites are Callimachus's mimetic hymns 2, 5, and 6 and Catullus 61.

vos Tempe totidem tollite laudibus
natalemque, mares, Delon Apollinis   10
    insignemque pharetra
        fraternaque umerum lyra.

hic bellum lacrimosum, hic miseram famem
pestemque a populo et principe Caesare in
    Persas atque Britannos   15
        vestra motus aget prece.

Sing of Diana, tender virgins, sing of long-haired Apollo, boys, and
Leto too, deeply loved by Jupiter supreme. You, [girls,] sing of the goddess who delights in rivers and woodland foliage, whatever stands forth
on chilly Algidus or in the dark woods of Erymanthus or of verdant
Gragus. [8] You too, boys, raise up with your songs of praise Tempe
and Delos, birthplace of Apollo, and his shoulder distinguished by the
quiver and his brother's lyre. When moved by your prayer, he will drive
away heartbreaking war and wretched famine and pestilence, away
from the Roman people and from Augustus their leader, turning them
instead toward the Persians and Britons.

Rather than inventing wholly alien practices, in poem 1.21 Horace is just
pressing further (and in an unexpected way) a feature that is at home in performed Greek hymns, namely, the various ways that hymnic speakers can call
attention to the act of singing. Parallels have been adduced for the chorus
enjoining itself to sing (e.g., Bacchylides 13.190; see Nisbet and Hubbard 1970,
ad 1.21.1 for further examples), and some forms of mismatch between time,
place, and speaker are quite common in choral lyric, though—and here is the
difference from Horace—these are momentary swerves within poems that construct and maintain an overall orientation to the moment of performance.[26]
We can see Horace doing something similar in poem 1.12, where he advertises
his adherence to tradition by starting with a close reminiscence of Pindar's Second Olympian Ode, a poem that also begins by asking who should be celebrated
(as if this moment stood outside the hymn proper). Pindar, however, answers

---

26. For example, Stehle (1997, 89) explains the apparent misfit in the opening lines of Alcman's
Partheneion (3 PMGF): "The speaker describes herself as waking and going to the *agon*, which must be
the location where she is already singing. It has been suggested that a solo singer sang the introduction to the song because it seems odd for performers to speak as though they had not yet begun to
sing. But the 'performative future' is well-attested." I am not arguing that this is the correct interpretation of these lines, but just showing an example of the complexities within the apparently smooth
performative mechanism of archaic Greek choral lyric.

this question (the victor Theron) within a few lines;[27] Horace first elaborates on the power of poetry to exalt names before asking again (lines 13–14) "what should I sing of before the traditional praises of Jupiter?" ("quid prius dicam solitis parentis / laudibus") as if the question were still open and thus extends the motif throughout most of the poem.[28] Therefore I think we should look at these moments where Horace makes the match between the poem and the performance more difficult than it needs to be (in fact, sometimes impossible), not as an effort to undermine Greek practice but as pushing to an extreme the slight illogicalities already present in the earlier forms.[29]

As I noted above, this technique of disrupting the performance occasion is just one way that Horace resists fully assimilating his poems to performed hymns. A second way is to invoke hymnic practices but avoid presenting the whole poem as hymnlike. This is a specific example of Horace's widely remarked tendency toward "discontinuity," that is, structuring his poems through leaps of thought or odd juxtapositions, and I will show here that the implications of this pattern are central for Horace's overall aesthetic.

To start with a prime example of poems that employ hymnic elements, we can do no better than the famous and controversial second ode of the first book. This poem begins with an extensive and harrowing description of the morass in which the Roman people find themselves after decades of civil strife. The first half of the poem addresses no one and never indicates a context of utterance or an identity of the speaker.

> Iam satis terris nivis atque dirae
> grandinis misit pater et rubente
> dextera sacras iaculatus arcis
> terruit urbem,
>
> terruit gentis, grave ne rediret   5
> saeculum Pyrrhae nova monstra questae,
> omne cum Proteus pecus egit altos
> visere montis

---

27. Granted, given Pindar's wide-ranging style, it would be hard to argue that this poem remains focused on Theron and his family, but it does not extend the serial question of who the *laudandus* will be beyond its opening lines.

28. Further instances in lines 21–24, 25, 33–36, 39.

29. There is, of course, one obvious model for the procedure of having the speaker seem to "stand aside" from the ritual performance: Callimachus's hymns to Apollo, Athena, and Demeter (*Hymns* 2, 5, and 6), the so-called "mimetic hymns." These poems (and Callimachus's whole experiment in hexameter hymns in the tradition of the narrative-heavy *Homeric Hymns*) clearly were an important influence for Horace, though he also takes Callimachus's practice in new directions and develops a specifically lyric species.

piscium et summa genus haesit ulmo,
nota quae sedes fuerat columbis,   10
et superiecto pavidae natarunt
    aequore dammae.

vidimus flavom Tiberim retortis
litore Etrusco violenter undis
ire deiectum monumenta regis   15
    templaque Vestae,

Iliae dum se nimium querenti
iactat ultorem, vagus et sinistra
labitur ripa Iove non probante u-
    xorius amnis.   20

audiet civis acuisse ferrum,
quo graves Persae melius perirent,
audiet pugnas vitio parentum
    rara iuventus.

Now the father-god has sent enough snow and frightening hail down to earth and has terrified the city by hurling thunderbolts at sacred citadels with his flame-red hand; he has terrified the human race, worried now that the dire age of Pyrrha will return, with its portents never before witnessed, when Proteus drove his whole flock of seals to visit the high mountains [8] and the race of fishes clung to the tops of trees (previously the familiar home of doves), and frightened deer swam through the sea that swamped everything. We have seen the Tiber gold with sand, its waters wildly flung back from the Etruscan bank, bent on the destruction of the Regia and Vesta's temple [16] as the river-god boasts of avenging Ilia (who makes loud complaints), and, devoted to his wife, strays beyond the left bank without Jupiter's approval. The new generation, thinned out by the sins of their ancestors, will hear of battles and of citizens who sharpened swords, which would have been better turned against the threatening Persians.

If we read the first three stanzas with no preconceptions about the content or aims of the poem as a whole, we find that these lines are absorbed in narrating a flood, at first unspecified as to place and time (the adverb "iam" in line 1 is the only element here that refers to the speaker's own perspective), and later associated with the famous mythological flood in the age of Pyrrha and Deucalion. This pattern holds through the third stanza, after which comes a sharp syntactic break; line 13 begins with "vidimus," and this stanza goes on to name Roman landmarks that identify the flood as taking place in Rome, thus offering a clear indication that the speaker is recounting a contemporary experience that he claims to have witnessed along with others.

I have belabored the description of these lines in such detail because only thus can we see that the most famous aspects of this poem—the invocation of the gods and the assimilation of Augustus to Mercury—are largely unrelated to the poem's opening movement. The first three stanzas come very close to the function of lyric Culler has labeled "epideictic" and has claimed to be the essence of lyric.[30] This epideictic opening does without the feature that is most characteristic of ancient lyric—the address to a present interlocutor, which situates the poem as a speech in a given setting—and thus comes close to owning its own status as a poem in a book with which the poet aims to communicate with readers. Even the next few stanzas, in which the speaker attests to his own act of witnessing ("vidimus") and makes clear that the flood is part of his own experience, do not break this spell by establishing a scene of storyworld speech, but pin down even more forcefully the impression that the real historical poet Horace is speaking to us through the text in his own voice.

It is also worth noting how central a role narrative plays in this opening section. The first five stanzas are completely given over to narration, and only the sixth stanza (a hinge to the poem's second part) turns to a moralizing prophecy of future generations.[31] This sixth stanza is remarkable for another reason as well: it introduces the topic of the civil war, which reorients the significance of the poem's narrative section. The earlier stanzas had linked the physical upheaval caused by flooding to the anthropomorphic motivations of the gods, but had not made human wickedness, still less the specific crimes of the Roman civil war, an explicit cause. The addition of this syntactically self-contained stanza (21–24) makes clear the rhetorical point of the long description of the flood.

We might have expected this epideictic mode to continue to dominate the poem, as it largely does in the Roman odes that open the third book.

---

30. Culler (2015, 35) describes lyric epideixis as "a non-mimetic enterprise . . . the presentation of assertions or judgments that are not relativized to a particular speaker or fictional situation but offered as truths about the world." So, for example, at the beginning of poem 1.2, what we get is the assertion "Now enough . . .," not the image of a man saying "Now enough. . . ."

31. The formal break with the previous stanzas is even softened a bit since the prophecy retains the third-person constructions that have dominated the early stanzas, though shifting into the future tense.

Instead, in line 25, the poem begins to shift into a performative mode, when it asks how prayer might save this doomed people.

> quem vocet divum populus ruentis   25
> imperi rebus? prece qua fatigent
> virgines sanctae minus audientem
>   carmina Vestam?
>
> cui dabit partis scelus expiandi
> Iuppiter? tandem venias precamur   30
> nube candentis umeros amictus
>   augur Apollo;
>
> sive tu mavis, Erycina ridens,
> quam Iocus circum volat et Cupido;
> sive neglectum genus et nepotes   35
>   respicis auctor,
>
> heu nimis longo satiate ludo,
> quem iuvat clamor galeaeque leves
> acer et Marsi peditis cruentum
>   voltus in hostem.   40

(1.2.25–40)

Which god should the people call upon in aid of the affairs of the tottering state? With what prayer should the holy virgins implore Vesta, unwilling to give ear to their songs? To whom will Jupiter give the role of expiating crime? Come at last, we pray, augur Apollo, wrapped with clouds around your gleaming shoulders; [32] or, if you should prefer to come, smiling Venus, encircled by winged Laughter and Desire; or [Mars] if you, as our ancestor, are willing to take thought for your descendants long estranged, when at last you have had your fill in the protracted game of war, you who take pleasure in battle-cries and polished helmets and the expression of the Marsian foot-soldier, fiercely facing the bloodied enemy.

In lines 25–30, the speaker does not yet begin to pray, but asks to which god and in what form prayer might be effective. Then, beginning in line 30, a series of gods is addressed in the second person as potential saviors, and each god's name is given in the form of the extended vocative phrase that is characteristic of hymns. What has happened over the course of a few stanzas is that a poem that started out as epideixis with no implied occasion or context has shifted into full-fledged prayer. This prayer still does not conjure up a detailed setting of religious observance, but in light of the corporate religious action that characterized Roman civic religion (unlike Christian prayer), it does frame the speaker in public, communal action. The final three stanzas (lines 41–52) unequivocally fit the pattern of poetic prayer, as they turn away from description of ravaged Rome and invest the poem fully in the act of humble and pious prayer.[32]

> sive mutata iuvenem figura
> ales in terris imitaris almae
> filius Maiae patiens vocari
>   Caesaris ultor,
>
> serus in caelum redeas diuque   45
> laetus intersis populo Quirini,
> neve te nostris vitiis iniquum
>   ocior aura
>
> tollat: hic magnos potius triumphos,
> hic ames dici pater atque princeps,   50
> neu sinas Medos equitare inultos
>   te duce, Caesar.
>
>   (1.2.41–52)

Or if, having changed your appearance, you, the winged son of Maia, assume here on earth the look of a young man and allow yourself to be called the avenger of Caesar, then may you be late in returning to heaven and may you linger here for a long time propitious toward Quirinus's people, and may a swift wind no take you away too soon, in disgust at our misdeeds. Here, rather, may you enjoy great triumphs and enjoy being called father and leader, and may you not allow the Parthians to ride unpunished with you as our leader, Caesar.

Equally striking in this poem is how little it prepares for its final phase of prayer in the first six stanzas and how scrupulously it follows the norms for prayer in its final stanzas.[33] This poem is a perfect example of how Horace

---

32. Of course, these final stanzas are famous for a different reason: they may technically preserve the distinction between humans and gods by claiming to be a prayer to Mercury rather than to Augustus, but the effect is in fact to treat the princeps as himself a worthy recipient of prayer. I take up further below the question of Horace's orientation to public, political concerns.

33. Cairns (2012, 165–67) argues that the genre of the poem is paean. It is useful to think of paean as one of the elements that go into this poem, but I don't think this generic identification (which has not seen much agreement since it was first made in 1971) solves the questions of disunity in this poem. It may give us a context for the narrative early in the poem, but if Horace wanted to

imports recognizable elements of Greek religious poetry, strictly obeying the rules that govern those forms but deploying them in unexpected ways. If his primary goal had been to re-create the aura of religious power that is generated by the actual performance of cult songs, Horace was certainly capable of writing poems that sustain over their length a clear and perceptible sense of being uttered in performance (as shown by the *Carmen saeculare*).[34] Instead he offers a significant number of poems that incorporate some elements of performed cult songs, but within contexts that don't unequivocally generate and sustain the illusion of performance.

At a minimum, these two techniques (disruption and discontinuity) are evidence against the assumption that Horace wanted his poems unproblematically to evoke the image of ritual performance. I think we can go further, though, and see that in these poems Horace tinkers with "story" and discourse; individual elements remain legible, and the poems themselves are not difficult to understand, but they refuse to make the production of discourse by the speaker line up neatly with the setting depicted in the storyworld. This is not just "crossing of genres"[35] or Horace's famously discontinuous style; although these poems exemplify both of those recognized practices, they also more specifically use such swerves to avoid producing any stable context of utterance. The sense of a well-defined consciousness expressing itself through these words is sustained throughout this poem, but the sense of this consciousness as embodied and placed in specific social, physical, temporal, and cultural coordinates is not sustained.

I suggest that what Horace accomplishes by writing such poems is to lay claim unapologetically to the ritually effective power of language and the communal authority associated with poetry performed in designated occasions, while asserting that such powers reside not in the context but in the poetry itself, specifically in the discourse. In other words, this is poetry that "performs" in books and for readers and does so without the fig leaf of pretending that the traditional performance context has somehow been transported across time and culture. In order to work out this argument more

---

evoke the genre of paean he surely would have done so more emphatically. See Miller (2009, 45–53) on the complex relation this poem (and the collection as a whole) constructs between Mercury and Apollo, who would have been the most obvious recipient of paean.

34. I do not mean to imply that the *Carmen saeculare* is a simple (or simple-minded) poem, produced by merely following the recipe for Greek hymns. As recent studies—e.g., Putnam (2000), Feeney (1998), Barchiesi (2002 and 2007), Lowrie (2009a)—have shown, there is a great deal of subtlety to this poem. Whatever twists or surprises it introduces, however, it does not disrupt the fundamental addressive structure (a chorus addressing the gods on behalf of the Roman people) that its opening stanzas so clearly initiate.

35. As Nisbet and Rudd (2004, xxvii) say about poem 3.11.

fully, it will be useful to analyze a variety of orientations of "story" to discourse. This is where the difference between hymns and dedicatory poems will be important.

If we think of hymns as invested in promoting the poem itself as a worthy offering, we will see that the poems influenced by this model are clustered in the first book of *Odes*, especially poems 1.2, 1.10, 1.12, 1.21, 1.30, 1.31, 1.32, and 1.35. Each of these poems contains at least one verbal expression for the performance of the poem itself (e.g., 1.2.30 "precamur," 1.10.5 "te canam," 1.12.25 "dicam"), though not always in a finite first-person form (e.g., 1.30.2–3 "vocantis . . . / Glycerae," 1.32.15–16 "mihi . . . / vocanti").[36] I am not claiming that the use of such a verbal expression is a litmus test for hymns (still less that the presence or absence of such an expression can confirm the performance history of a poem), but just pointing out that these poems that might be thought of as hymnlike on other grounds share this feature that accentuates the performative aspect of poetry.

This is particularly striking because poems of this type are largely lacking in the other two books of Horace's first lyric collection. Poem 2.19, the only example in the second book, is a hymn to Bacchus that tips visibly toward the narrative/descriptive function of hymns and in fact contains no element of prayer or request except for the request to be spared the full force of the god's disruptive power (lines 7–8).[37] In book 3 there are many religiously oriented poems; they either present ritual instruction (e.g., 3.23 in which the speaker advises Phidyle) or are focused on an offering other than the poem itself, especially sacrifice (3.13, 3.18, 3.22). Significantly, none of the poems in these two classes (instructive or dedicatory) contain a verbal expression for singing (or praying) the poem itself.[38] There are a few poems in the third book that come closer to the model of hymn that was developed in the first book (especially 3.4 and the lighter-toned 3.11 and 3.21),[39] but the only poem that really fulfills that expectation is poem 3.25, which is again a hymn to Bacchus, though in this case turned to the purpose of praising Augustus.[40]

---

36. Poem 1.35 (the so-called hymn to Fortuna) is an exception; this poem, like 1.2, is almost wholly invested in epideictic description until its final stanzas where it comes closer to the model of prayer ("serves . . . Caesarem," etc. 1.35.29–40). Unlike poem 1.2, however, it opens with an unambiguous address to a divinity ("o diva") and an extended vocative phrase, though it maintains its distance from hymn form by never explicitly naming this divinity.

37. It does contain a self-reflexive expression for song, though a slightly circuitous one: "it is right for me to sing" ("fas . . . est mihi . . . / cantare," lines 9–11). This poem almost seems to be exaggerating both the strategy of ironic detachment (in its first stanza) and the strategy of real-time "ecstatic" engagement (in its second stanza).

38. I will discuss below the one exception: "me dicente" in 3.13.14.

39. These three poems also lack any performative verbal expression for singing.

40. Verbs of singing in 3.25: "audiar meditans" (4–5), "dicam" (7), "loquar" (18).

I give this overview not to propose a hard-and-fast categorization of different kinds of poems in *Odes* 1–3, but given the consensus view that the three books are carefully constructed, it seems significant that the self-reflexive poems are clustered in the first book, with one example in each of the other books.[41] I would argue that along with the other forms of likeness and difference that Horace uses to organize the arrangement of the odes into three books, he saw meaning in the distinction between religious poems that generate a "story" focused only on their own performance (the category I have been referring to as hymnlike) and religious poems that ground their discourse in some more physical, more social, more plot-like version of "story." This latter category is what I am calling dedicatory, and it will be useful now to look at these in greater detail.

Poem 3.22 resembles a relatively simple and straight-faced hymn, like poem 1.10 in praise of Mercury.

> Montium custos nemorumque, virgo,
> quae laborantis utero puellas
> ter vocata audis adimisque leto,
> diva triformis,
>
> imminens villae tua pinus esto,   5
> quam per exactos ego laetus annos
> verris obliquom meditantis ictum
> sanguine donem.

Virgin goddess, guardian of mountains and groves, you who give ear when called three times by girls in labor and who rescue them from

---

41. Another exception to this overall pattern should be noted. Poem 3.1 starts off the Roman odes—a sequence clearly patterned for maximum visibility and impact—with what at first glance looks like the most strongly performative language anywhere in the collection: "Odi profanum volgus et arceo. / favete linguis: carmina non prius / audita Musarum sacerdos / virginibus puerisque canto" (3.1.1–4; I shun the uninitiated masses and keep far from them. Silence, please! As priest of the Muses, I sing for unwed girls and boys a song never before heard). This stanza not only highlights the speaker's singing but calls into being a full ritual context, with the communal participants and the speaker's authoritative status. The powerful performative effect of this stanza is somewhat modified by the designation "priest of the Muses," as it takes the speaker one step away from a ritual in the civic religion. As the poem continues, however, this context of performance is quickly shown to be an image, a metaphor for authoritative address through poetry. The rest of this long poem operates in an unambiguously epideictic manner and never returns even obliquely to the possibility of live performance so memorably presented in the first stanza. Thus this poem is a good example of the technique by which hymnlike forms are inserted into a poem but not allowed to define the poem. This bait and switch here in 3.1 also turns out to be the perfect introduction to the Roman odes that are largely unaddressed (3.4 addressed to Calliope and other Muses, 3.6 to generic "Romanus") and epideictic, providing almost no encouragement to imagine scenes in which these poems might be spoken or sung.

death, triform goddess, let the pine tree leaning over the country house be yours, so that I may happily honor it, as the years go by, with the blood of a boar that practices its sidelong blow.

The poem offers no backstory and characterizes the speaker only in relation to his religious action and the apparently humble homestead in which this action takes place. Two aspects of this religious action, however, invest the poem with more "story" than the hymns I examined above. The dedicatory nature of it implies that the words of the poem are linked (even perhaps subordinated) to actions in the storyworld. Further, the obviously private nature of this act creates a situation almost like that of the conversational technique I analyzed in the previous chapter: unlike the conversational outbursts of Propertius's Ego, these words have the special status of ritual, but like those outbursts it takes place without an audience,[42] and thus the words of the poem are making available to others an otherwise private act in the life of an ordinary person.

I argued above that poem 1.2 inserts full-fledged prayer language into a poem that seems to be founded on quite different principles. In the case of poem 3.22, the first stanza gives no hint that the poem will contain a dedicatory utterance, detailing instead the powers of Diana in typical hymn form.[43] In the second stanza, on the other hand, there is no mention of Diana's powers or her role aiding women in childbirth; instead we get an emphatically performative dedication that points up the exact moment of transferring the tree into Diana's possession ("tua pinus esto," line 5).

Each of the stanzas of this tiny poem offers perfectly correct forms of religious lyric performance, but while they are not at odds in any way, they aim the poem's energy in quite different directions. The first stanza fulfills our expectations for hymn in the sense that the poem, together with its performance, itself constitutes the offering, while the second stanza situates the poem as the ritual recording of the dedicatory act. Note that the first stanza invokes only the bare minimum of storyworld context (as I have shown above is consistent with hymnic form): someone is praying to Diana. Only in the second stanza does this uncontextualized voice take on the contours of space, time, and intent: it is a man standing near a pine tree that leans over a house, a man whose piety is marked not just by this individual action but by his desire to extend it into the future, as he will repeat every year the sacrifice of a boar to this tree. There is very little characterization here beyond

---

42. The poem actually does not rule out that this act could be a communal ritual, but it does nothing to secure or even encourage that perception.

43. See Syndikus (2001, 190–92).

the man's piety and his apparently humble, rural circumstances, but the second stanza reorients the trajectory established by the first stanza, giving the speaker body and place.

In the second stanza we also get a "story"-based analogue for the ritual transcendence that characterized the first stanza: the hymnic language of the first stanza is one way of yoking a specific action in time (this performance, this ritual) with a transcendent and always-available ritual present; the second stanza focuses on the act of dedication and emphasizes that this act is meaningful both in itself and as an individual instantiation of the long string of dedications that will unfold over the years. I noted in poem 1.10 the minimal but important assertion of the singer's action ("te canam," line 5); here the speaker is similarly brought into focus ("ego laetus . . . donem," lines 6–8), but the action that makes him visible for us is not the act of singing (an act that inheres in the poem itself) but the act of ritual sacrifice, which is performed in the storyworld rather than in the discourse. This act is made as much as possible like the act of hymnic praise (in its repeatable nature and in the way that the boar is endowed with its own virtue and value), but it is ultimately a different kind of action, and this difference accords with the difference in poetic expression in the two stanzas.

This poem also stands apart from the hymnlike poems discussed above in that it courts an identification with inscribed dedicatory epigrams.[44] It does not exactly align itself with that genre, well known to Roman poets of Horace's period,[45] but it certainly gestures toward such poems. For the purposes of my argument, this halfway link to writing is important because it calls attention to one of the authenticating practices through which a private act of dedication could be preserved and made visible to a wider audience.[46]

---

44. Henderson (1999, 114–44) acknowledges the poem's toying with its written status as part of a larger argument about the Augustan deployment of piety in the service of civic ideology. Key to Henderson's argument is the way that the poem both segregates a small-scale private ritual (such as the one this poem depicts) from the large-scale rituals of civic religion and yet also metonymically links private and public piety "in their sliding scale" (121; see also 140–43).

45. Syndikus (2001, 190) compares this poem to the dedicatory epigrams in the sixth book of the Palatine Anthology. He finds that this poem agrees with those examples on many points of form and content, but ultimately judges Horace to have used that pattern for purely poetic, rather than religious purposes. Nisbet and Rudd (2004, ad 3.22.5) note the lack of deixis in referring to the pine and the subjunctive "donem" as ways that this poem "avoids the formulae of genuine inscriptions."

46. My point here rests on the differences between performance and writing. Lowrie (2009a, 78–81), on the other hand, uses this poem to demonstrate how, in parallel to the ways that Horace's apparently choral hymns actually preclude performance, a seemingly epigrammatic poem can resist actual inscription. "The tree's mediation between poet and goddess—he would really offer the putative sacrifice to Diana, not the tree—parallels the chorus's intervention between poet and Palatine deities in *Odes* 1.21. A layer of deferral keeps each poem from cultic felicity, whether or not inscribed or sung." I share this view but am offering an argument that seeks to push this analysis further,

I would suggest, in fact, that this poem evinces a poetic practice that differs markedly from that demonstrated above in the case of hymns, but is no less distinctively Horatian. While the hymnlike poems analyzed above line up public life with performance and with the inherent efficacy of discourse, poem 3.22 brings together privacy, writing, and the significance of "story" as a counterpart to (not substitute for) discourse.

The description of the boar in poem 3.22 ("verris obliquom meditantis ictum," line 7) is brief but carries great visual power as well as the power to make us conscious of the lifeblood that will be spilled for this sacrifice. In these ways, it resonates with the more extended description of a sacrificial victim offered in the famous address to the spring of Bandusia (3.13). That poem too focuses on an apparently private, even solitary act of sacrifice undertaken in the rustic hinterlands of Rome. Although built on this common pattern, the two poems have very different effects.

O fons Bandusiae, splendidior vitro,
dulci digne mero non sine floribus,
  cras donaberis haedo,
    cui frons turgida cornibus

primis et venerem et proelia destinat—   5
frustra, nam gelidos inficiet tibi
  rubro sanguine rivos
    lascivi suboles gregis.

te flagrantis atrox hora Caniculae
nescit tangere, tu frigus amabile   10
  fessis vomere tauris
    praebes et pecori vago.

fies nobilium tu quoque fontium
me dicente cavis inpositam ilicem
  saxis, unde loquaces   15
    lymphae desiliunt tuae.

O spring of Bandusia, more glittering than glass, worthy of sweet wine and flowers, tomorrow you will be honored with the gift of a young goat, whose forehead now swells with its first horns, foretelling love

---

beyond Lowrie's claim that such devices "generate indecision" (quotations from 2009a, 79). While I think there are good reasons to investigate writing and performance as parallel practices, it is also worth calling attention to the ways that the specific poems I am examining here make visible and relevant the disjunction between writing and performance.

and battles—in vain, for this offspring of the playful herd will dye your chill-cold streams with its red blood. [8] The fierce season of the blazing dog-star cannot touch you, you offer a lovely coolness to the oxen tired from the plow and to the wandering herd. You too will become one of the famous springs, as I sing of the ilex-tree leaning over the hollow rocks, from which your babbling waters leap down.

While poem 3.22 first offers the impression of a "weirdly context-less" hymn,[47] followed by the embodied image of a man performing sacrifice, poem 3.13 begins with an apparently dedicatory invocation of the spring,[48] before becoming in its final stanza one of Horace's strongest statements of poetry's performative power to ennoble and immortalize ("fies nobilium tu quoque fontium / me dicente," lines 13–14). In other words, the poem begins by foregrounding poetry's role as a supplement to sacrifice and ends up trumpeting the status of the poem itself as an efficacious offering. This poem seems built on the same Horatian impulse as poem 3.22, the impulse to juxtapose these two different concepts of the relation between religious language and religious action, but it inverts the order in which they are invoked.

This poem, however, takes two further steps in exploring the role of "story": it stretches to the breaking point the authorizing link between ritual action and speech, and it invests the physical aspects of this storyworld with the utmost worth. The act of sacrifice here is both more physically detailed (the red blood mixing with the chill clear water) and, surprisingly, more unreal since the whole sacrifice is being conjured up as what will happen *tomorrow*, rather than presented as being enacted in real time with the poem itself.

It may seem like a small change to insert "cras" (line 3), especially since the future tense is often at home in hymns and prayers (cf. the so-called "performative future," such as "dicam," 1.12.25). But in fact this adverb fundamentally changes the poem. No longer can we understand the speaker's words as the real-time performance of dedicatory vows; instead these words become a description of a future event, with the present context of utterance now left unaccounted for. The speaker's words have the representational power to conjure up what they describe rather than the performative power to accomplish some act by speaking. Unlike poem 3.22, which seeks as far as possible to align the moment of speaking with the ritual action, this poem

---

47. The phrase comes from Feeney's (1998, 43) analysis of Catullus's poem 34.

48. Even before we get to the specification of the sacrifice ("cras donaberis haedo," line 3), the spring is described in terms of the offerings it is worthy of ("dulci digne mero non sine floribus," line 2).

divides them and yet still insists on the special, unique / repeatable quality of both the language and the ritual action.

If we focus on the first and last stanzas, we see reflexes of typical dedicatory and hymnic expression, respectively: the first stanza invokes the spirit of the spring and announces the sacrifice, while the last stanza emphasizes the action of the singer ("me dicente," line 14) in rendering this offering appropriately special for this purpose. We should note that the "story" in these two stanzas is limited to establishing that the speaker is making a sacrifice to a woodland spring (with some detail as to the spring's setting in the last stanza); it provides no information about the speaker or the situation. The two middle stanzas, however, are full of vividly rendered physical detail, which brings into the reader's visual imagination first the goat itself, then the sacrifice, and then the cool pleasures of the spring. The effect of this description is somewhat paradoxical, since it conjures up the goat and the spring in all their physical specificity, even though the poem has made clear that it is describing not a present scene but an imagined future.

This odd form of specificity is perhaps nowhere more clear than in the poem's strangely sympathetic evocation of the future that the goat will not have, the lusts and battles that it was destined for "in vain" ("frustra," line 6). Not only is this image arresting for the rare opportunity it offers to see blood sacrifice from the point of view of the victim, but given this poem's off-kilter relationship to performance, it seems the very concept of futurity is being explored here—a combination of predictable order (in which young animals are sacrificed) and the almost palpable presence of other temporal regimes in which the kid can go on to have this lusty future even while its blood also stains the spring's waters. By splitting off poetic expression from its strictly performative function, these two futures can coexist—the kid's existence as a full-grown goat and as a sacrifice laden with ritual meaning. By putting the sacrifice into the future, the poem makes both these events equally real and equally unreal—both exist in the poetry but not in any world, not even in the storyworld.

The final stanza of poem 3.13 has been read (rightly, in my opinion) as a comment on the poet's own power to celebrate and memorialize. The juxtaposition of the present "desiliunt" (line 16) and the future "fies" (line 13) again demonstrates this poem's distinctive temporal structure in which the present consists of physical description (here, the motion and sound of the water), while the future tense encompasses the effects of both poetry and ritual.[49] We are used to the notion of lyric taking place in an eternal present,

---

but what this poem creates is an eternal future: the poem avows its identity as an event in its own right, but distinguishes that lyric event from the ritual and performative event on which it might have seemed to depend. The lyric event points forward to a ritual event always on the brink of coming into existence, but never *now*. Thus this poem invokes the expected alignment of lyric with ritual and performance but also distances the moment of lyric speech from the grounding that such a context would have afforded. In this reading, then, the poem's final claim of commemorative power ("fies nobilium tu quoque fontium / me dicente," lines 13–14) is even more ambitious than it might have seemed: Horace is not just likening poetry to sacrifice (in the manner of seeing choral song as a ritual offering), but declaring that poetry's power is independent of that authorizing frame.

Poems 3.22 and 3.13 are similar in introducing a greater element of "story" (or, more precisely, elements of "story" that go beyond an image of the ritual performance itself), but "story" has quite different effects in the two poems. In poem 3.22, the "story" that we get taps into elements of the setting that have powerful thematic effect: the image of the Italian countryside,[50] and the piety implied by the speaker's scrupulous and deferential behavior. Thus, while this poem (contrary to the practice of poem 1.21, for example, where we were given a clear view of projected choral performance but no indication of a specific festival context) does use "story" to pinpoint the speaker and his actions, it does so only in ways that are themselves readily understood as supporting the poem's thematic meanings, rather than encouraging us to imagine a "plot" that has brought the speaker to this moment.[51] In poem 3.13, "story" is taken in a few different directions: the rich physical description of the spring and its environs, but also the imagined biography of the sacrificial victim and, most implicitly, the characterization of the speaker as one who can marshal the forces of poetry to ennoble the spring. The first two of these uses of "story," however, are clearly marked as the product of the third: it is the speaker as poet who brings into existence the spring and the goat. Thus the overall effect of "story" in this poem is also thematic rather than mimetic and lines up with the poem's overall impact, which is to awe readers with

---

50. Whether we see the setting of this poem as specifically Horace's Sabine farm (of which there is little indication in the poem itself, though within the context of the collection this becomes a valid inference) or just the countryside in general, each of these options carries with it strong and well-defined themes.

51. There actually is a history of reading for the plot here: Nisbet and Rudd (2004, 257) retail several scholarly attempts to establish the identity and parentage of a child born on the Sabine farm on behalf of whom this poem/sacrifice would have been produced.

poetry's powers to generate something that is separate from reality but more like a superreality, a better, fuller version of reality.

Poem 3.18 offers yet another variation on what it means to combine hymnic and dedicatory language and, further, how "story" can operate within such a poem.

Faune, Nympharum fugientum amator,
per meos finis et aprica rura
lenis incedas abeasque parvis
    aequus alumnis,

si tener pleno cadit haedus anno   5
larga nec desunt Veneris sodali
vina creterrae, vetus ara multo
    fumat odore.

ludit herboso pecus omne campo,
cum tibi nonae redeunt Decembres;   10
festus in pratis vacat otioso
    cum bove pagus;

inter audacis lupus errat agnos,
spargit agrestis tibi silva frondes,
gaudet invisam pepulisse fossor   15
    ter pede terram.

Faunus, lover of nymphs who flee you, may you enter my land and sunny fields gently, and go on your way with kindness toward the little nurslings, if as the year draws to a close a tender young goat falls and there is no lack of wine for the mixing bowl, companion to Venus, and the ancient altar smokes with rich scent. [8] The whole herd plays in the grassy field, when your December festival returns, the merry villagers celebrate in the meadows and even the ox is released from work; the wolf wanders among the lambs, now made bold; the woods scatter rustic leaves for you; the ditchdigger rejoices to stomp the hated earth in triple rhythm.

At first glance this poem seems to be a straightforward dedicatory prayer to accompany the sacrifice of a kid. But, as I observed for poem 3.13, this poem's construction also opens up a slight gap between the act of the sacrifice and the poem's own performative unfolding, in this case by phrasing the sacrifice in the conditional. The first stanza describes the kind of solicitous care that Faunus's worshippers hope for in present subjunctives, to be understood as equivalent to the imperative ("incedas abeasque," line 3). But the sacrificial action on which this fostering behavior is made to depend is expressed as a simple (present indicative) condition: "si tener pleno cadit haedus anno," line 5 ("if a tender kid falls as the year comes to a close").[52] There is nothing in this structure that would rule out speaking this poem as one sacrifices a kid at the altar of Faunus, but unlike the strictly performative language we saw in poem 3.22 ("tua pinus esto," line 5), the language of this poem has more in common with description than with enactment.[53]

Beyond its conditional syntax, this description of the sacrifice has further implications, since it avoids a performative first-person verb (cf. 3.22.8 "donem"). In fact, unlike all the other poems I have considered so far, this poem contains no first-person verb, either of singing or of dedicating.[54] The possessive phrase "per meos finis" in line 2 prepares us for the more usual procedure in which the speaker's action, as either performer or dedicator, is registered within the poem, but this turns out to be a false promise. I would link this somewhat surprising feature to the poem's overall investment in description, which fails to specify the speaker's relation to the scene. Even second-person forms get comparatively short shrift in this poem, appearing most strongly in the first stanza and then acknowledged later only by two instances of "tibi" (lines 10, 14), within a poem dominated by third-person, indicative description.

This descriptive orientation, only very minimal in the first two stanzas, takes over completely in the last two stanzas, which offer an idealizing view of rustic prosperity and rustic rites, bringing into focus both the rich security of the animals (lines 9, 11–12, 13) and the pleasure the human inhabitants

---

52. In itself the use of an if-clause in prayer is completely unremarkable. Pulleyn (1997, 16–38), starting from Chryses's prayer in *Iliad* 1.37–42, finds that the prayer form that Chryses uses, which Pulleyn terms *da-quia-dedi* ("if ever I have roofed over for you a temple . . ., fulfill for me this wish . . ."), is distinctively Greek. He notes in passing (17) that promising the gift in the future (*da-ut-dem*) is very common. But he gives no examples of (or considers) the formulation we have in this poem, which uses the present indicative. I am arguing not that such a form is impossible in a prayer, but that it slightly reduces the sense of temporal coincidence between speech and ritual. Nisbet and Rudd (2004, ad loc.) also note the parallel with Chryses's prayer and suggest "the present tense underlines that the sacrifice recurs every year," supporting my sense that there is a slight pull away from the specific occasion.

53. Nisbet and Rudd (2004, 220) on the poem's latter half, which describes the festivities: "a more realistic cult hymn would not describe an occasion that was due to occur at some distance in the future."

54. Actually, poem 3.13 does not contain a first-person verb of singing or dedicating, but it uses the second-person passive verb "donaberis" in line 3 and the participle construction "me dicente" in line 14, which closely replicate the effect of first-person verbs.

take in these festivals.[55] Key to this image, as we saw in poem 3.22 ("exactos . . . annos," line 6), is the notion of repetition ("cum tibi Nonae redeunt Decembres," line 10), which naturalizes in storyworld terms a feature common to both ritual and lyric, that is, that these individual animals and worshippers are both themselves and the present instantiation of a series of festive participants through the ages.

The final stanza gives a particularly poignant twist to the poem's ambiguous relation to performance. The closing image highlights the role of dance in religious festivals. Dance is an appropriate note on which to close this poem, which has been much more concerned with communal ritual than the other examples we have looked at. But rather than invoking the ideal of dance as a graceful offering performed by the young and beautiful, Horace specifies here dance as performed by a laborer ("fossor," line 15) and conflates his three-step dance with a nonritual expression of anger or frustration, as he "rejoices to stomp the hated earth" (lines 15–16). Thus this poem, which has mostly been invested in idealized images of natural beauty, harmony, and abundance, closes with a pointedly human and unidealized image, one that reorients our sense of festive expression away from a perfect timeless world to a world in which festivals are a special loophole in the texture of ordinary life. We might even say that this final image introduces a bit of backstory, since it prompts us to imagine the life of this laborer and the battle he wages every day (except on festival days) with the hard and unforgiving earth.

This final swerve does not radically change the poem as a whole, but it does provide a small countercurrent of specificity within a poem that is largely dedicated to a description of ritual, the utterance of which is unanchored to any specific moment or context. The image of the laborer does not establish the same kind of context that would be established by setting this poem as a speech in the moment of ritual performance (by, e.g., using deictics and a first-person performative verb); rather it establishes a different kind of specificity and a different kind of context, one closer to the textured representation of everyday life we see in other genres. This laborer need not be a specific person with a specific history in order to function in this poem as a counterweight to the idealizing and generalizing images that precede it. It is particularly salient that Horace not only brings in this low-status worshipper and gives us a sense of his state of mind, but that he uses this character as a way of reframing ritual action—what looks like dance in honor of the god (and in fact still is dance, whatever else it may also be) is also the

---

55. The poem shifts away from subjunctive verbs after the first stanza and uses only indicative verbs for the rest of the poem.

kind of action with which people express their emotions in ordinary life, as if ritual is both a special, set-apart realm in which only certain actions "count" and a conversation with the gods and the natural world, in which actions like stamping the ground or laughing have their ordinary meanings.

Since these formal patterns show Horace disrupting solemn traditional forms, it seems appropriate to ask whether we can see in these instances ideological or other impulses that might explain the kinds of innovations Horace pursues. It would be hard not to notice, for example, that the poems that seem closest to hymns are also the poems most likely to include praise of Augustus. Others have argued that Horace's inclination to avoid reproducing ritual contexts in a consistent way allows him to use the prestigious genre of hymn for its obvious value as praise poetry while maintaining a certain autonomy that keeps the poem (and the poet) from being merely a made-to-order glorification of the ruler.[56] There is certainly some appeal to this notion, and it may well be true. I would add, however, that in the broader perspective provided by my argument, which allows us to see Horace undermining the solidity of performance contexts not just in poems praising Augustus but as an overall approach to adapting Greek poetic forms, the effect that this practice produces may not be catalyzed by motives of political resistance or a desire to declare his autonomy. What I am suggesting here is the formal counterpart to Oliensis's argument made on the ground of thematic readings of poems such as 1.37 and 3.14, which put pressure on the "Augustan" (in every way) closure of the civil wars: "Horace's political resistance may be nothing more than an after-effect or side-effect of his poetic resistance. It may be, that is, not the cause but one consequence of this need to assert his poetic authority" (1998, 150).

What I have tried to describe here may not be exactly a form of poetic resistance, but it is a certain kind of poetic stubbornness, which prevents Horace from fitting his poetry into the grooves that have been laid down by the tradition, even though he signals his reverence for that tradition in a variety of ways. The specific way that these poems frame their innovations makes it clear that Horace knows very well what traditional religious poems

---

56. None of the arguments I have in mind are naïve in their conception of either poetics or politics. E.g., again Lowrie (2009a, 92): "Horace invariably sidesteps immediacy. This feature gives his poetry aesthetic independence and keeps it from embracing fully the occasional moment." Santirocco (1986, 131) proposes that in the third book, Horace achieves a harmony between political and private conceptions of the poet's duty. Roman (2014, 201–20) describes a realm of aesthetic autonomy constructed in the odes, which simultaneously acknowledges its dependence on the Augustan order and declares its separateness. Formulating the question slightly differently, Athanassaki (2014) interprets the difference between Pindar's use of occasion and Horace's as reflecting the unique status of Augustus.

look like but chooses not to reproduce them. Especially because religious poetry is so thoroughly implicated in other forms of civic authority (even if Horace did not take the extra step of aligning hymnic form with praise of Augustus) this poetic stubbornness is indistinguishable from an expression of political resistance. This similarity makes it difficult (perhaps even impossible) to tell whether the assimilation between the two kinds of resistance is superficial or is the index of a deeper kinship, still more to know which form of resistance is the driver.

The assimilation between poetic and political resistance might happen in any case, but when we look at the particular form that Horace's departures from tradition take, it is not surprising that these poems have raised questions of autonomy and political resistance.[57] I find it striking that spatial metaphors dominate the discussion of Horace's management of his poetic agenda in the context of Augustan politics.[58] This notion of a space or gap or distance between Horace and some envisioned Augustan orthodoxy fits well with my overall argument in this book, that the historical poet's agency is expressed not (only) through visible elements in any poem, but especially through what Edmunds calls "a deeply implicit, *external* . . . intentionality" (2001, 34; emphasis added), which I understand to be the intention to produce poetry and circulate it. One aim of my argument is to show the ways that this implicit, external intentionality is reflected and subtly acknowledged, not just through metaphor or theme, but through poetic structure. I do not believe that this practice maps on to any specific political or ideological or ethical content, certainly not consistently across corpora. I have argued that the kinds of swerves that Horace introduces into the received generic patterns can legitimately be read as the trace of authorial intent, but have also tried to shed light on this process to show that it can be understood as an element of poetic production more generally and need not be interpreted as a strategy for introducing "hidden meanings" that subvert an otherwise anodyne operation of the poem. Thus the fact that the poems give readers the impression of an artistic

---

57. One other reason why these questions have been raised, of course, is that the difference between Roman political culture and post-Enlightenment liberal democracy makes readers feel that they have to apologize for/undo Horace's praise of Augustus (see Lyne 1995). Fowler (2009) is an outlier in this respect, making central to his argument modern readers' discomfort with the kind of power visible in Augustus and in Horace's representation of his rule.

58. To cite only a few recent and compelling examples, Roman (2014, 204): "What allows, anchors, and counterbalances this newly public orientation of Horatian poetry [in the odes] . . . is precisely the sequestered grove of *Odes* 1.1. . . . Horace speaks all the more persuasively to the extent that he speaks, or sings, from the independent space of his vatic authority." Lowrie (2009a, 91): "Horace habitually keeps his distance from overt praise poetry, through the *recusatio* and surrogate *laudator* of *Odes* 4.2, or other devices."

consciousness that stands slightly aside from the position of the speaker certainly could be evidence of political critique on Horace's part, but it also could be evidence that Horace is marshaling all his most innovative poetic skills to render his praise of Augustus as powerful as possible.

Catullan Invective as Performance

The performative element in Catullus builds on some of the same assumptions we saw in Horace's odes, but it differs significantly both in the forms of performance that are used as models and in the ways those models get reworked into poems. What the two poets share is an assumption that performance implies both a communal context (sometimes made palpable in the poems through an internal audience, but not always) and the specially efficacious language through which performance brings into existence what it depicts.[59] As Horace does, so too Catullus capitalizes on these two assumptions to create poems that naturalize the poetic discourse within the story-world situation, thus aligning the stance of the poem's speaker with that of the historical poet, though the degree and kind of alignment vary. But beyond these central and important similarities that justify treating the two together under the rubric of "performance," it is equally useful to explore the differences. Most significantly, the forms of performance that Catullus gravitates toward are not those of solemn ritual (poem 34 is an exception), but the forms of ritualized behavior that take place within the interstices of everyday life, and, secondly, that he develops the storyworld in a way that makes it a true counterweight to the allure of the poetic discourse, as it vies for our attention.

Poem 42 offers a memorable instance of Catullus's signature style, as it combines aggressive force with humor and an apparently self-deflating image of the poet's authority.

> Adeste, hendecasyllabi, quot estis
> omnes undique, quotquot estis omnes.
> iocum me putat esse moecha turpis,
> et negat mihi nostra reddituram
> pugillaria, si pati potestis.   5
> persequamur eam et reflagitemus.

---

59. Or at least attempts to have this generative effect, subject to the norms of felicity that govern specific forms and acts of performance. I will explore in this section ways that Catullus is more interested in raising the possibility of infelicitous performance than Horace is; this quality fits with Catullus's well-known orientation toward social risk and conflict.

quae sit, quaeritis? illa, quam videtis
turpe incedere, mimice ac moleste
ridentem catuli ore Gallicani.
circumsistite eam et reflagitate: 10
"moecha putida, redde codicillos,
redde, putida moecha, codicillos!"
non assis facis? o lutum, lupanar,
aut si perditius potest quid esse.
sed non est tamen hoc satis putandum.   15
quod si non aliud potest, ruborem
ferreo canis exprimamus ore.
conclamate iterum altiore voce
"moecha putida, redde codicillos,
redde, putida moecha, codicillos!"   20
sed nil proficimus, nihil movetur.
mutanda est ratio modusque vobis,
siquid proficere amplius potestis:
"pudica et proba, redde codicillos."

Come here, you hendecasyllables, all of you from all sides, as many
as exist. That shameful whore thinks I'm a joke and says that she
won't return my writing tablets—can you believe it? [5] Let's pursue
her and hound her. Who is she, you ask? She's that one you see walk-
ing in a shameless way, laughing like a mime actress, annoyingly, with
a mouth like that of a Gallic puppy. Stand around her and make your
demand: [10] "You disgusting whore, give back the tablets; give back—
you disgusting whore—the tablets!" Oh, so you don't care a bit? O
filth, O brothel, or if anything can be more depraved. But we must not
think this sufficient. [15] If nothing else is possible, let's raise a blush
on the dog's brazen face. Shout again in a louder voice, "You disgusting
whore, give back the tablets; give back—you disgusting whore—the
tablets!" [20] But we're not getting anywhere, she is unmoved. You've
got to change your strategy and your approach, if you're going to be
able to make progress. "Modest and respectable woman, return the
tablets."

Commentators often put this poem in social historical context by mention-
ing the archaic legal form *flagitatio*.[60] This practice, a form of public dunning,
is the perfect example of what I mean by "social ritual," since it draws on the

---

60. Usener (1901), Fraenkel (1961).

resources of performative language and form (the very announcement of the debt has legal effect) but also because its public nature (witnessed by the community) is central to its power. Clearly poem 42 makes use of this social practice, but for my purposes I want to register not only Catullus's choice to bring it into his poetry but also his choice to frame this poem as a kind of commentary (or parable) on the relation of poetry to this kind of efficacious social use of language.

A quick comparison to poem 25 can help to sharpen our sense of the specific strategy of poem 42.

> Cinaede Thalle, mollior cuniculi capillo
> vel anseris medullula vel imula oricilla
> vel pene languido senis situque araneoso,
> idemque, Thalle, turbida rapacior procella
> cum diva +mulier aries+ ostendit oscitantes,[61]   5
> remitte pallium mihi meum, quod involasti,
> sudariumque Saetabum catagraphosque Thynos,
> inepte, quae palam soles habere tamquam avita.
> quae nunc tuis ab unguibus reglutina et remitte,
> ne laneum latusculum manusque mollicellas   10
> inusta turpiter tibi flagella conscribillent,
> et insolenter aestues, velut minuta magno
> deprensa navis in mari, vesaniente vento.

Thallus, you boy toy, softer than bunny fur or than goose down or than a little earlobe or than an old man's penis, droopy and cobwebbed with disuse; but you, the same Thallus, also more voracious than a swirling storm-blast . . ., give back the cloak you stole from me, and the Spanish cloth and the Bithynian tablets;[62] you idiot, you show off these things as if they were heirlooms. [8] Now release these from your talons and return them to me, so that your downy little flank and your soft little hands don't get horribly scrawled over by the

---

61. At line 5, Thomson prints "cum laeva nummularios offendit oscitantes," an emendation that depends on a very speculative identification of Thallus. I have quoted here instead Mynors's Oxford Classical Text edition (1958), which remains close to the transmitted text and obelizes the phrase "mulier aries." None of the proposed emendations are persuasive; I leave this line out of the translation.

62. There is no general agreement as to what the word "catagraphos" means. I apply here Thomson's speculation that they might refer to writing tablets, but I will not make use of this tantalizing coincidence with poem 42 since the identification is so sketchy. Other commentators assume that, in keeping with the "pallium" and "sudarium," this must be some kind of fabric, perhaps "figured" (with embroidery vel sim.) as the *Oxford Latin Dictionary* suggests.

scorching lashes of the whip and so that you don't get tossed around in a strange new way, like a little tiny ship caught in a great ocean, as the wind rages.

Poem 25 could be paraphrased as representing the words spoken by someone confronting Thallus, accusing him of stealing a cloak, and demanding its return.[63] While the practice of *flagitatio* clearly influences poem 42, it wholly accounts for the form of poem 25. Both poems emphasize the kind of verbal features we associate with the Roman concept of *carmen*[64]—especially repetition (of sounds, of whole words, of phrases), piling up lists of outrageous and hyperbolic images—and thus both poems point obliquely to the relationship between poetry and other powerful verbal formulas at Rome. Poem 42 offers something like the backstage preparation for *flagitatio*: it shows a poet gathering his hendecasyllables around him, giving them instructions, and dictating to them the incantatory insult with which the desired effect is to be accomplished. While the poem addressed to the hendecasyllables takes as its central scene the orchestration of such a verbal action, the poem addressed to Thallus poses as a moment of real verbal exchange taken from the flow of life (as a response to the theft of the cloak).

Although poem 42 seems more unreal (certainly the personification of poetic lines violates the norms of naturalism), what is at stake here is not the differentiation between nonfictional and fictional, but the divergent ways in which the two poems situate the ritual of *flagitatio* in relation to the action of the poem itself. Poem 25 bases its status as poetry on the fact that the elaborations of language that define *carmina* in Latin operate within the sphere of legal language as well as poetic language; we don't know what actual *flagitationes* would have sounded like, but we do know that in other areas of the law, Romans respected the effects of stylized language. Certainly

---

63. For a different view of what "theft" might mean in this context, see Young (2015, 64–74). She emphasizes the coexistence in this poem of a performative authority that "actually fashions Thallus into the *cinaedus* the speaker claims him to be" and the countervailing force by which the poem acknowledges Thallus's justified right to the stolen objects as his (Greek) cultural patrimony, thus turning the poem into a comment on its own furtive relation to Greek poetic forms. "The poem briefly opens up the self-reflective question of whether Romans had any legitimate claim to Spanish napkins or Greek poems. It opens with this question only to dismiss it with a poetic *performance* that poses brute force as the only guarantor of legitimacy. This poetic tour de force shows its author to be in full command of his invective performance and it suggests that Catullus's skill at manipulating this form legitimates his own claims to rightful ownership of Greek objects, whatever they may be" (73; emphasis added).

64. Meyer (2004, 44–72) gives an excellent analysis of the *carmen* style (characterized especially by "repetition; accumulated pleonastic synonyms . . .; detailed and precise identification of what is wanted or required; and the use of assonance and alliteration to create something that would sound rhythmical and impressive" (45).

this poem takes that basic principle much further than one would expect in a *flagitatio* performed in the Roman street, but again, we should remind ourselves that this poem is not an attempt to pass for ordinary social speech but poetry that claims to share its origin with the speech rituals of real life.[65] Poem 42, on the other hand, is exactly the opposite of this: rather than collapse the impulse for poetry into the impulses that drive social speech, this poem dramatizes the invention of poetry, as if giving us the backstory of how a poem like poem 25 came into being. This poem makes a claim for the relationship between poetry and the semiritualized uses of language in social life (as poem 25 does), but the whole energy of poem 42 is put into showing the effort and strategy that go into aligning these two forms of stylized language, rather than taking that alignment as natural or inevitable.

I am tempted to see poem 42, even with all its whimsy, as perhaps the closest thing we have to an artistic self-portrait of Catullus. There are other poems—the dedication to Cornelius Nepos that opens the collection (1), the abusive rebuke of Aurelius and Furius for their misreading (16)—that might seem to come closer to a realistic portrait of Catullus as poet, but in poem 42 we see the basic components from which his distinctive artistic practice is built: a poet, himself disengaged from any actual slanging, instructs his hendecasyllables to energetically and hyperbolically taunt others (over the ownership of writing implements), and in the end shows that flattery of a woman and obscene insult of a woman are equally useful elements in his palette.[66] Just as important, this poem also leaves open the question of poetry's real social effect—does the elaboration native to poetic discourse strengthen the poem's performative effect or defang it?[67]

What intrigues me about poems 42 and 25 and about their coexistence in Catullus's corpus is that they demonstrate that Catullus makes central to his poetic practice the language rituals of everyday life, but that he also quite

---

65. Fitzgerald (1995, 101–3) on poem 25 makes much of the idea that because Thallus is characterized as a pathic and "soft" in every way, the profusion of "soft" language here (esp. diminutives, which Fitzgerald claims, citing Ross 1969, to be marked as both the language of pathics and the language of the urbane) is a form of theft that the poet perpetrates against Thallus. Fitzgerald also gives due attention to the punishment envisioned in this poem: "Combining preciosity with violence, Catullus threatens to cover Thallus' body with scribbles (conscribillent, 11) a form of writing that reflects both the anger of Catullus and the sinuous softness of Thallus" (103).

66. I am not persuaded by Fitzgerald (1995, 100–101) that this poem cedes control to the woman: "Clearly, the theft here is implicated with a struggle for the control of discourse, and in this poem the poet appears to lose the struggle, for the target of invective who does not recognize the rules of the game escapes his power."

67. Cf. Richlin (1992, 105–6) on the relation between political invective and its literary twin: "without [the motive] of seeing a politician shamed by his rival, the motive can only be pleasure in the hearing or reading of the invective itself. Thus this invective is an art form."

clearly marks the choices and strategies that go into transforming such rituals into poetry. Catullus's distinctive way of handling these instances of social performance lies at the heart of his poetry, and especially of its apparently seamless combination of his own social life with a transcendent realm of art. I think this feature can help to explain why readers of Catullus feel unusually close to him (as if he is whispering his secrets to each individual reader alone) and also unusually conscious of our inability to access the brute facts of his social world (as if his writing so fully takes his world for granted that there is no point in explaining or naming). He shows us the artistic work that goes into transforming language rituals into poetry, but he also aestheticizes social life, equating the practices of social intercourse with the choices a poet makes in formulating language that both arises from social life and is intended to have a social effect.

A quick look at another, modified *flagitatio* may help to clarify how the form operates in Catullus. Although it has not been discussed primarily under this label, poem 12 could be seen as a *flagitatio* that has been adapted to the intercourse of polite society.[68]

> Marrucine Asini, manu sinistra
> non belle uteris: in ioco atque vino
> tollis lintea neglegentiorum.
> hoc salsum esse putas? fugit te, inepte;
> quamvis sordida res et invenusta est.   5
> non credis mihi? crede Pollioni
> fratri, qui tua furta vel talento
> mutari velit: est enim leporum
> differtus puer ac facetiarum.
> quare aut hendecasyllabos trecentos   10
> exspecta, aut mihi linteum remitte,
> quod me non movet aestimatione,
> verum est mnemosynum mei sodalis.
> nam sudaria Saetaba ex Hiberis
> miserunt mihi muneri Fabullus   15
> et Veranius; haec amem necesse est
> ut Veraniolum meum et Fabullum.

Asinius Marrucinus, you use your left hand in a distinctly unpretty way: while we're joking and drinking, you steal the napkins of those who

---

68. Fitzgerald (1995, 100) does note the similarity. Richlin (1992, 144–45) notes the predominance of poems about theft in Catullus's invective.

are not paying attention. You think this is smart? You're out of it, you idiot. It's an act as dirty and clumsy as possible. [5] Don't believe me? Believe your brother Pollio, who would be willing to pay an enormous sum to undo your theft, since he is a young man full of charm and wit. And so, either expect to get three hundred hendecasyllables [10] or give me back my napkin. I'm fond of it not because of its monetary worth, but because it is a souvenir of my friend. Fabullus and Veranius sent to me as a gift these Spanish cloths; I must love them just as much as I love Fabullus and my dear Veranius.

As poem 25 does, this poem opens with its addressee's name, makes the charge of theft, demands the return of the stolen item ("remitte," line 11), and threatens revenge/punishment if it is not returned. The elements of accusation and threat sit oddly, however, in this poem, which is also at pains to depict the companionship of this urbane society. In fact, this poem has often been used as a prime exhibit in defining Catullus's concept of urbanity. The poem is practically a phrasebook of the relevant vocabulary.[69] Emphasis has fallen on the positive definition of *urbanitas* through the figures of the speaker and Pollio (lines 6–9), with Asinius Marrucinus seen only as a negative exemplum. This explains why the *flagitatio* aspect of this poem has been given short shrift: to see this poem as primarily a demand for the napkin and denunciation of the thief would cut against the poem's own apparent impulse to play down the value of the napkin or the ability of the thief to disturb the party.

Given the set of values that scholars have generally agreed are asserted in this poem (aestheticism, friendship, noneconomic exchange), it is striking that the speaker should resort to the semiofficial form of *flagitatio*, which implies public and civic norms rather than the private judgment of a group of like-minded friends.[70] One answer (elaborated particularly by Nappa 2001)

---

69. Positively valued terms include "belle" (2), "salsum" (4), "leporum . . . facetiarum" (8–9) and the key nouns "sodalis" (13) and "muneri" (15). Negatively valued terms here include "inepte" (4; cf. 25.8), "sordida . . . invenusta" (5). Krostenko (2001) points to the density in this poem of "the lexemes of social performance" and says that "they are the characteristic language of a cultural model that Catullus employs so he can make his own use of the expectations the model raises" (241). He also argues that Catullus here displays the logic of the language of social performance, i.e., that it issues from (and therefore gives evidence of) a society that makes aestheticism its defining characteristic, but unlike Cicero's use of that vocabulary this poem shows social authority to rest not with those who have distinguished themselves by action in civic life but with those for whom "aestheticism replaces, and does not augment, politics" (246).

70. Young (2015, 55–63) reads the contrast between public and private differently, as acknowledging the ways that the private life of the elite is implicated in "broader themes of colonial expansion and material expropriation."

is that the contrast between public and private is key to showing in the end that the poet is on one side with his right-minded friends, while Marrucinus is outside that charmed circle. This makes sense as far as it goes, but I am intrigued by the fact that Nappa's explanation does not take up the way that Catullus's poetry is implicated in the quasi-legal structure of *flagitatio*, since it is positioned as the punishment the thief is to expect if he does not return the napkin (lines 10–11).

The threat to send a spate of hendecasyllables links this poem more closely to poems 25 and 42, where poetry is implicated as punishment. This happens only implicitly in poem 25, with the image of the flail "writing" on Thallus's oh-so-soft body, but both poems are governed by the notion that the very poem we are reading, which exposes the theft, *is* the punishment. *Flagitatio* is based on the idea that publicity itself is a form of punishment or at least a form of pressure that will produce the desired outcome. If this is so, then poem 12 seems to offer a contradiction in terms, a private *flagitatio*.

Poem 42 embraces the notion that Catullus's poetry arises out of the speech rituals of everyday life, but also that the poetry works its aesthetic effects on those rituals rather than taking them as they are. Poem 12, on the other hand, segregates two forms of social speech, which feed into the poetry in different ways: a form of aestheticized conversation, that is, the effortless production of witticisms by the in-group, and a form of public declaration that draws on civic and institutional authority for its power. Each of these forms is built on a combination of socially efficacious speech and poetic form, but in inverse ways (one is an aestheticized version of conversation that turns it into an artistic object and the other is a social act made possible by the special formal qualities of *carmen*). Even more striking, the specific poetic form most closely identified with Catullus—the hendecasyllable— is associated with both of these forms (with the first as its unacknowledged metrical translation of conversation and with the second as the explicitly named punishment).[71] So this poem does two contradictory things: it offers its own hendecasyllabic lines as an elevated (poeticized, aestheticized) version of everyday speech—lifting conversation into the realm of art—but also

---

71. Pliny's letters tell of his work in hendecasyllables and carefully situate it as something between dabbling and real publication (see esp. 4.14, 7.4, with comments by Marchesi 2008, chap. 2, and Roller 1998), thus seemingly claiming that hendecasyllables occupy a space somewhere between social life and "real" poetry. (More broadly on the associations of hendecasyllables with informality and release from constraints, see Morgan 2010.) See also Pliny 5.10, in which he claims to have used his hendecasyllables as a kind of *flagitatio* to extract from the unwilling Suetonius writings that the author himself was unwilling to publish. The language describing Suetonius's revisions and preparations for publishing is reminiscent of Catullus 1 and 22.

explicitly identifies hendecasyllables with the stylized forms of language that circulate in the poet's own contemporary environment and have in that context real social (and possibly even legal) effects. Meter here operates both to separate poetry from everyday speech and, counterintuitively, to bolster the link between the two.

In these three poems (42, 25, and 12) *flagitatio* as a social form gets nearly but not quite aligned with Catullus's poetry. Poems 42 and 12, in very different ways, point to the power of hendecasyllables as poetry that has effect in social life and implicitly associate this form with Catullus's verse, but at their most literal level maintain a gap between the socially embedded form and Catullus's own poetry. Poem 42 does this by depicting the poet crafting the abusive speech and by closing with a twist that emphasizes the role of strategic rhetorical choices in shaping the poetry. Poem 12 does this by juxtaposing two examples of hendecasyllables—the conversational/convivial and the performative/ritual—and refusing to comment on their similarities or differences. Poem 25, on the other hand, does seem to align Catullus's poetry with *flagitatio*, that is, pretends that the poem as it appears in the book is a record of (or representation of) an act of social speech in which stylized language is used to bring about specific social effects.

Flagitatio is a very specific social/legal ritual at Rome and appears in all its specificity in poems such as 25, 42, and 12. But it also shares a boundary with a much broader and less concretely defined verbal practice that fundamentally shapes Catullus's poetics: invective. Unlike *flagitatio*, which is defined by specific form (the claim of theft, followed by the use of words like "remitte") and is (depicted as) motivated by the desire for a return of the stolen goods, invective is a verbal action intended to have social traction but less obviously recognizable in a particular prescribed form and less clearly aimed at producing a concrete action.[72] Certainly, what the Romans called invective belongs to a broad ancient category of blame poetry and often to the specific genre of *iambos*, though it is unclear whether that term should be understood to be defined for Roman poetry by meter, by style, or by content.[73] This is a type of literature that most sharply poses questions about what kind of communication is assumed for poems published in

---

72. Richlin (1992) remains fundamental as a study of the various forms invective takes in and outside literary texts.

73. For the particular case of *iambos* in Catullus, see Heyworth (2001), Fain (2008, 31–33). Morgan (2010, 84–97) suggests that the unsettled identity of hendecasyllables (their origin and metrical analysis were debated in antiquity) allows them to possess both an "iambic" and an "ionic" character. Ruffell (2003) surveys the whole category of Roman verse invective and its relation to subliterary popular forms.

collections: is their publication assumed to be an even more powerful variation on speech, since it can carry its effects beyond the present audience to
readers at a distance (in both space and time), or does the publication in a
written collection extract the poetry's critique from the push and pull of real
social life and make it an artistic object?[74]

Poem 37 is not only one of the most aggressive poems in a famously
aggressive corpus, but also a poem that combines to a surprising degree the
brutality of a threat with filigrees of poetic imagery.

Salax taberna vosque contubernales,
a pilleatis nona fratribus pila,
solis putatis esse mentulas vobis,
solis licere, quidquid est puellarum,
confutuere et putare ceteros hircos?   5
an, continenter quod sedetis insulsi
centum an ducenti, non putatis ausurum
me una ducentos irrumare sessores?
atqui putate: namque totius vobis
frontem tabernae sopionibus scribam.   10
puella nam mi, quae meo sinu fugit,
amata tantum quantum amabitur nulla,
pro qua mihi sunt magna bella pugnata,
consedit istic. hanc boni beatique
omnes amatis, et quidem, quod indignum est,   15
omnes pusilli et semitarii moechi;
tu praeter omnes une de capillatis,
cuniculosae Celtiberiae fili,
Egnati, opaca quem bonum facit barba
et dens Hibera defricatus urina.   20

You sleazy drinking tavern and you the comrades there, at the ninth
column from the temple of Castor and Pollux, you think you're the
only ones who have dicks, you're the only ones who get to fuck all the
girls in the world and to judge other men as old goats? [5] Or maybe you
think that because you lugheads are sitting there all packed together
by your hundreds that I won't dare to stuff mine in the mouths of the

---

74. Just to be clear, I am engaged here not in a historical analysis, asking what kind of influence
such poems actually had in their contemporary environment, but in a literary analysis, asking how
the poems themselves frame the continuities and discontinuities with the forms of social speech and
action that they portray.

whole lot of you, two hundred at a time. Well, think again, because I'm going to scrawl over the façade of your whole tavern with pricks. [10] Because my girlfriend, who has slipped from my embrace—a girl loved as no other girl will ever be loved, a girl for whom I have fought serious battles—she's sitting there with you. All you excellent gentlemen love her, and what's worse, [15] even all you small-time guys and street-corner fuckers; you, above all, you from the long-haired race, you the son of rabbit-breeding Celtiberia, Egnatius, whose dark beard makes him look like one of the right kind and so do his teeth, brushed with Spanish piss.

It starts off in a vein that implies a strong version of social instrumentality: a direct address with a rhetorical question that basically has the effect of challenging the interlocutors: "solis putatis esse mentulas vobis?" (line 3).[75] The opening address, including as it does the drinking house itself and its denizens, is a direct challenge and yet made slightly distanced or unreal by including the tavern as a personified addressee. And if we think that this is merely a convenient way to sum up the group of rivals the speaker is addressing, we will still need to take account of the fact that this poem's explicit threats are parceled out to the "sessores" (lines 7–8) and to the "taberna" itself, in the arresting image of lines 9–10: "totius vobis / frontem tabernae sopionibus scribam." Just as he threatens to irrumate the men sitting there, in an exact parallel he also threatens to sexually violate the face (*frons*) of the drinking house.[76] In light of this, I think this poem has a stronger claim to make about the status of poetic language than is often acknowledged; this claim is not disguised as a sexual threat but made within the very contours of that threat.[77]

In the poem's first half, the "poetic" language consists of the personification of the tavern and various artful repetitions of exact forms ("solis . . . solis," lines 3–4), the same word in multiple forms (esp. *puto* in lines 3, 5, 7, 9), and sound patterns, such as the prefix "con-" ("contubernales" line 1,

---

75. Also the geographical reference of line 2 ("a pilleatis nona fratribus pila") is a perfect example of how ambiguous such reference is in Catullus: does the poem assume that we know which tavern this refers to (and so is written for a contemporary circle), or does this reference with the speaker's apparent assumption that readers will recognize it construct the sense of the concreteness that grounds readers' experience of the storyworld (cf. Barthes's reality effect)?

76. Cf. Quinn (1970, ad loc.).

77. In several ways, my reading of poem 37 is consonant with that offered by Wray (2001, 80–87), especially since he seeks to explicate the poem's representational strategies and resists privileging the Lesbia narrative as a way of understanding this poem's role in the corpus. I find unconvincing, however, the claim that the comic stock character of the *miles gloriosus* is key to this poem and that the poem's exploration of performance depends on this intertext.

"confutuere" line 5, "continenter" line 6).[78] In short, these lines have the qualities associated with *carmina* (in the sense of legal/ritual/magical formulas),
and the expansive address that takes up the first line heightens the sense of a
ritualized address, an almost official "challenge" to the denizens of the bar.

Beginning in line 11, the poem shifts not only in focus but also in form as it
turns to a narrative of what has brought the speaker to this point: the promis-
cuity of his beloved "puella." Note that the sentence in lines 11–14 dispenses
with any second-person forms, and thus with the strongly addressive logic that
governed the opening half of the poem. And with the addressive structure,
so too the performative quality of the poem fades. This mininarrative (lines
11–14) seems unanchored to the brutal, aggressive challenge that the poem
as a whole presents. It substitutes tender (e.g., "quae meo sinu fugit," line 11)
and simple language for the performatively amped-up bluster of the poem's
opening and closing lines, and it allows itself to be read (though does not
enforce such readings) as either self-addressed, addressed to no one, or even
addressed outward to readers.[79] Further, line 12 of this poem ("amata tantum
quantum amabitur nulla") echoes very closely line 5 of poem 8 ("amata nobis
quantum amabitur nulla"). This strongly resonant intratextual allusion not
only revives the more tender, emotionally vulnerable speaker of that poem,
but also points us back to another poem in the corpus that shook up our
assumptions about the very notion of address as an engagement with others.

Poem 37 juxtaposes an apparently straightforward example of social performance (the wronged lover threatens his rivals in a way that showcases
his elite masculine authority) with a form of poetic expression that is not
for public consumption, a form that aligns itself with self-communion, intimacy, the words that are whispered softly under the breath to oneself or a
close companion. This latter poetic form exchanges the storyworld audience
(here the "sessores") for the role of the reader;[80] instead of situating the
poem's meaning in light of the social situation happening in the storyworld,
it is reframed as happening at the meeting point of poet and reader in the
discourse itself.

As important as this reorientation is, it does not take over the poem.
The for-us moment (marked out by allusion and by narrative form) in lines

---

78. Wray (2001, 81) notes all these repetitions.

79. This turn is signaled by "nam" in line 11, and thus implies that this narrative is offered as an
explanatory context for the speech that began the poem; this strengthens the impression that readers
are the audience here.

80. The intratextual allusion operates at a level that is meaningful for the reader of the collection, but not for any conceivable internal audience.

11–14 is just part of the complex orchestration of various poetic impulses that shape this poem. Beginning with "hanc boni beatique" in line 14, the poem returns to the addressive and performative form that governed its opening lines. Again we see the stylistic features associated with *carmina*: an alliterative and near-synonymous pair ("boni beatique"), repetition of the second-person address ("omnes . . . omnes," lines 15–16), coinages and other extravagant, multisyllabic language ("pusilli," "semitarii," "cuniculosae"). Notably absent from these lines, however, is the language of threat or any other instrumental language, such as the rhetorical questions and imperatives we saw earlier. Instead these lines are purely descriptive: they assert a claim ("hanc . . . omnes amatis") and then go on to elaborate at great length the identity of these men, finally singling out Egnatius for special treatment.

This structural shift (away from threats and toward description) gives the final lines a very different tone from what came before. These final lines look like the kind of invective in which the description of others' flaws seems intended as much for the entertainment of the audience as for the rebuke of the addressee. Although we might be tempted to say that the shift to jocular description of others' bad habits is a generic shift (to something like satire or epigram, bracketing metrical considerations), it is also importantly a structural shift that reorients the relation of "story" and discourse. The opening half of the poem with its emphatically performative stance implied that we were witnessing an event in which the speaker confronts his rivals, thus strongly foregrounding the storyworld and the not-for-us dimension. The narrative section in lines 11–14 and the "satiric" closing lines that describe the "sessores" rather than threaten them (though, importantly, still in the second person, not third), on the other hand, imply that the weight of the poem has shifted to its discourse and the reception of that discourse by readers. These latter two sections emphasize the operation of discourse in distinctive ways with distinctive implications. The narrative section, with its inward, almost meditative turn and its marked allusion, takes an ahistorical readership as its audience, while the final, descriptive, lines seem to operate on the model of invective as it circulates within a community, defaming and discrediting individuals. (This effect only makes sense if the audience knows the individuals targeted and can react to the invective by withholding their respect.)

In demonstrating that Catullus's invective practice shares conceptual ground with the more specific social/legal ritual of *flagitatio* I am seeking to work out more precisely why readers sense that his poetry is embedded in his own social world to a degree far beyond anything we get from

Propertius and Horace. One measure of this impression is the (now dated) scholarly assessment of Catullus that depended on labels such as "intimacy," "sincerity," or "spontaneity."[81] Even though scholars have mostly given up the practice of reading this corpus as a sort of poetic diary of Catullus's desires and disappointments, there persists (for good reason) the conviction that these poems are shaped in important ways by the forces in Catullus's social and emotional life, that poetic decisions in this corpus are made as much with an eye to establishing the poet's own status as in the service of aesthetic achievement. Certainly, readers of Horace and Propertius regularly interpret their work in light of the need to respond to the historical upheavals of their period and to articulate a stable position for their own political and social identities.[82] But Catullus's poetry gives the impression that such an identity is constructed not only as an effect of the poetry in reception, but within the very fabric of the poetry itself; even though no one would believe that these poems retail real conversations the historical poet engaged in, there is a sense that the social intercourse we see in the poems is, in an indefinable and perhaps even illogical way, linked to his real life.

For example, Wray (2001) offers a study of the poet that is exquisitely attuned to the formal texture of the poetry and to Catullus's complex allusive relation to the tradition, but interprets these literary attributes in light of the overall goal to produce a convincing "performance of manhood." He argues that, in the mid-first century, the clash between two models of masculinity—one shaped by the traditional norms of *mos maiorum* and the other by the ideals of Rome's newly cosmopolitan culture—plays out through the durable Mediterranean pattern of a "poetics of manhood," as formulated by anthropologist Michael Herzfeld.[83]

> Catullus's response to this double bind . . ., the response he performs in his poems, was resolutely centrifugal . . .: the speaking subjects of his poems occupy, from moment to moment, stances of hypermasculine aggression, of provocatively effeminate delicacy, and stances at points in between or located on other axes. The real Catullus, the Catullan self, is not to be found outside the poems, or behind them like a masked actor, or above them like a puppeteer. He is all of the speaking subjects

---

81. E.g., Quinn (1982), which makes intimacy a key critical term. See also Fitzgerald's (1995) approach to the surface/depth dichotomy as a way of critiquing this older view.

82. Roman (2014) is a recent and large-scale example.

83. See Wray's conclusion (2001, 206–9).

of the poems, and none of them. Catullus's honor, his manhood (and its poetics), can be said to rest upon that proposition.[84]

(Wray 2001, 209)

The overall goal of my formal analysis is to delineate the structure of Catullus's poetry (especially the way it constructs and deploys a storyworld as distinct from the poetic discourse) in order to show *how* it does what Wray describes. How do these varying voices and stances get constructed in the poems? How are they able to be perceived as mutually exclusive while also ultimately redounding to "Catullus's honor, his manhood (and its poetics)"? It is exactly Catullus's distinctive handling of "story" and discourse that produces this effect. Like Horace's use of the performative technique in the *Odes*, Catullus's emphasis on performance aligns the special qualities of poetic discourse with the speaker's verbal action in the storyworld and thus strongly aligns the poetic speaker with the historical poet. Unlike Horace's performative technique, however, which emphasizes the kinds of ritual that are set apart from ordinary social life, Catullus selects those aspects of performance that are at home in social life. In fact, what is distinctive about these forms of performance (and a major source of their power) is that they do not insert themselves into a ready-made context, such as a religious ritual, but depend on the performer's own ability to transform an ordinary social interchange into a moment of high-stakes performance.[85]

And yet, this strong orientation toward the storyworld as the matrix within which the poems take on meaning does not prevent Catullus from pursuing a different form of invective, one that seems more at home in a book. While the great majority of poems that could be labeled invective take the shape of a second-person address, there is a smaller group that makes that address less prominent (e.g., poem 39, which consists of a third-person description of Egnatius until line 9, where he is addressed for the first time). Some poems take this principle even further, notably poem 59 ("Bononiensis Rufa"), which consists of a third-person description of Rufa's alleged sexual misconduct, but embeds within that description an appeal to the community as witnesses ("quam . . . / vidistis," lines 2–3). Thomson (1997, 345) likens this poem to a "defamatory pasquil" and suggests that the opening is

---

84. This claim can be productively compared to those of Miller (1994) and Selden (2007), both of whom in very different ways develop a notion of the literary / rhetorical multiplicity (noncoincidence) of Catullan speakers.

85. As is well brought out by Wray's use of Herzfeld's model; see also Richlin (1992, 57–80) for an analysis of the workings of Roman sexual humor that discusses various psychological, sociological, and anthropological theories for these effects.

"based on a *graffito*, such as those found on the walls of houses in Pompeii" (cf. Quinn 1970, 262).[86] I do not believe that we can securely trace the ancestry of this particular poem, but its form is suggestive for thinking about ways that the performative power of invective (and its implied claim to be voicing the judgment of the community) could be associated with writing, not just with oral performance.

Writing makes this verbal assault public in a different way, with consequences for how the audience is perceived. Catullus uses this approach less often, but it is worth noting that the clearest examples involve invective against women and, surprisingly, the most powerful men of the day. Poem 57 is a no-holds-barred political invective against Julius Caesar and his associate Mamurra. It uses the most uncompromising language to detail the indiscriminate sexual voraciousness of these two men (whose partners include each other), but it is not framed as the second-person address we might have expected.

> Pulcre convenit improbis cinaedis,
> Mamurrae pathicoque Caesarique.
> nec mirum: maculae pares utrisque,
> urbana altera et illa Formiana,
> impressae resident nec eluentur: 5
> morbosi pariter, gemelli utrique,
> uno in lecticulo erudituli ambo,
> non hic quam ille magis vorax adulter,
> rivales socii et puellularum.
> pulcre convenit improbis cinaedis.   10

Those two shameless whores suit each other perfectly, Mamurra and the queer Caesar. No surprise, since they are equally stained, one from city life and the other from life in Formiae,[87] and the stains have sunk right in and won't be washed away. [5] What a pair of disease-ridden twins, fancy little scholars sharing the same couch, each one is more sexually voracious than the other, rivals and yet also partners in pursuit of women. Those two shameless whores suit each other perfectly.

---

86. Another poem that closely (though not exactly) parallels this form is poem 41 ("Ameana puella defututa"), again critiquing a woman's sexual habits and scrounging lifestyle, though this poem also includes second-person address to the woman's relatives, advising them to get help for her apparent madness.

87. Formiae, a small city near Rome, is referred to by Horace (*Sat.* 1.5.37) as Mamurra's city; cf. poem 43, in which the woman is insulted as being "the mistress of that bankrupt guy from Formiae."

Poem 57 is consistent in style with the performative invective poems that I have analyzed above. It opens by naming its targets and labeling them with the indecent charges made against them ("improbis cinaedis," line 1; "pathico," line 2). It also continues the patterns we have seen in making full use of metaphorical and imagistic language, here the language of pollution ("maculae . . . impressae resident nec eluentur," lines 3–5), of disease ("morbosi," line 6), and of gluttony ("vorax adulter," line 8). We also see the familiar Catullan forms of linguistic elaboration, especially diminutives ("lecticulo" and "eridituli" appear side by side in line 7; "puellularum," line 9). Thematically, the poem emphasizes the notion of pairing, how alike and well-suited to one another Mamurra and Caesar are, and this in turn implies another kind of pairing, as the poem shows them sharing a bed (or reading couch?).[88]

Perhaps the most striking stylistic feature of this poem, and one that it shares with the famous assault of poem 16 ("Pedicabo ego vos et irrumabo"), is that the first line is repeated as the last line.[89] I will discuss poem 16 further in the next chapter, but here it can help us to see by contrast that poem 57 may be aggressive in arrogating the right to point fingers, but unlike poem 16, it makes no threat and in fact is framed as a third-person description, rather than as a second-person address. It is as if the poem itself is both the threat and its fulfillment: publicly voicing such assertions about men like Julius Caesar in language like this is the act of aggression itself.[90]

There is a paradox at the heart of poem 57: its overall effect is of the most direct and unvarnished verbal assault, but when we look closely at the syntax and structure it seems strangely detached. This poem comes as close as possible to replicating the familiar model of second-person invective (note, for example, how the dative names in the second line—"Mamurrae pathicoque Caesarique"—approximate the structure of address in poem 16's vocative phrase "Aureli pathico et cinaede Furi," 16.2) but in fact delivers

---

88. Fitzgerald (1995, 85): "The obscene confusion of the pairing in this poem reflects a political scandal in which the hierarchy and competition that should work to control the behavior of individuals has broken down." Cf. Konstan's (2011) political reading.

89. Other poems (36, 52) that use this form of ring composition all feature second-person address.

90. The anecdote preserved in Suetonius (Jul. 73) tells us that even though verbal abuse was considered a normal part of the political culture in the late republic, there could be examples that crossed the line (either because of the outrageousness of the libel or because of the stature of the victim or perhaps the difference in stature between victim and perpetrator). It also gives us evidence of the high standing of Catullus's family in Verona, since the sign of Caesar's forgiveness is that he returns to his habit of visiting Catullus's father's house.

a more impersonal and abstract assault, addressed to no one and with no implied setting or occasion.

Or rather, it takes as its setting not a moment of confrontation in the storyworld but its real situation as a poem in a book. We are dealing with a small set of poems here—the two *graffito*-like insults to women (poems 59 and 41) and poem 57—so certainty is elusive, but it seems possible that we see Catullus developing here a form of insult poetry that shifts its center of gravity away from the implied storyworld occasion (the speaker confronting his victim, backed up by communal judgment) and toward the half-acknowledged power of insults that circulate in writing. Why would this form be used especially against women and against the "unicus imperator" (one and only military leader, as Caesar is called sarcastically in 29.11)? It may be that second-person invective (represented as a face-to-face action) operates on the assumption of at least a loose form of egalitarianism, the kind of egalitarianism that characterized the oligarchic elite.[91] Women fall outside this "set" in one way, but the appalling fact of Julius Caesar's (self-proclaimed) special status puts him outside that circle in another way.

This speculation can be supported to some degree by an analysis of poem 28. This poem, an invective against an associate of Julius Caesar, shares something of the paradoxical quality of poem 57: it does make use of a second-person addressive structure, but destabilizes it in specific ways.

> Pisonis comites, cohors inanis,
> aptis sarcinulis et expeditis,
> Verani optime tuque mi Fabulle,
> quid rerum geritis? satisne cum isto
> vappa frigoraque et famem tulistis?   5
> ecquidnam in tabulis patet lucelli
> expensum, ut mihi, qui meum secutus
> praetorem refero datum lucello?
> o Memmi, bene me ac diu supinum
> tota ista trabe lentus irrumasti.   10
> sed, quantum video, pari fuistis
> casu: nam nihilo minore verpa
> farti estis. pete nobiles amicos!
> at vobis mala multa di deaeque
> dent, opprobria Romuli Remique.   15

---

91. I acknowledge, however, that some of the targets of second-person invective seem to be treated like outsiders rather than as fellow members of the oligarchy. See especially Young's (2015, 64–74) discussion of poem 25, which turns on the implications of Thallus's Greek name.

Companions of Piso, staff with empty pockets[92] and suitably light baggage, my dear Veranius and you, my Fabullus, what's up with you? Have you had enough of freezing and starving with that no-account? [5] Has any tiny bit of profit shown up in your ledger, just like the "profit" I got from serving my praetor, when I chalked up everything I paid out as profit? O Memmius, you well and truly fucked me over at your leisure with that whole beam of yours. [10] But, as far as I can see, you two are in the same boat since you've been stuffed right up by a prick of the same dimensions. "Pursue friends in high places!" But may the gods and goddesses give you many evils, you disgraces to Romulus and Remus.

Poem 28 has a clear vocative address in exactly the form and position we would expect it: "Verani optime tuque mi Fabulle" (line 3). Most of the poem does make sense as an address to these two comrades, but on closer inspection (again) the structure is less straightforward. In lines 9–10 we have an abrupt apostrophe to Memmius, the praetor with whom Catullus says he served in Bithynia (see poem 10). These lines make logical sense, carrying forward the parallel of his own experience with that of his friends introduced in lines 6–8, but it is striking that they should be phrased in the second person as an apostrophe. This "turning away" is made even more shocking by its content, which is a graphic second-person description of sexual humiliation suffered by the speaker.[93] This claim puts the speaker into the position of the powerless victim and, significantly, he chooses to voice this in the second person, a form that echoes the form of a public accusation and yet also forces the victim to voice his own humiliation.[94] Rendering his mistreatment in this way crystallizes the force of invective as genre: invective is

---

92. A phrase borrowed from Thomson (1997, ad loc.).

93. The same thought is expressed in the third person (and with less detail) in poem 10, when it describes Catullus and his colleagues as "those who had a fucker for a praetor, one who did not care at all for his cohort" ("quibus esset irrumator / praetor, nec faceret pili cohortem," lines 12–13). Fitzgerald (1995, 69–70) argues that the level of detail in poem 28, especially as it renders the quality of a leisurely lingering over this sexual assault ("bene . . . ac diu . . . / . . . lentus," lines 9–10), "causes the language of aggression to teeter over into the language of pleasure," and as a result, "the extreme expression of Catullus's humiliation turns into, or becomes indistinguishable from, the description of pleasure—a free-floating, textual pleasure that is hard to attribute definitively and exclusively to Memmius or to Catullus and the reader who dwells on his words." The notion of "a free-floating, textual pleasure" (and thus "a more ambiguous distribution of roles," 70) supports my claim that the supposedly clear-cut roles in this scenario become unmoored as the poem goes along, though I am more skeptical than Fitzgerald that Catullus can use this ambiguity to reassert his own invulnerability (by foregrounding "the pleasurable materiality of his own poetry," 70).

94. And, as Fitzgerald (1995, 69) notes, reverses the usual pattern in Catullus of *irrumatio* being associated with silencing the victim.

predicated on the speaker having been wronged (usually as a representative of the community rather than as an individual), but deploying his resources to accuse and punish the wrongdoer. But we have to remind ourselves that this clear-cut moment of invective address occurs as an apostrophe within a poem addressed to friends whose troubles the speaker apparently sympathizes with.

Poem 28 contains yet another oddity of address. The last two lines offer a curse in the second person plural. Of course the vitriolic content of these lines means that the curse is meant for the two corrupt governors, Piso and Memmius, but the poem does not make clear at a structural level that the plural addressee of these lines is different from Veranius and Fabullus to whom second-person plural verbs have been addressed earlier in the poem.[95] These final lines lack a definitive vocative, except for the descriptive "opprobria Romuli Remique."[96] Poem 28 offers us the opposite of poem 57: there we saw a relatively straightforward invective assault, which on closer inspection turned out to be a curiously abstract third-person description; here we have a second-person invective outburst shoehorned into a poem that is addressed to someone else.[97]

The shifting forms of address in poems 57 and 28 do not undermine the invective effect (certainly Caesar didn't feel that Catullus's poems were toothless, according to Suetonius), nor do the complexities they introduce into the poem make it "merely literary." But it is important to register how these poems underplay the implied social setting (i.e., the storyworld occasion)

---

95. It is generally agreed that the singular imperative in line 13 ("pete nobiles amicos") marks this phrase as implicitly quoting typical advice (see, e.g., Quinn 1970, ad loc.). This "quoted" phrase is thus set apart, but since it is embedded within the second-person plural address to Veranius and Fabullus, it does nothing to ease the transition to the new plural addressee in the final lines.

96. The curse at 3.13–14 ("at vobis male sit, malae tenebrae / Orci") is sometimes cited by commentators as a parallel to 28.14–15, but this comparison only strengthens the impression that poem 28 blurs the boundary between the addressees of the rest of the poem (Veranius and Fabullus) and the recipients of this curse. The example in poem 3 both includes an explicit vocative and follows a long section (lines 3–12) describing the sparrow in the third person (not, as in poem 28, direct address in the second person).

97. A brief overview of poem 29 ("Quis hoc potest videre") shows that it offers yet another version of an almost unaccountable combination of direct engagement and obliquity. This poem features two different forms of indirection: First and at the largest scale, the poem's invective force is leveled against Mamurra, but instead of attacking him directly it takes the tack of asking why Caesar tolerates his behavior, thus implicating both of them but significantly distinguishing them (both in the actions described and in the structural role each plays in the poem) rather than treating them as a pair of twins, as in poem 57. Second, the poem starts off as a general, unaddressed question ("Quis hoc potest videre," line 1) and then addresses "Romulus" (lines 5, 9)—either an apostrophic address to the city founder or more probably a sarcastic pseudonym for Caesar (or Pompey?).

that might have been expected to give them their aggressive weight and traction. They seem to rely instead on their coherence as poems in a book—the lines hang together as an expressive whole, but not as a performance aimed at a specific target before a crowd. One could argue that these formal complexities turn "real" political invective into something like a museum piece just for show. It seems equally possible, however, that this reliance on (and acknowledgment of) the poem's status as circulated in a book could be evidence for Catullus's sense of confidence in the power of his circulated poems and that these poems are, if anything, a *more* serious blow to reputations, since the critique comes now not in a storyworld but in Catullus's own "voice" as transmitted through writing (and for a potentially wider audience). He is in fact, though in a very different way from Horace, accentuating the discourse as the place where author and reader meet.

 Chapter 3

Poetry That Says "Ego"

Cui dono lepidum novum libellum
arida modo pumice expolitum?
Corneli, tibi: namque tu solebas
meas esse aliquid putare nugas.

(Catullus 1.1–4)

To whom am I giving my charming new book, freshly polished with dry pumice? To you, Cornelius, because you have generally thought my little trifles to be worth something.

Quaeritis, unde mihi totiens scribantur amores,
    unde meus veniat mollis in ora liber.
non haec Calliope, non haec mihi cantat Apollo:
    ingenium nobis ipsa puella facit.

(Propertius 2.1.1–4)

You ask me why I write so often of my love affairs, why my book is soft upon the lips. It is not Calliope or Apollo who sings these poems for me: my girlfriend herself creates my talent.

Two poems, opening two collections of passionate poetry. Each poem explicitly positions the poetic speaker as the author of written collections rather than of orally performed songs. Each poem also partially undercuts this acknowledgment of its written status, however, by shaping this moment of inauguration as an address, as if the speaker's voice can stand outside the book it is presenting. In these shared characteristics, the two poems situate themselves in the contemporary world of their authors and first readers and display their consciousness of their status as literature (as opposed to ritual script, prayer, song, transcribed conversation, etc.).

These similarities are extremely important for understanding the kind of poetry produced by these two authors and others of this period, but the differences between these two poems are equally important. Notice that while both poems conceive of themselves as parts of written collections with contemporary readerships, Catullus diminishes the distance between the book referred to in these lines and his own collection in which it appears, while Propertius situates the speaker more emphatically within the experiences and motivations of the storyworld, by claiming that the poetry is almost mystically generated by his beloved girl's beauty and charm. Even in the first couplet, where Propertius's poem gestures toward the world of book-rolls and readers, it still maintains a slight gap between the speaker's book (implicitly published before this moment) and his present response to questioners.

The two previous chapters have established a set of practices by which first-person poetry can suggest varying degrees (and kinds) of alignment between the speaker depicted in the poem and the historical poet. Although scholars have frequently taken up the question of whether the "I" of the poem represents the speaker, my approach differs from others in basing the argument not on the poetry's content (e.g., attitudes expressed, personal characteristics such as age or social status), but on its structure. In the current chapter, I am building on those results by examining in more detail a subset of each author's corpus to gain a better understanding of whether / how the speaker is identified with the poet.

This question has more than formal implications. In any context, and perhaps especially in the second half of the first century BCE in Rome—a period that was a political watershed and also laid the groundwork for new patterns of literate culture—the question of how to define poetry as consequential speech is a thorny one. Does poetry's consequence consist in its special discursive patterning or solely in its content? Do figurative language and other forms of indirection magnify, alter, or even undermine the consequences we attribute to poetry? And, most relevant for the questions of this book, is the poem's "statement"—to the extent that poems make statements—to be understood as parallel to statements the poet might make in his own life?

It is not my intention to develop an algorithm that would claim to sort out the effective social or political interventions poetry makes from merely decorative or inconsequential acts. On the contrary, my analysis has convinced me that these three poets, and quite possibly Latin first-person poets more generally, are spurred on in their experiments by the tantalizing ways that these various first-person forms avoid any reductive division between the "real" and the "literary." In particular, the fact that all three poets find various ways of playing speaker and poet off against one another—sometimes suggesting their identity, sometimes rejecting the link or accepting it only in a limited way—shows that they are sensitive to the difference between speaking *in* poetry (as the speaker does) and speaking *through* poetry (as the poet does). When we take account of the fact that these poets are also conscious of their unknowable future readers—readers who will have no access to the poet as social being and will know him only through the text—the likelihood of finding either a smooth alignment or clean break between speaker and poet becomes even slimmer. I would argue that what these collections represent is not an answer to the question of how one speaks in/through poetry, but an exploration that teases out and makes visible the various forces that shape this complex question.

Against the backdrop of the conversational and performative techniques as I have analyzed them in previous chapters, I have chosen to focus here on a specific subset of poems that will shed light on the practice of each poet. For Propertius, I will show how the well-recognized contrast between his first book and second book can show him serially experimenting with different relations between the Ego and himself; significantly, in book 2, the concerns of the poet as poet (not as lover) come to the fore and partially close the gap that had been opened up in the first book.[1] For Catullus, I will home in on several poems that depict poetry functioning in ways that it would have functioned for the poet himself (as a gift between elite men, as an opportunity for competitive display, as a bond between friends). For Horace, I will explore how he exploits the implications of sympotic poetry (which lies on the boundary between ordinary and special, between private and public) to negotiate his self-presentation as a poet.

---

1. In keeping with the current consensus, I believe that "book 2," as transmitted, probably contains material that was originally published in more than one collection, but it is convenient to continue to use this term and the traditional numbers assigned to individual poems. I assume that all the poems included in this book were made public after the publication of the first book, and so represent a new stage in Propertius's poetic career, but beyond that I am not assuming any particular date or serial organization of these poems. The patterns I describe below for book 2 become even stronger and more visible in book 3. Thus, where other scholars have described book 3 as marking a major turn in Propertius's practice, as he sidelines the story of the lovers in favor of a wider range of topics and more publicly oriented stance, I would argue that the shift happens earlier and that book 3 is an intensification of the practice inaugurated in the poems discussed here.

The Propertian Ego in Book 2

It has long been understood that in book 2 Propertius modifies the practices he used in his first book, with the result that the Ego's poetic ambitions are taken more seriously and the poems focus less intensively on his masochistic relationship to Cynthia. To put this shift into context, we should note that in each of the first two books, the first-person form avoids the full identification it seems to promise between the agent in control of the discourse and agent who acts in the storyworld. Book 1 is able to maintain its counterintuitive structure by allowing the discursive level of the poetry and its public circulation to be acknowledged only implicitly; it keeps its focus on the verbal exchanges of private life, and it offers an image of poetry as parallel to social speech rather than as publicly circulated poems. Book 2 reflects more centrally and more explicitly its own status as publicly circulated poetry, as suggested in the opening lines I quoted above. It carries over from book 1 the mesmerizing character of Cynthia, but now, instead of participating in the all-encompassing "elegiac voice," she is more sharply delineated as a fictional character—through address, through physical description, and through alignment with the mythological world—and segregated within the storyworld.

The comparison of these two books shows that a close alignment of the speaking voice in the poetry with the artistic agency of the poet (the kind of alignment that has usually been meant by the term "the lyric I") is not the only way to marshal the poetic resources made available by a scene of address. Book 1, in refusing to align the Ego and the historical poet, creates effects that are both artistically sophisticated and emotionally resonant. (To put it bluntly, book 1 shows that "story" does not make poetry simpleminded or unsubtle.) The challenge of book 2 is to re-create this effect but on entirely different terms. Propertius's solution is to accentuate two aspects of Cynthia that might seem to be mutually exclusive: he builds up the reader's sense of her as a well-defined character (her "mimetic" dimension, in Phelan's terms), in contrast to the powerful but hazy presence she had in the first book, and he reinforces her thematic meanings through the more explicit invocation of mythology (a decidedly public form of knowledge) to depict her as a known quantity.[2]

---

2. Wyke (2002, 49) argues that in book 2 Cynthia loses the realist aspects of her character developed in book 1 (the factors that make readers want to see her as a real woman outside the text) and instead "is depicted as matter for poetic composition not as a woman to be wooed through writing." I will show in what follows that while I disagree that Cynthia in book 1 is a realist character, her characterization in book 2 accentuates the ways that she serves the artistic purposes of the poet and

Close to the beginning of book 2, we see a physical description of Cynthia that is unparalleled in the earlier book.

> fulva coma est longaeque manus; it maxima toto
>   corpore, ut incedit vel Iove digna soror,
> aut ut Munychias Pallas spatiatur ad aras,
>   Gorgonis anguiferae pectus operta comis.
>
> (2.2.5–8; Heyworth 2007a)

Her hair is tawny brown and her hands long; she is statuesque through-out her whole body in her walk, as the sister worthy even of Jupiter walks or as Pallas proceeds to Athenian altars, her chest covered with the Gorgon's snaky hair.

Particularly striking in these lines is the combination of detailed physical description and comparison to goddesses: this juxtaposition is emblematic of the strategy of this book as a whole, which brings Cynthia down to earth, making her more concrete and less elusive, and at the same time exalts her into divine company, making her more obviously "matter for poetic compo-sition" (Wyke 2002, 49). In other words, she is more unambiguously marked as a fictional character and as the product of Propertius's artistic design, in contrast to the implicit way this fact is established in book 1. Reconfiguring Cynthia and her powers in this way has implications for the Ego and his vul-nerabilities. The use of mythology subtly implies that just as the poet stands outside the realm of myth and makes use of it for his own purposes, the "story" of Cynthia and her sway over the Ego is a similar kind of resource to be deployed, rather than the very context within which the Ego speaks. Cynthia may be as uncompromising and unpredictable as she was in book 1, but here she is clearly limited to the storyworld, while the Ego is now more strongly aligned with the poet and so can claim a certain kind of control over her.

One of the concrete changes that support the overall shift in practice between the two books is a striking decrease in the number of poems that define the moment of speaking in strongly dramatic terms, face-to-face with an interlocutor. As a result, any detailed impression of the storyworld as the matrix within which the poems arise is significantly weaker. In book 2, we see more poems that lack address or use apostrophic forms of address, but

---

therefore, though from a very different angle, I agree that her status as a "written woman" is high-lighted. Sharrock (2000) constitutes another important contribution on the operations of realism in Propertius; see 275–82 for an analysis of mythology in the second book that pays close attention to the specific myths invoked and their relation to the elegiac plot.

the most important new pattern in this book is address that shifts within poems, thus undermining the sense of dramatic unity of each poem.[3] It is within this overall nondramatic use of address that Cynthia is addressed more often—she is addressed in twenty-three of thirty-four poems, though we should take into account that many of these poems have multiple address-ees.[4] At first glance, addressing her more frequently might seem to bind the Ego and Cynthia more closely together in the storyworld. But because of the way address is handled in this book—less strongly linked to a stable dramatic scene—addressing Cynthia frequently does little to counteract the fact that we see fewer instances here of the Ego talking about Cynthia to another man (a pattern well represented in book 1),[5] and thus he seems less present in the storyworld and more strongly associated with the discourse. So the overall effect of book 2's pattern of address is that it bolsters the reader's impression of Cynthia's storyworld existence but does not do the same for the Ego.[6]

Book 2 also changes the pattern of address to male addressees. It contains only two addresses to real Roman men (Maecenas in 2.1.17 and 73, Augustus in 2.10.15),[7] and instead we see more frequent address to the beloved woman, more frequent use of apostrophe, and two forms of address that have no parallel in the previous book: addresses to singular or plural unspecified masculine addressees (e.g., "amice," 2.8.2; "credule," 2.25.21; "mortales," 2.27.1),[8] and addresses to men with Greek names (Demophoon in 2.22 and Lynceus in 2.34; note also the use of Panthus for a rival in 2.21). Each of the first two books, then, uses a distinctive pattern that has implications for how the Ego is related to the poet. In book 1, the fact that many of the poems are

---

3. While some of these instances of shifting address might be artifacts created by the unstable boundaries between poems in this book, this certainly does not explain all or even most of the cases. See, for example, poem 2.5, which begins with a conversational opening addressed to Cynthia (including three vocatives in the first two couplets), and then turns in lines 9–16 to something like self-addressed rumination ("crede," line 10; "nec tu non aliquid . . . dolebis," line 15), then goes back to addressing Cynthia ("tu . . . vita") at lines 17–18 and maintains this focus for the rest of the poem.

4. It is notoriously difficult to decide what constitutes a "poem" in this book. I am using here the number thirty-four as the total for this book, which is the traditional number, but editors have usually decided that there are (traces of) more than that.

5. Sharrock (2000) demonstrates the importance of this practice for the realist effects in the first book.

6. Book 2 also shows a decreasing interest in the conversational technique, and when it is used it is more likely to feature Cynthia as addressee; see 2.5.1–8, 2.7, 2.16, 2.18B, 2.19, 2.20, 2.21, 2.22.43–50 (Goold makes these lines the beginning of 2.17), 2.24.

7. This adds to the evidence that 2.10 might be a programmatic poem for "book 2B" or whatever we are going to call the collection that seems to have been mashed together with book 2.

8. There actually are cases of generalizing addresses in book 1, but they are made more specific by an extended description; see, for example, 1.1.31: "vos remanete, quibus facili deus annuit aure."

addressed to real Roman men seems to imply that these conversations take place in the poet's own world, and yet they downplay the Ego's equivalence with Propertius through the conversational technique and related practices. In book 2 the fact that many of the poems are addressed to the fictional beloved and/or to multiple addressees emphasizes the poet's creation of a storyworld, with the result that the poetic discourse in this book more obviously has its source in the historical author.

So we see in Propertius's second book yet another possible relation between "story" and discourse. Like Horace's *Odes*, this collection comes close to representing the real agency of the author in producing the poems, rather than melding that external agency together with storyworld actions and motivations (as Catullus does in the polymetrics) or expressing that agency implicitly as Propertius did in his first book. Unlike Horace's *Odes*, however, this book of poems offers a storyworld that consists not just of isolated moments, but of a fairly well-developed plot that unifies the poems through repeated motifs and consistent characterization of the key figures. Ultimately, this book is still more devoted to "story" as an engine of poetic effects (in contrast to Horace's *Odes*), though it uses that element differently from Propertius's first book.

The opening poems can give us a sense of the differences between book 1 and book 2. Although it deals with metapoetic issues quite fully through metaphor and allusion, poem 1.1 never refers to the Ego's poetic endeavors and instead characterizes him exclusively by his surrender to Cynthia. This poem is far from a simple cri de coeur, and especially complex in its addressive structure and use of mythology.[9] In its use of storyworld events and motivations to characterize the speaker and to account for his speech, however, it is a reliable index of what I have shown above is the dominant structure of book 1, where the Ego seems largely unaware that his own words constitute a poem for readers.

The contrast with poem 2.1 could not be more obvious. Although both opening poems begin by situating the speaker in storyworld experience, in the second book that experience consists of responding to readers' reception of a book of his poems. He does link his poetic career to his experience of

---

9. I find it particularly interesting that this poem uses two features that slightly marginalize the force of direct address: it delays the first vocative by opening with four couplets of unaddressed narration, and it serially addresses several different interlocutors (Tullus in line 9, witches in line 19, friends in line 25, and successful lovers in line 31). Thus, although the poem highlights the content of the storyworld, it does little to naturalize this speech as communication within that world. These features produce an effect similar to that of the conversational technique (i.e., that the poet is in control of the discourse but the storyworld will occupy the visible space of the poem), but it allows the controlling hand of the poet to be somewhat more strongly highlighted, as is appropriate for a programmatic poem.

love, but he does so by positioning the "puella" as parallel to the gods who inspire poets. I quoted the first two couplets at the beginning of this chapter; the lines that follow (lines 5–16) give an extensive catalogue of the mistress's features (e.g., her silken dress, her tousled hair) and show how Cynthia will function in this new book by "translating" each feature from the realm of physical description (i.e., from her storyworld existence) into an aspect of the resulting poetry.[10]

> sive illam Cois fulgentem incedere vidi,   5
>   totum de Coa veste volumen erit;
> seu vidi ad frontem sparsos errare capillos,
>   gaudet laudatis ire superba comis;
> sive lyrae carmen digitis percussit eburnis,
>   miramur, facilis ut premat arte manus;   10
> seu compescentis somnum declinat ocellos,
>   invenio causas mille poeta novas;
> seu nuda erepto mecum luctatur amictu,
>   tum vero longas condimus Iliadas:
> seu quidquid fecit sivest quodcumque locuta,   15
>   maxima de nihilo nascitur historia.

If I have seen her go forth gleaming in the silk of Cos, there will be a whole book of that cloth; or if I have seen her tousled hair scattered across her forehead, she rejoices to walk proudly, on account of the praise her hair has received; or if she has struck out the lyre's song with ivory fingers, I am amazed by how skillfully she applies her nimble hands; or if she lowers her eyes as they resist sleep, I as poet discover a thousand new themes; or if she wrestles with me naked, having cast aside her clothes, then indeed we compose long *Iliads*; whatever she has said or done, the greatest possible story arises out of nothing.

Further, this description is studded with gestures to the poetic tradition ("de Coa veste," line 6; "lyrae," line 9; "Iliadas," line 14), and—in a move with no parallel in the previous book—the speaker uses the word "poeta" of himself with a first-person verb: "invenio causas mille poeta novas" (line 12).[11]

---

10. Here too, as in 2.2.5–8 quoted above, the emphasis is on external physical appearance and/ or behavior, not on Cynthia's personality or attitudes, thus again underscoring her concreteness as a character rather than showing her influence over the Ego.

11. The only occurrences of the word "poeta" in the previous book come close together in poem 1.7, at lines 21 and 24 (Goold transposes 23–24 to after 14), where the Ego uses it as a term that other people will call him in the future when they recognize the usefulness of his poetry in love affairs.

What the opening movement of this poem establishes is not that the Ego is a poet (that was clear in the first book), but that his poetry is now positioned to draw on the resources of the storyworld for the purposes of his own poetic agenda, an agenda that involves both contemporary readers and the poetic tradition. In other words, the Ego's poetry now comes much closer to the shape of Propertius's poetry.

Although poem 1.1 begins with four couplets of unaddressed narrative—telling the woeful tale of the Ego's fall from autonomy into submission—the rest of the poem plays with different versions of second-person address: first, an address to Tullus (line 9) in the first line of a mythological exemplum, and then a series of apostrophes in the second half of the poem.

> Milanion nullos fugiendo, Tulle, labores
> saevitiam durae contudit Iasidos.
>
> (1.1.9–10)

Tullus, Milanion wore down the rage of harsh Atalanta by never avoiding difficult tasks.

Notably, Tullus is not characterized in any way, and nothing in these lines (either in content or form) connects Tullus to the tale of Milanion's struggle.[12] In handling both the address and the exemplum in this way, Propertius offers a glimpse of a poetic logic that associates mythology with poetry's role in the cultural life of elite men and therefore is more closely aligned with the motivations and actions of the historical poet than with those of the Ego. In book 1 this logic is honored only by using moments such as these as a kind of leavening within the overall texture of the book, an element that is sufficiently visible to support the otherwise oblique reference to the poet's agency but not developed as an object of interest in itself.[13] It is significant that this instance appears so prominently in the opening poem, but it is equally significant that the practice seemingly inaugurated here is not continued in the rest of the poem. The combination of the unaddressed personal narrative with which the poem begins and this exemplum (with its address to Tullus) fulfills the demands of this programmatic poem in a specific way: in

---

12. Sharrock (2000, 269) suggests that Milanion acts as a foil for Tullus, but this is because he is "another man invited into the poem, invited to join in the manly business of looking at Cynthia," not because of any characterizing touches.

13. Poem 1.20 is both the strongest instance of this pattern and almost an explicit comment on its principles. This poem segregates the didactic address to Gallus into its opening and closing couplets, thus forming a neat frame around the mythological panel that makes up the bulk of the poem.

content these lines establish the "facts" of the storyworld, but in form they allow the historical poet to demonstrate his control.

The remaining lines of poem 1.1 are programmatic in a different way: they maintain the focus on storyworld events, but they also introduce what will turn out to be the dominant formal pattern of this book by highlighting moments of address: to witches (19–24), to well-meaning friends (25–30), and to happy lovers (31–38). These addresses in the second half of the poem make ample use of second-person forms (especially imperatives and pronouns) and characterize their addressees, and thus emphasize the speaker's storyworld milieu (in contrast to the effect created by the isolated address to Tullus in line 9). Unlike most of the addresses in this book, however, these addresses follow one another in a quick series, and so function as apostrophes rather than establishing any contexts of utterance.[14] Overall, the use of address in this poem meets two distinct programmatic needs: first, in lines 9–18, mythology and the mention of Tullus direct our attention to the historical poet and his milieu, then in lines 19–38, the multiple apostrophes emphasize the importance of the speaker's storyworld situation but without fully adopting the conversational technique. Since that technique implies that the speaker is unaware of the poetic status of his words, it can hardly be at home in a programmatic poem.

Tracing the pattern of address can give us insight into poem 2.1 as well. The opening couplet is striking in this respect, almost the inverse of what we saw in poem 1.1. It is very emphatically a second-person address (it even could be considered conversational, with its implication of in medias res), but it characterizes its addressees not at all (beyond the fact that they know about the speaker's poetry), and the only aspect of the storyworld these lines portray is the speaker's public status as a poet. While poem 1.1 began with a bit of unaddressed narration (as if silently acknowledging the need of readers to have the storyworld introduced), this poem opens as if thrusting us into the midst of a debate, but the content of that debate is poetic style. Further, just as the mode of narration accounts for very little of book 1 after its first few couplets, so too the immediacy implied by beginning this book with "you ask me why . . ." ("quaeritis, unde . . .") turns out to be an instance of misdirection, since book 2 is designed on very different principles.

But of course there is a much bolder and more famous instance of address in this poem: at lines 17 and 73, the speaker turns to Maecenas.

---

14. Unlike the apostrophes of poems 1.17 and 1.18, in these cases the poem itself does not thematize the unreal quality of the address. I take that as supporting the role these addresses play here in giving body to the storyworld.

The first of these instances enacts the topos known (by modern scholars) as *recusatio*, by which the poet excuses himself from grand public praise poetry, usually on the grounds of unfitness.[15] Here the speaker says (to paraphrase lines 17–26), "if I were capable of writing heroic poetry, my subject would not be myth or earlier Roman history, but Augustus's triumphs and your own." As in the address to Tullus in poem 1.1, here too the address to a powerful elite man comes yoked with reference to mythology, but poem 2.1 uses the mythological material to directly characterize the addressee. The speaker here implies that Maecenas and Augustus have a stature that would justify their celebration in mythological terms. In other words, Maecenas is woven into the texture of this poem in a way that Tullus is not in 1.1.

The terms of this address, then, make clear that this poem centers on a poet thinking about his art, not a lover bewailing his sad lot. This difference from Propertius's first book is underscored in the poem's next section, which enumerates in uncomfortable detail what it would mean to celebrate the deeds of Augustus and Maecenas. The examples of battles and exploits (27–34) are stated in a way that highlights rather than softens the brutality of the civil wars. Even more pointedly, the battle of Perusia is included, the very episode to which the final two poems of book 1 refer.[16] What has changed between the two books can be gauged by the fact that in poems 1.21 and 1.22 the forthright engagement with the sorrows of the civil war was rendered without any reference to the speaker's role as a poet, while here in poem 2.1 the question that is explicitly asked is how the speaker's envisioned poetry would report these events.

Undoubtedly, the second book comes closer to unifying the speaker with the historical poet and substituting momentous contemporary events for the endless iterations of disappointed love that constitute book 1. And yet, this second book does not jettison the love plot and the storyworld of private life.[17] Poem 2.1 continues after this *recusatio*, first to justify the speaker's choice to remain focused on "small" genres by invoking the authority of

---

15. For a recent discussion of *recusatio* as a phenomenon of the Augustan period, see Roman (2014, 163–69); for Roman's analysis of this specific poem, see 169–76.

16. "eversosque focos antiquae gentis Etruscae," line 29; cf. "ab Etruscis . . . aggeribus," 1.21.2; "Gallum per medios ereptum Caesaris enses," 1.21.7; "montibus Etruscis," 1.21.10; "Perusina . . . sepulchra, / Italiae duris funera temporibus," 1.22.3–4.

17. Although I mean it in a slightly different sense, I agree with Roman (2014, 173) that the "autonomist strategy" of this poem "allows Propertius to display his connection with Maecenas, while remaining within his elegiac realm."

Callimachus (lines 39–46) and then to return to the material of the first book, namely, the speaker's powerlessness before his beloved and before Love itself (lines 47–70). Significantly, however, this return to familiar ground is also a departure from the manner of the earlier book. While the sentiments are familiar, there is no implied storyworld occasion or addressee for thoughts like this:

> una meos quoniam praedatast femina sensus,
>   ex hac ducentur funera nostra domo.
> omnis humanos sanat medicina dolores:
>   solus amor morbi non amat artificem.
>
> (2.1.55–58)

Since one woman has taken possession of my senses, from this house my funeral procession will be conducted. Medicine heals all human pains: love alone has no affection for the doctor that might cure its disease.

While in poem 1.1, such expressions (linking the Ego's own trials to universalizing claims) might have been addressed to the friends who seek to save him, in this poem they occur at the same discursive level of the poem as the *recusatio* and expressions of allegiance to Callimachean aesthetics. The context in which these lines appear is particularly notable, since they are sandwiched between two runs of mythological exempla, and thus they are reviving the amatory plot within a profoundly different poetic structure.

The boldest moment in this poem's attempt to lay out a new strategy comes in its final lines, where the amatory glory peculiar to book 1 collides with the more usual public conception of glory. In book 1, the theme of death and burial was used to portray the notion that the Ego was preeminent in his own (topsy-turvy) world, as he prays to receive the homage of his devoted lover. The last four couplets of this poem (lines 71–78) replay that pattern, but here Maecenas performs the role previously given to Cynthia, by mourning over the Ego's grave and speaking an appropriately "story"-oriented eulogy.

> quandocumque igitur vitam me fata reposcent,
>   et breve in exiguo marmore nomen ero,
> Maecenas, nostrae spes invidiosa iuventae,
>   et vitae et morti gloria iusta meae,
> si te forte meo ducet via proxima busto,   75
>   esseda caelatis siste Britanna iugis,

taliaque illacrimans mutae iace verba favillae:
"huic misero fatum dura puella fuit."[18]

(2.1.71–78)

And so when the fates demand back my life and when I am just a short
name on a bit of marble, you, Maecenas—hope and envy of Roman
youth and a rightful glory for my life and my death—if by chance your
path leads you by my tomb, stop your British chariot with its engraved
yoke and tearfully cast such words as these over the silent ashes: "this
poor man died because of a hard-hearted girl."[19]

This surprising move demolishes the mimetic and thematic functions that
mourning scenes performed in the first book, where they underscored the
Ego's desires and delusions. By introducing the indubitably real Maecenas
into this scene, Propertius demonstrates precisely that his poetic skill allows
him to produce "impossible" juxtapositions. This final gesture, then, is
emblematic of the way that amatory material works throughout this poem
and, largely, throughout this book: it is strongly marked as fictional, as under
the control of the historical poet, and as capable of being used strategically,
to force this fictional world into collision with the figures and events of the
real contemporary world without being absorbed into that orbit.

Direct address to Cynthia is fundamental to Propertius's second book.
We can begin to explore its effect by examining two poems that create quite
similar effects in spite of the fact that they are built on very different premises. Poem 2.7 is unusually explicit about its contemporary Roman context, referring to the abrogation of a marriage law and explicitly raising
the question of whether Caesar's power is the kind of power that can rule
over lovers. Poem 2.20, on the other hand, seems almost to place the lovers in the mythological world itself; not only does it include a high density
of mythological material, but this material is integrated into the conversational texture of the poem to an unusual degree, especially in the opening lines where it appears in a second-person question ("quid fles abducta
gravius Briseide?"). The storyworld situation presented in the two poems is
roughly similar and stands in contrast to the Ego's more masochistic stance
in other poems: 2.7 seems to take for granted that Cynthia will want to stay
with him and would be upset if he married, while in 2.20 he is celebrating

---

18. Following his usual practice for quotations of characters' voices, by which Propertius avoids
making them into metrically independent units (either a full hexameter or a full couplet), he places
this quotation in a pentameter.

19. This translation borrows some phrases from Goold (1999).

the fact that for seven months she has allowed him in her bed (lines 21–28). Importantly, neither poem refers to the speaker's status as a poet or refers to poetry at all (unless we consider any reference to mythology to be also a reference to poetry). Each of these poems is also slightly more conversational than is the norm for this book.

The use of the conversational technique in poem 2.7 can give us a clue to the poem's large-scale structure.[20] The conversational elements are clustered in the first couplet and the last:

> Gavisa es certe sublatam, Cynthia, legem
> qua quondam edicta flemus uterque diu.
>
> (2.7.1–2; Heyworth 2007a)

You rejoiced, indeed, Cynthia, that the law was abrogated, the law over which we both wept for a long time when it was proclaimed.

> tu mihi sola places; placeam tibi, Cynthia, solus:
> hic erit et patrio nomine pluris amor.
>
> (2.7.19–20; Heyworth 2007a)

You are the only one for me; Cynthia, may I be the only one for you. This love will be worth more than even the name of father.

There are some conversational elements elsewhere in the poem,[21] but the combination of such elements (e.g., the backward glance in lines 1–2 or the strong *ego–tu* links in line 19) with Cynthia's name in the vocative in both of these couplets gives these lines a claim to the kind of dramatic scene that we saw so often in book 1. The rest of the poem, by contrast, is framed mostly in third-person syntax and, even more tellingly, offers sentiments that look more like public proclamations than like the effusions of a lover. This is an excellent example of how Cynthia functions in the second book: she is part of a coherent storyworld that has obvious thematic weight (here, the contrast between the pleasures of love and the duties of patriotism), but the Ego seems less tethered to this context and speaks through the poem to a broader audience. It is important to Propertius's style in this book that the conversational technique is not completely abandoned, but it is equally

---

20. I am referring here to Heyworth's (2007a) text rather than Goold's; the biggest difference between the two is that the couplet transmitted as 6.41–42 (beginning "nos uxor numquam") is placed by Goold before 7.1 (following Luck 1964) and by Heyworth after 7.6 (following a previously unpublished emendation by Sandbach).

21. *Ego–tu* links appear in the couplet 6.41–42, which both Goold and Heyworth place in this poem. Heyworth also reads another vocative Cynthia in line 11.

important that it encloses Cynthia in the storyworld while allowing the Ego to stand partly outside it.

Poem 2.7 contains almost no mythological material;[22] poem 2.20, on the other hand, comes much closer to the normal practice of book 2 in making the heroines of myth as central to the poem as Cynthia herself. This poem maximizes two elements that might seem to contradict each other, mythological exempla and *ego–tu* links, and thus offers a key demonstration of how Propertius attempts in this book to render the lovers' tale through a less personal lens.

In the first four couplets, Propertius uses a series of mourning heroines to represent a storyworld scene in which the Ego addresses Cynthia while she cries; in these lines the pragmatic question "why are you crying?" is expressed in the second person as we would expect, but also voiced in a more universalizing key through these mythological images and through third-person description of Philomela and Niobe.[23]

> Quid fles abducta gravius Briseide? quid fles
>   anxia captiva tristius Andromacha?
> quidve mea de fraude deos, insana, fatigas?
>   quid quereris nostram sic cecidisse fidem?
> non tam nocturna volucris funesta querela   5
>   Attica Cecropiis obstrepit in foliis,
> nec tantum Niobae, bis sex ad busta superbae,
>   lacrima sollicito defluit a Sipylo.
>
>   (2.20.1–8; Heyworth 2007a)

Why do you cry more intensely than Briseis taken away from Achilles? Why do you fearfully weep more sadly than Andromache in her captivity? Madwoman, why do you harangue the gods about my deceit? Why do you complain that my good faith has lapsed? The mournful bird of Attica [i.e., the nightingale] does not amid the Athenian leaves clamor so loudly with her nighttime complaint, nor does even the weeping of Niobe, whose pride brought her twelve children to their deaths, flow down so fully from sorrowful Sipylus.

---

22. Exceptions: Jupiter's inability to part lovers (lines 3–4) and the mention of Castor's horse (line 16) to suit the hyperbolic ambitions of the soldier of love.

23. In a notable reversal from the pattern of the first book, in these lines the words "queror" and "querela" are used of the woman's pointless lamentations rather than the man's. Cynthia's speech in poem 1.3 is the only instance of such usage in the first book. See above in chapter 1 for a full discussion of "queror" in relation to the elegiac voice.

Although these lines include second-person verbs, there are no other second-person forms (e.g., pronouns), and the only visible first-person form is the possessive adjective "mea" in line 3. By rendering the second-person address relatively strongly (including a vocative at line 3) and intertwining this address with mythological content, these opening couplets underscore Cynthia's position in the storyworld and her status as parallel to mythological figures, while the Ego's position is left largely uncharacterized except as speaker of these lines. Further, the opening question "why are you crying?" would seem well-suited to the conversational technique, but the anaphora of "quid" undercuts that effect. These first few couplets are emblematic of the counterintuitive combination of storyworld engagement with stylistic elements that seem to pull the Ego halfway out of that world.

Like poem 2.7, this poem stresses one pattern in its opening and closing lines and another in the middle. In the case of poem 2.20, the middle of the poem has perhaps the strongest concentration of *ego–tu* links of any poem in the second book, while the final couplets return to mythological material rendered in a more personal form, as we saw in the opening lines. In lines 9–28, almost every line contains multiple first- and second-person pronouns, often juxtaposed for maximum effect.[24] In lines 9–12 the mythological material is carried over from the previous section, but after that the imagery is strictly private and personal, telling a story of unalloyed devotion. The diction, the sentence structure, and the content in lines 13–28 all seem at odds with the mythological opening to this poem: on all these levels the poem presents these lines as the words by which one lover assures the other of his undying faith.

In the poem's final turn it reintroduces mythological material (the punishments of the underworld and Aeacus as judge), but in contrast to the opening couplets, here mythology is used to characterize the Ego, not Cynthia. Whatever meaning we attach to the specific design of each section, it is significant that this poem compartmentalizes its style and content in this way: the first and last sections use mythology to define the addressee and speaker respectively, while the middle section uses a strong interlinking of first- and second-person forms and represents the lovers as themselves, not as mythological types. This poem seems to experiment precisely with the question of how far the different modes of mythology and intense dramatic interchange can be unified simply by the "story" of the poem: the

---

24. Just a few examples: "in te ego et aeratas rumpam, mea vita, catenas," line 11; "quod si nec nomen nec me tua forma teneret," line 19. There is also a higher proportion of first-person verb forms here, especially in lines 12–16 and 26–28.

man asks the woman why she is weeping, then protests his devotion to calm her fears. Unlike the dominant practice in the first book, which kept storyworld events central to the overall effects of each poem, here we see a poem that uses its "story" almost like an external frame to hold together the disparate parts. The varying discursive modes this poem brings together provide as much (perhaps more) of its interest as the emotional struggle between its characters.

I cannot hope in this compressed overview to do full justice to the wide range of poetic strategies represented by the poems included in Propertius's second book. Without oversimplifying the effect of these poems, I have tried to show that two seemingly contradictory patterns characterize this group. They mostly continue the focus on the story of disappointed love that the first book introduced, complete with the abject lover and his domineering mistress. But the effect of this substantive pattern has been radically changed from the first book by a new formal pattern that governs its representation. Readers have often noted the weightier engagement with the poetic tradition in this second book, especially obvious in poem 2.34. I suggest, however, that this willingness to talk explicitly about poets and genres is only the most obvious marker of a more subtle and more fundamental change: this book jettisons the strategy of making the Ego something like a fictional character in a novel, who doesn't realize the larger frame within which his words and actions take on meaning, and instead associates him more closely with the real discursive agency wielded by the historical poet.

That shift opens up new possibilities for generating artistic effects out of storyworld events (especially by exploiting the alignments between the storyworld and the world of myth). I would argue, however, that the impression sometimes voiced that this book becomes too repetitive stems from a limitation of this new procedure. The endless reiteration of the cycle of hope and disappointment, when rendered in book 1 through the Ego whose understanding does not rise above his own experience, manages to convey emotion compellingly while also offering ambitious poetic effects that go beyond the mimesis of an individual psyche. That strategy in book 1 also displayed a certain wit, with its sly way of pointing to the poet's skill while seeming never to acknowledge his existence. In the second book, the same small set of events and reactions is now rendered from a more distanced perspective and so deprived of their emotional intensity, while the poet figure now appears more obviously to ask for our approval. There are some outliers in this book, poems that take a more essayistic approach (such as 2.12 and 2.34, which position the Ego as an uninvolved observer, more in keeping with his discursive role), but for the most part this book tries to meld together the distance of the poet with the experience of the lover who must discover the same truths again and again. Ultimately, this combination proves unsustainable, and in the next book Propertius maintains the alignment between Ego and poet but engages with a wider variety of topics and embraces more fully a perspective from outside the storyworld.

The Catullan Ego as Writer and Reader

Even though Propertius's second book moves the Ego closer to the position of the historical poet, it still shows only limited interest in representing the nuts and bolts of a poet's life in first-century Rome. In Catullus's polymetric collection, by contrast, poetry performs a celebrity cameo: in this work, poetry often appears as itself, mirroring its action in the poet's contemporary world, where poems functioned as gifts, as identifiers of in-groups, as bonds between friends, as political and personal slanging. The single most important anchor of this strategy is the choice to render the voice of the speaker (internal to the poem) not just as a poet, but as closely aligned with the production of the very discourse we are reading. This positioning is the polar opposite of the treatment of the Ego that characterized Propertius's first book, where the Ego has a poetic vocation but is segregated from the discursive control of the poems we read. But Catullus's speaker is also quite different from the epideictic position that operates at times in Horace's *Odes*. In Catullus's polymetric poems, the speaker's focus on his own (story)world forces us to take seriously their addressive form. In this section, I will offer readings of a few poems that most clearly demonstrate Catullus's distinctive way of creating tension between the external perspective (that of the historical poet and readers) and the internal perspective (that of the storyworld); not surprisingly, these poems center on depictions of reading and judging poetry.

The first poem enacts most vividly this combination of internal and external perspectives.

> Cui dono lepidum novum libellum
> arida modo pumice expolitum?
> Corneli, tibi: namque tu solebas
> meas esse aliquid putare nugas
> iam tum, cum ausus es unus Italorum   5
> omne aevum tribus explicare cartis
> doctis, Iuppiter, et laboriosis.
> quare habe tibi quidquid hoc libelli,

qualecumque quod, o patrona virgo,
plus uno maneat perenne saeclo.   10

To whom am I giving my charming new book, freshly polished with
dry pumice? To you, Cornelius, because you have generally thought
my little trifles to be worth something, already then when you alone
among the Italians dared to unfold a universal history in three book-
rolls, a learned and painstaking work, by Jupiter! And so, have for
yourself this bit of a book, such as it is—o patron Muse, may it last
evergreen more than a single age.

I noted at the start of this chapter that this poem, especially when compared to the introductory poem of Propertius's second book, represents the
speaker as very close to the actual position of the author of the collection, as
a man who has completed a book of poems that he hopes will have an enduring life in spite of their apparent triviality, and who is well connected among
the literary men accustomed to produce much more ambitious works. But
the very impulse to represent this "documentary" view within a poem testifies to the fact that this is not merely a recording of the social facts but an
artistic strategy. And the choice to foreground this strategy so forcefully in
the first poem is an index of the distinctive way that Catullus makes use of
his own authorial persona as a feature of his poetry.[25]

Recent commentators have drawn attention to the potential gap between
the opening question and the more fully described scene of dedication that
follows (beginning with naming the dedicatee in line 3: "Corneli, tibi"). Until
we get the explicit vocative in line 3, this question floats strangely unanchored.[26] What is striking to me is the way that the opening question frees

---

25. While my approach is oriented slightly differently, focusing on the question of what the
poetry tells readers about the poet, I have benefited from recent studies of this poem (and more
broadly the representation of books in Catullus) that discuss the question of how much the physical
book (or any specific copy) coincides with the poetry itself (e.g., Fitzgerald 1995, Roman 2001 and
2006), and the significance of patronage for this scene of dedication (e.g., Farrell 2009; on patronage
and books more generally, Stroup 2010). Feeney (2012, 33) comes closer in conception to the question I am asking here: "what does Catullus make of the relationship between the maker (the poet),
the made things (the poems), the made object in which the poems have their existence (the book),
and the objects or persons which the poems represent?" I agree with his conclusion that references
to the material book in Catullus's polymetrics "call attention to the constructed, made, nature of the
poetry and to the fictive dimension inextricable from its modes of representation" (44), and in what
follows I will try to push this formulation further.

26. Its unplaceable quality is enhanced by the oddness of a first-person singular question in the
present indicative: "to whom am I giving?" encapsulates the combination of internal and external
perspectives that the first-person speaker of this poem embraces. Farrell (2009, 175, n. 23) suggests,
in light of this poem's reference to Meleager's poem dedicating his *Garland* (*A.P.* 4.1), that the question could be addressed to the Muse, that is, to a divine and transcendent embodiment of the poetic

itself from the social matrix depicted in the rest of the poem to occupy a different zone, a zone where there is important contact (between poet and Muse, between the book and the reader, between Catullus and Meleager), but this contact exists outside any temporal and social context. This poem very successfully evokes the social world of its author—where dedications were social performances and where a slim collection of poems would seem negligible in comparison to a three-volume history—but it is equally success-ful in conjuring up the possibility that Catullus's words are capable of force even apart from this context.

And yet it is within these first two lines that the book is imagined in all its physical specificity. Here the poem juxtaposes the book at its most concrete and the notion of poetry reaching out toward the reader at its most abstract. This provocative opening is well suited to a poem that feels simultaneously very real (an image of the author dedicating this very book) and almost fantastic since it offers us from within the book an image of the scene that will take place when the book is circulated. This poem both embodies and comments on what Nita Krevans has called the coexistence of poet and editor and has shown to be one of the defining characteristics of Hellenistic and Roman poetic books. Krevans uses the word "poet" for the voice that inhabits the storyworld and speaks within poems, and "editor" for the agency that brings the poems together and offers them to readers; thus the "poet" is the anchoring agency of the internal perspective, and the "editor" is the anchoring agency of the external. Here, the poem comes as close as is possible to depicting the editor, though not at the expense of the "poet" or internal speaker.[27]

---

tradition and its authority. Stroup (2010, 220–21) builds on Fitzgerald's (1995) observation that this poem highlights the coexistence of the single copy of the book that is handed over to Nepos and the collection of poems that transcends any individual copy and suggests that the opening question allows itself to be read on two distinct planes: "If we listen to the 'poetic' voice (that is, the voice of 'Catullus the poet'), then the dedication is framed as an exchange between textual allies [i.e., Catul-lus and Nepos]. . . . If, on the other hand, we listen to the 'poematic' voice—the voice of the poem that has arisen from that of the poet—c. 1 is written in such a way that it seems to give itself, and the *libellus* it represents, to all subsequent readers, to each individual who, for a moment, can identify with the *tibi* of line 3."

27. My argument here is consistent with Krevans's observation: "Like Meleager's title metaphor of the garland, the appearance of the book calls attention to the collection as a whole, *and to Catul-lus's role in melding the individual poems into a unit*" (1984, 312; emphasis added). Krevans's overall argument about this poem (312–16), however, focuses on the question of how the poem creates links to previous works and how it uses the form of *recusatio* to signal Catullus's distinctive way of balancing out the unity of the collection against the singularity of individual poems: "the *recusatio* is an appropriate poem to introduce a polygeneric collection, because the poems can unite under the umbrella of anti-epic while retaining individual associations to the occasions that provide lyric sub-genres" (316). Krevans also notes that the poem does not name the poet or describe the book's

Alongside all the other programmatic statements that have been detected in this poem,[28] it also provides an effective introduction to Catullus's aesthetic by forcing into an unstable proximity the internal perspective of the speaker and the external perspective of the author. The anchor of this strategy is the emphasis on the physical book. As others have noted, the poem preserves a distinction between the individual well-groomed copy that Nepos will receive and the book as the collection (which will take on different physical characteristics in individual copies).[29] The choice to zoom in on the look and texture of the book, however, also presents an image as close as possible to the actual experience of the reader, mirroring the action of the reader as s/he takes up the book. Importantly, this almost hyper-literal effect is not at odds with the more figurative effects that have long been seen here: the metaphorical freight of the book's slightness, neatness, newness, etc., only serves to heighten the miraculous fact that the book is both an amalgam of paper and ink and the locus of contact between poet and reader, transcending historical boundaries. What makes this poem so powerful and so pitch-perfect as an introduction to Catullus is the tension between an internal perspective, in which the scene of dedication forms the center of interest and we as readers are positioned only as incidental, and an external perspective, in which the whole scene is arrayed for our benefit and the poem comes *this close* to depicting our very own reading of the book.

The physical existence of books turns out to be the pivot around which Catullus arrays internal and external perspectives throughout the polymetrics. The book is both the literal object that allows poems to circulate apart from the voice and social presence of the author and a symbol of the ambiguously (im)personal quality of poems circulated in this manner. Therefore images of the book in Catullus get at the heart of the reader's experience of this corpus: the feeling that we have privileged access to the poet through the poems even while realizing that what we really have access to is the poetic discourse itself, not to the poet or his life. Beyond just grounding the "documentary" view of poetry, his practice of depicting books is key to Catullus's exploration of a range of ways that the voice

---

content beyond vague terms like "nugae" and "quidquid" (313), even though it goes into so much detail about the book's *external* appearance.

28. Certainly the poem also contains a manifesto for Callimachean slightness and craft over bigness and raw power. For a recent recap of this poem's metapoetics, see Feeney (2012, 35–36).

29. For interpretations of this distinction, see Fitzgerald (1995), Farrell (2009), Stroup (2010), Kennedy (2014).

within the poems works in relation to (and sometimes at odds with) the implied perspective of the poet.[30]

Poems 14 ("Ni te plus oculis") and 22 ("Suffenus iste") engage in this tension between internal and external, even though in each poem the speaker acts as a reader of other authors' work, rather than introducing his own. Like poem 1, these poems are set in the world of elite social intercourse that provides the framework for both writing and reading. All three poems are also united in their portrayal of the content of poetic books chiefly in terms of style rather than in terms of the ideas, attitudes, claims, or feelings represented in the poems or evoked in their readers. In other words, while these poems foreground issues of judgment and reception, we learn very little about the content of any of the poems in these collections. These three poems represent poetry collections as physical objects, as socially significant gifts (e.g., able to construct or bolster relationships), and as opportunities for readers to exercise (and advertise) their own aesthetic discrimination, but they do not represent them as a vehicle for finding out more about the authors or for discovering what those authors think or feel. These poems seem to propose that poetry collections have important social functions, but none of those functions depends on the content of the poetry, just on its style. In these scenes of literary reception in the story-world, the twin facets of style and social function take precedence over the idea that reading poetry might involve a kind of access to or communion with the author.

And yet this physical/social depiction of books is complicated in each of these poems by the very fact that these representations of poetry appear within poems and a fortiori within a poetic collection that makes the construction of a consistent authorial persona across poems one of its most obvious strategies. In poem 1, as I discussed above, the very fact that Catullus appears both as the internal speaker handing over a papyrus roll to Cornelius Nepos and (implicitly) as the author of the collection that this poem inaugurates implies a relation between author and poetic content that will not allow us to ignore the impression that someone is trying to communicate with us through this poem. This poem, then, offers the somewhat contradictory proposals to take poetry as a physical, social, and aesthetic object and to take it as a form of contact with the author. In poems 14 and 22, the speaker is positioned as the reader of other poets rather than as the author of his own work, and so the tension between internal and external gets expressed

---

30. A few of the poems that treat poetry as a physical object (poems 35, 36, 50) will be discussed in the next chapter rather than here.

differently. And, as I will discuss below, poem 16 ("Pedicabo ego vos") brings this contradiction to an unparalleled pitch, though it also departs from the pattern created by the other three poems.

Poem 14 emphasizes the way that aesthetic judgment functions like gossip to identify like-minded individuals for one another and bind them together.

> Ni te plus oculis meis amarem,
> iucundissime Calve, munere isto
> odissem te odio Vatiniano:
> nam quid feci ego quidve sum locutus,
> cur me tot male perderes poetis?   5
> isti di mala multa dent clienti,
> qui tantum tibi misit impiorum.
> quod si, ut suspicor, hoc novum ac repertum
> munus dat tibi Sulla litterator,
> non est mi male, sed bene ac beate,   10
> quod non dispereunt tui labores.
> di magni, horribilem et sacrum libellum!
> quem tu scilicet ad tuum Catullum
> misti continuo, ut die periret
> Saturnalibus optimo dierum!   15
> non non hoc tibi, salse, sic abibit.
> nam, si luxerit, ad librariorum
> curram scrinia; Caesios, Aquinos,
> Suffenum, omnia colligam venena,
> ac te his suppliciis remunerabor.   20
> vos hinc interea valete abite
> illuc, unde malum pedem attulistis,
> saecli incommoda, pessimi poetae.

If I did not love you more than my own eyes, dear sweet Calvus, I would hate you with a Vatinian hatred for that gift you sent. For what have I said or done that would give you a reason to kill me with so many poets? May the gods send many evils to that client of yours who sent you such a lot of wretches! But if, as I suspect, it is the schoolmaster Sulla who has given you this clever new gift, then I have no problem with that—in fact, I think it's great that all the trouble you've taken for him has not gone to waste. [11] Good gods, what a truly awful and execrable book! And yet you sent it right away to your friend Catullus, so that he should die on this best of days, Saturnalia. You won't get away with this, smart aleck. For, as soon as it's light, I'll run to the booksellers' shelves; I'll collect all the poisons—poets like Caesius and Aquinus and that Suffenus—and I'll pay you back with these as torments. [20] In the meantime, goodbye to all of you, go back to the place from which you brought your evil foot, you pests of our time, terrible poets!

The poem begins with an address to Licinius Calvus (who also appears in poems 50, 53, and 96), establishes a storyworld relation of warm affection between speaker and addressee, and also introduces this speech as part of a cycle of gift and countergift.[31] In other words, before we know that this is a poem about poetry we know it is a poem about the complex rules surrounding friendship and status among elite men. This poem as a whole most closely hews to the line I sketched above, by focusing on the social effects of poetic collections rather than analyzing the content of such collections. Even here, though, the poem's diction calls attention to the way that readers might be tempted to conflate collections and their authors. It uses the term "poeta" and the names of authors as metonyms for the collections ("tot . . . poetis," line 5; the proper names in lines 18–19); within the overall logic of the poem, this usage operates, as Stroup (2010, 82) argues, to rob those authors of the status enjoyed by the speaker and addressee. This very effect, however, relies on the notion that what is being rejected here is not just the book but the author and his claim to social status. So even though this poem evinces very little interest in the contents of poems as an index of the author behind them, it maintains a bond between poet and book.

Poem 22, on the other hand, puts front and center the question of the relation between poet and book, though again it characterizes Suffenus's poetic misdeeds as crimes of style, and we learn nothing of the topics, conceptions, or attitudes of these poems.

> Suffenus iste, Vare, quem probe nosti,
> homo est venustus et dicax et urbanus,
> idemque longe plurimos facit versus.
> puto esse ego illi milia aut decem aut plura

---

31. Although it is possible to read the relation between speaker and addressee here as genuinely hostile, the trend in recent decades has been to take the harsh language as teasing. Those who see the poem as replicating good-humored banter between friends are more likely to prefer the reading "salse" over "false" at line 16, though considering how much negative language there is elsewhere in the poem, even the reading "false" does not require that it be read literally. Stroup (2010, 78–82) argues strongly for seeing the relation within which this exchange takes place as occurring between equals (in contrast to the poets of lesser status than Catullus and Calvus, whose work gets used as fodder for their game of one-upmanship).

perscripta, nec sic ut fit in palimpsesto   5
relata: cartae regiae novae libri,
novi umbilici, lora rubra, membranae,
derecta plumbo et pumice omnia aequata.
haec cum legas tu, bellus ille et urbanus
Suffenus unus caprimulgus aut fossor   10
rursus videtur: tantum abhorret ac mutat.
hoc quid putemus esse? qui modo scurra
aut siquid hac re scitius videbatur,
idem inficeto est inficetior rure,
simul poemata attigit, neque idem umquam   15
aeque est beatus ac poema cum scribit:
tam gaudet in se tamque se ipse miratur.
nimirum idem omnes fallimur, neque est quisquam
quem non in aliqua re videre Suffenum
possis. suus cuique attributus est error;   20
sed non videmus manticae quod in tergo est.

Varus, that Suffenus, whom you know well, is a charming man, witty
and sophisticated, and writes a huge amount of poetry. I think he's
written out ten thousand lines or more, and not (as is usually done)
on palimpsest; he uses proper book-rolls of brand-new best quality
paper,[32] brand-new bosses, red bands, parchment covers, the whole
thing ruled with lead and smoothed with pumice. When you read it,
that neat sophisticate Suffenus seems instead to be some goatherd or
ditchdigger—so strange and changed is he. [11] What should we make
of this? A man who just now seemed to be a wit (or if there is anything
more clever) becomes more hickish than a hayseed farm as soon as he
comes into contact with poetry, nor is he ever so happy as when he is
writing a poem: such joy does he take in himself and so much does he
marvel at himself. Of course, we all make the same mistake, and there
is no one whom you could not perceive as a Suffenus in some respect.
Each person has his own peculiar failing; but we don't see the part of
the knapsack on our backs.

In contrast to the opening poem's free-floating question ("cui dono?"), in
this poem the speaker begins by addressing Varus and then expresses distress
over Suffenus's failed volume of poetry—so luxuriously produced and yet so

---

32. See Thomson (1997 ad 22.6) for this interpretation of "cartae regiae novae libri."

lacking in the urbane wit that characterizes the author in his social life.[33] The first line here is very much in the conversational mode, since it combines the vocative address with a hint of shared experience ("quem probe nosti"), which produces by implication a whole social network complete with gossip. This sets us up to expect a poem that will emphasize an in-group dynamic, highlighting the bonds of knowledge, taste, and judgment that connect the speaker and Varus, from which we as outsiders are excluded (as we saw in poem 14). But after this first line, Varus disappears as an addressee (his name never reappears and the only second-person forms—"legas"[34] in line 9 and "possis" in line 20—are generalizing, equivalent to English "one"), and there are no indications that his attitudes or judgments are being solicited. So the poem starts off as if the speaker is sharing his opinion with a friend who also knows Suffenus, but then seems to turn all but explicitly to the reader, who has no knowledge of this amateur poet and who will require background information and description.[35]

The poem raises two interlocking questions that involve different aspects of the relation between internal and external: First, does a poet's social demeanor (Suffenus is "venustus," "urbanus," "bellus") automatically get expressed in his writing? Second, does the quality of the book's physical materials correlate with the quality of the poems? Both questions imply a simplistic view of poetry as aligned with the author's social existence; in the case of the second question, this view depends on a notion of "value" that is fungible between the social and the literary. It is not surprising, then, that the poem answers with firm negatives across the board, but the airing that these questions receive here suggests that there is a certain appeal to these simple equations. The speaker seems to come to the negative answer in each case against his own instinct, as if needing to convince himself that it really is true that a witty "scurra" can be a clumsy poet and that a physically

---

33. Varus's most notable appearance in the corpus is in the odd anecdotal poem 10 (on which see McCarthy 2013). Possible identifications include Quintilius Varus (mourned by Horace in Odes 1.24) and Alfenus Varus (who could be the addressee of Catullus 30). Feeney (2012, 42) seconds Nisbet (1995) in suggesting that Varus and Suffenus are the same person, a possibility that cannot be ruled out but that I find the poem does very little to support.

34. Fordyce (1961, ad loc.) notes that it is unusual for the generalizing second person to include the pronoun "tu" as it does here. See further discussion and bibliography on this point in Feeney (2012, 40, n. 52).

35. The headnotes of commentators reflect this shift. Fordyce (1961, 146): "The opening address to Varus which disguises literary criticism as a letter to a friend is a piece of hellenistic technique." Quinn (1970, 156): "We can treat Poem 22 as a historical document . . . it touches . . . on questions of critical theory about which the *poetae novi* were intransigent. . . . The matter is lightly put, but seriously meant."

beautiful book can contain rubbishy poetry.[36] Thus, even though this poem argues against the simplistic view, the notion of a simple, organic link that would unify the poet's social existence and the value of material objects with the qualities and value of the poetry retains a certain attraction.

The object of desire that this poem describes (and finds elusive) is none other than the reader's sense that reading poetry secures us some access to the poet. But while this poem demolishes the simplistic sense of poetry as "a natural function or reflex of the nature of the poet" (Feeney 2012, 40–41), both the design of this poem and the design of the whole collection (marked here by intratextual allusion to poem 1) still seek to maintain the sense that poetry does offer some form of contact with the poet—not direct and not simple, but rather conditioned by the special attributes of poetry. This more complex, ironic effect—in which the speaker's argument is partially countered by the poem's presentation of it—is in fact an example of the very proposition that the author of the collection, not the speaker, is the person with whom the reader communicates by reading these poems.[37]

We can read off from this poem statements about what poetry is or how it relates to social actions and truths, but in order to do so we need to ignore the poetic form—not just the meter and the playful exuberance of the language, but the structural choice to frame this poem as a moment of social speech. I noted above that the addressive structure of this poem, the sense that the speaker is really exchanging views with Varus, is visibly weaker than in many other Catullan poems, but that fact should make us even more conscious of Catullus's choice to retain the addressive structure here. This paradoxical relation of social language and poetry—that they can be neither completely severed nor completely aligned—and the implications of that paradox for the relation between speaker and poet are, I believe, central to Catullus's work. He never seems to be content with the notion that poetry lacks social meaning and social traction, but will also never allow us to assume that the two forms of action in language can be stably aligned. This is the reason for his

---

36. I am persuaded by Farrell's argument (2009, 171–72) that the intratextual allusions that associate Suffenus's sharp-looking book with the description Catullus gave of his own in poem 1 make this poem in part an expression of the anxieties the author has about the reception and impermanence of his own work.

37. It is possible that this sense of irony is also what produces the somewhat puzzling proverb with which this poem closes. The speaker in this poem, like most Catullan speakers, has been confident and unapologetic in his judgments, but then closes with a recognition that Suffenus's inability to be a good judge of his own poetry is a common failing. The unusual humility of this line belongs to the speaker (who does not realize the ironic position the poem has placed him in), but also to the author, who has constructed a poem that both strengthens and weakens the proposition that the poet's own views are expressed in his/her poetry.

distinctive focus on the storyworld as the conditioning matrix of his poetry, and for his persistent play with internal and external perspectives.

No poem in the corpus more fully enacts this paradox than the famously aggressive poem 16.

> Pedicabo ego vos et irrumabo,
> Aureli pathice et cinaede Furi,
> qui me ex versiculis meis putastis,
> quod sunt molliculi, parum pudicum.
> nam castum esse decet pium poetam   5
> ipsum, versiculos nihil necesse est;
> qui tum denique habent salem ac leporem,
> si sunt molliculi ac parum pudici,
> et quod pruriat incitare possunt,
> non dico pueris, sed his pilosis   10
> qui duros nequeunt movere lumbos.
> vos, quod milia multa basiorum
> legistis, male me marem putatis?
> pedicabo ego vos et irrumabo.

I'll fuck you in the ass and in the mouth, you queer Aurelius and you slut Furius, you two who have decided that I am not quite proper sexually because my little verses are a bit on the soft side. For a respectable poet ought to be modest himself, but there's no reason for his poetry to be so; [5] poems only have wit and charm if they are a little on the soft side and not quite proper sexually and if they can stir up a tingling, not in boys, I mean, but in hairy men who can hardly move their stiff loins. Because you read about many thousands of kisses, you think I'm not man enough? I'll fuck you in the ass and in the mouth.

The internal perspective here is that of a poet who is defending his manhood, having been charged with writing poems that are excessively soft and insufficiently modest. The external perspective is rooted in the ironic choice to include in the corpus a poem that shares the usual addressive mode, but uses this address to stake out a poetological claim about the noncoincidence of speaker and historical poet. More than any other poem in the corpus, this poem highlights the irresolvable tension between these two perspectives.

Central to this poem's paradoxical relation of internal and external is the fact that the storyworld elements (anchored by the address to Furius and Aurelius) are foregrounded and yet at the same time made to seem mere instruments in the poem's strategy. Furius and Aurelius seem both to matter in their own right and to be stand-ins for misguided readers. The poem as a whole does not go very far toward presenting a social scene in which these words are spoken, but it still frames the speech very forcefully as a social act. The poem offers a further, complementary paradox by equating poetry with physical action, when it claims that some poems are powerful enough to incite erections in grown men, thus making poetry something like a real actor in the social and physical world of its readers. Therefore in addition to the other more obvious paradoxes this poem presents—that its chaste and modest speaker is threatening to rape his detractors,[38] that it is a poem telling us not to believe what is said in poetry[39]—it also seems to be making contradictory claims as to the social embeddedness and social traction of poetry.

This poem ratchets up the stakes from poem 22 in several ways: it not only strengthens the addressive quality of the poem, but uses the performative technique to heighten the sense of the speaker facing his addressees in real time and haranguing them in language that is meant to draw on both the powers of verbal patterning and the powers of communal standards pronounced by an authoritative speaker.[40] Even more tellingly, this poem explicitly aligns the poetry under discussion with Catullus's own corpus, by referring to the "many thousands of kisses" of poems 5 and 7 (or perhaps poems to Juventius, such as 48 and 99). Like poem 1, this poem claims to give a view of the collection from the outside, but unlike that opening poem, in this case the speaker's language injects into the poem the disparaging views of others, thus offering a new twist on the combination of internal and external perspectives.

Thus poem 16 strains to an almost unsupportable pitch the essential paradox presented in poem 22: Can a poem claim that it is illegitimate to assume the poet's views from poetry without collapsing under its contradictions?

---

38. See Richlin (1992, 13) and Selden (2007, 515). Although I am not foregrounding it here, there is also an important line of criticism on this poem that focuses on its sexualized power relations, rather than on how this poem grapples with questions of language, meaning, and speech, including Fitzgerald (1995, 49–52).

39. "The logical problem with the poem, and the feature that makes it a riddle when one treats the logic rigorously, is that one must make an assumption that contradicts the poem in order to get meaning out of the poem": Batstone (2011, 248).

40. Beyond the obvious element of the elaborated vocative (in lines 2–3), this poem underscores its performative status by repeating its threat in the first and last lines and by bookending this repeated line with paired first-person singular future indicatives. It also (implicitly) constitutes the poem itself as punishment, as we saw for *flagitationes* in the previous chapter. Richlin (1992, 13) associates this punishment with the sexual aggressiveness of the poem itself: "The poem itself in reality achieves a kind of public verbal rape."

This poem embraces that failure,[41] and yet also draws into this logical conundrum the attributes of social speech, not as a way of moving beyond the failure but as yet another way to explore it. In other words, while Culler's notion of epideixis ("presentation of assertions or judgments that are not relativized to a particular speaker or fictional situation," 2015, 35) implies that such purity increases the power of a poem's assertions, Catullus's artistic instincts pull him in the opposite direction, toward thickening the texture of the storyworld exchange. Not only does he use address and the performative technique to give greater mimetic weight to the speaker, the addressees, and the implied context,[42] but he also frames the question under debate as a question about proper manly sexual behavior, and so renders the stakes of this argument in terms of the speaker's social life and social identity. So my contribution to the endless debate about this poem (and I really do believe it will be endless) is to say that it stands as an extreme example of the principle that consistently defines the polymetrics and their deep investment in "story": as sophisticated and supple as Catullus is in demonstrating the ways that poetry transcends merely referential, merely constative, merely ends-oriented language, he keeps bringing it (and us) back to language defined, in part, by its use in social settings.

The Horatian Ego in Symposium

My readings of Propertius and Catullus in this chapter have focused on poems that offer some glimpse of the authors' own position as poets in contemporary terms. It is characteristic of Horace's first collection of *Odes* (books 1–3) that it excludes any similar kind of reference: he never even describes this poetry as written, still less does he revel in descriptions of book-rolls or readers' reactions.[43] One can of course find Horace engaging with books, readership, recitation, etc., in his other collections, but my goal is to analyze the strategy of self-presentation within the exotic ecosystem that Horace invents in the *Odes* rather than to fill in its highly strategic gaps by turning to other evidence.

---

41. I agree with Selden that in this poem the performative and the constative fight to a standstill: "In c. 16, Catullus not only confirms the opposition of performative to constative language, but designates their mutual resistance as the generative principle of his work" (2007, 527).

42. The commentators provide examples of how the addressive frame of this poem lends itself to the construction of narrative, e.g., "Es war dem C. zu Ohren gekommen, daß . . ." (Kroll 1968, ad loc.).

43. Horace does depart from this pattern in the fourth book of *Odes*, using the word "chartae" (pages) twice to refer to his own poetry (4.8.21 and 4.9.31).

With that in mind, I have chosen to focus here on a well-defined subset of the odes, the poems that place themselves (scenically) at drinking parties and (historically) within the tradition of Greek sympotic poetry. This lyric subgenre has an iconic stature as the birthplace of lyric, and even of "the lyric self"—that is, the idea of lyric as a privileged poetic form for expressing an otherwise ineffable subjective experience and identity. Central to this conception of lyric's unique association with subjectivity is the impression not only that sympotic poems are simultaneously artful and socially efficacious (as I argued in the previous chapter for performed lyric generally), but that this multivalent power is produced within the bounds of a moment of private life, thus endowing these poems with an intense coloration of privacy and spontaneity.

I argued above that archaic Greek poetic practice was organized to get as much mileage as possible out of the impression that the scene is a real event in the world to which the poem is responding, rather than an element internal to the poem and designed for thematic utility. Such poems are most successful when they can simultaneously give the impression of responding to an external scene and making that scene meaningful and emotionally resonant beyond any significance it would have as a moment of real life. Unlike the relation of religious ritual to hymns, however, the "occasions" around which sympotic poetry is organized are set in a boundary zone between special and ordinary, transcendent and concrete, universal and contingent.

What happens to this alchemy of event and theme in literate poetry? Perhaps even more decisively than in the case of literate hymns, literate poems that extol the pleasures of wine-drinking, song, friendship, sex, and revelry have been seen as sad latecomers, always trying to recapture the intensity and authenticity of "real" sympotic poetry but only betraying the emptiness of their own gestures. I think literate sympotic poems have been judged even more harshly than literate hymns because, beyond laying claim to a socially embedded status, sympotic poems also claim to preserve a moment of pure unmediated pleasure, an untaught enjoyment of life. In terms of the analysis I have been developing, while hymns avail themselves of the special status that inheres both in the moment of performance and in their own elevated poetic style, sympotic poems edge more toward the conversational—not in the manner of the outbursts scripted for Propertius's hot-headed Ego, but as language that is less conscious of its own formal perfections and its own thematic density, and more centrally engaged with the people and happenings of the storyworld. The twin labels of "private" and "spontaneous," while recognizably inaccurate even within the prestigious tradition of Greek sympotic poetry itself (which relied on the reperformance of poems by famous poets), still have the power to express what is most valued in that tradition. Therefore, in addition to the charge that is laid against literate hymns—that they are "fictional" in inventing the occasions they pretend to celebrate—in the case of literate sympotic poems, the lack of an external occasion makes these poems seem even more distant from their lively Greek models.

While Horace's sympotic poems offer us nothing like the alignment of authorial agency with speaking position that we get in Catullus's opening poem, his distinctive treatment of this famous lyric subgenre is one of the places in this collection where he most clearly leaves his fingerprints. Specifically, his sympotic poems are designed to register the implicit claim this form makes for its spontaneity and privacy, rather than participating in that assumption or seeking to strengthen it. In what follows I'll examine first a few poems that seem most obviously to adhere to the expectations for sympotic poems by situating themselves as real-time speech/song within an unfolding party (1.27, 3.19, and 2.7). The first two of these poems are robustly "mimetic" (in the terminology of Albert)[44] but make use of their scenic context for purposes other than establishing a dramatic frame for the speaker's words; the third (2.7) is equally emphatic in its sympotic identity but creates more distance between the speaker's words and the scenic context it describes. These three poems (discussed in this order below) also allow us to gauge the effect of contemporary reference. The unspecified cultural/historical context we see in poem 1.27 shifts to allow a slight nod to Roman historical context in poem 3.19; poem 2.7, however, positions itself in the midst of the most fraught tensions of public life in the 20s BCE: it depicts a drinking party that takes its celebratory impulse from the desire for reconciliation after the civil war. Horace's approach in poem 2.7 is an example of the broader principle I am trying to demonstrate in his sympotic poems: he makes his own biography the matrix within which public and private are interrelated, but just as he maintains a distance between discourse and the scenic context in the other poems, here too he makes it clear that this biographical material is subordinated to a discursive agenda. This pattern obviously has political consequences in the age of Augustus and especially

---

44. Albert (1988) is a study of Greek and Roman poems that seem to respond to a scene in real time, reacting as events unfold. The term "mimetic" has been influential, most obviously in discussions of Callimachus's *Hymns* (of which the hymns to Apollo, Athena, and Demeter exemplify this technique). While my argument obviously has a similar focus, I have tried to develop a more thorough-going analysis of the relation between story and discourse and therefore rarely use this term. For Albert's analysis of Horace's ode 1.27, see 127–32.

if one of your closest "private" friends is Maecenas. Therefore I will close this section by looking closely at two poems that integrate Maecenas into Horace's sympotic practice (1.20, 3.8).

Poem 1.27 not only situates itself as speech unfolding within the bounds of a symposium, but uses several features to heighten its apparent spontaneity. The poem opens in a way that implies that the speaker is addressing present companions and trying to intervene to prevent imminent chaos.

> Natis in usum laetitiae scyphis
> pugnare Thracum est: tollite barbarum
>   morem verecundumque Bacchum
>   sanguineis prohibete rixis.
>
> vino et lucernis Medus acinaces   5
> immane quantum discrepat: inpium
>   lenite clamorem, sodales,
>   et cubito remanete presso.

It is a Thracian habit to fight with cups that were made for pleasure; be done with that barbarian behavior and keep modest Bacchus far from your violent quarrels. The Persian dagger is wildly at odds with wine and lamps; muffle your unseemly shouting, my friends, and stay with your elbow pressed on the couch.

The poem immediately calls attention to the physical scene and focuses our attention on the speaker's desire to have an effect on his companions. These elements are muted in comparison to the conversational style we saw in Propertius's first book (especially by the *gnomai* with which the speaker prefaces each of his requests to his rowdy companions, in lines 1–2 and 5–6, and by the elevated diction). Still, the "story"-oriented nature of these stanzas is underscored by the content of the speaker's pleas, which not only point to the sympotic context but imply that the party is getting out of hand and, thus, rather than conjuring up the idealized symposium, present a specific unpredictable drinking party. So while these stanzas are full of the expected sympotic vocabulary, it is more important that they create an ongoing *scene* rather than (or, in addition to) using the symposium as a topic or theme.

The next few stanzas continue building the impression that the poem allows us a window into a moment of spontaneous (and even potentially disorderly) social life, by focusing attention on the speaker's attempt to wheedle a secret (the identity of his lover) from one of his drinking companions. Again here we see an almost textbook iteration of sympotic themes as the poem makes a game or challenge of the drinking, reveals erotic vulnerabilities, and amps up the teasing quality of the exchange. These stanzas deepen the impression that Horace is here demonstrating his knowledge of (and reverence for) the Greek sympotic tradition and especially its trademark, the ability to produce an elegant, resonant, beautifully crafted poem for readers while seeming to be wholly absorbed in the emotional and sensuous life of the symposium itself. If anything, this poem is perhaps more focused on "story" than is the norm for Greek sympotic lyric (and elegy), but again that quality seems to imply that Horace realizes that the impression that the speaker is responding to an ongoing external event is the lifeblood of such poems and what differentiates them from his own literate practice.

This description holds true for *almost* the whole poem. There is a moment in the fifth stanza that, at first glance, seems just to underline the spontaneity of the speaker's utterance, but on closer inspection turns the poem in a new direction.

> quidquid habes, age
> depone tutis auribus. a miser,
> quanta laborabas Charybdi,
> digne puer meliore flamma.
>
> (1.27.17–20)

whatever you have, come on, place it in my trusty ears. Oh! poor you! what a Charybdis you are up against, though you are a young man worthy of a more elevated passion.

Between "auribus" and the exclamation "a!" in line 18, we are meant to understand that the young lover has whispered his secret into the speaker's ear, after which the speaker goes on to commiserate with him. This structure, like the features of the poem considered above, underscores the poem's investment in the storyworld, but it differs from the usual practice of Latin first-person poetry in a fundamental way. As readers we are very comfortable with the notion that such poetry transmits certain aspects of the storyworld (the setting, the identity of the interlocutor) while remaining largely focused on thematic and other effects, and therefore does not give a comprehensive view of the scene. In that sense, this poem is doing nothing out of the ordinary. Where this poem differs from most first-person poems, however, is that the hitch between these two words in line 18 reminds us forcefully of the poem's own selective process by which the storyworld gets filtered through discourse—in short, reminding us that the storyworld is made accessible to us only through the discourse and only for the purposes to which the discourse puts it.

As I suggested earlier, we can gauge the "specialness" of the lyric speech act by the fact that even when it is clearly situated in a social scene, the speaker's utterance is rendered as a continuous stream with no interruptions or responses from others. This seemingly practical detail can stand as an index of the counterintuitive power of the lyric voice, its power to mediate between its social and aesthetic identities (as a speech and a poem). In contrast to the lyric norm, in which any potential rift between these two aspects is minimized, in this poem Horace engineers a subtle but immediately comprehensible way to make the discourse call attention to its independence from the scene.[45]

The upshot of this tiny gesture radically changes the meaning of a poem that is otherwise markedly obedient to the norms for sympotic poetry. What happens (or doesn't happen) between the two words in line 18 silently points to a physical action in the storyworld that the discourse is selectively excluding and thereby shatters any sense that this poem is trying to pretend that it is responding to external event rather than creating (or being) its own event. I would nominate this poem as the most characteristic expression of Horace's sympotic aesthetic, since it pushes almost as far as possible the rhetoric by which spontaneous speech over the wine bowl also constitutes an artful poem, but also reveals that such seamlessness (and the implied distant echo of archaic performance culture) is not at all what Horace is interested in.

Perhaps the ode that comes closest to poem 1.27 in its apparent zeal for portraying real-time sympotic revelry is poem 3.19, which begins with a rebuke to a long-winded pedantic drinker before indulging in toasts and finally ends with a warning against waking up the neighbors.

> Quantum distet ab Inacho
>   Codrus pro patria non timidus mori,
> narras et genus Aeaci
>   et pugnata sacro bella sub Ilio:
>
> quo Chium pretio cadum   5
>   mercemur, quis aquam temperet ignibus,
> quo praebente domum et quota
>   Paelignis caream frigoribus, taces.
>
> da lunae propere novae,
>   da noctis mediae, da, puer, auguris   10

---

45. See McCarthy (2013) for a more detailed discussion of this poem.

Murenae: tribus aut novem
    miscentur cyathis pocula commodis.

qui Musas amat imparis,
    ternos ter cyathos attonitus petet
vates; tris prohibet supra   15
    rixarum metuens tangere Gratia

nudis iuncta sororibus:
    insanire iuvat: cur Berecyntiae
cessant flamina tibiae?
    cur pendet tacita fistula cum lyra?   20

parcentis ego dexteras
    odi: sparge rosas. audiat invidus
dementem strepitum Lycus
    et vicina seni non habilis Lyco.

spissa te nitidum coma,   25
    puro te similem, Telephe, Vespero
tempestiva petit Rhode:
    me lentus Glycerae torret amor meae.

You discuss how many years came between Inachus and Codrus, who was not afraid to die for his homeland, as well as the race of Aeacus, and the wars fought at holy Troy; what price we pay for Chian wine and who will warm the water, and at whose house and at what time I can escape this cold weather worthy of the Paelignian mountains— on these subjects, you say nothing. Hurry up and pour one in honor of the new moon, pour one in honor of midnight, slave, pour one in honor of Murena the augur. The cups are mixed with three or nine generous ladlefuls. [12] Let the poet who is devoted to the Muses in their uneven number, struck out of his wits, ask for nine; the Grace, joined in dance with her nude sisters, fears quarrels and forbids us to take more than three ladlefuls. It's good to go crazy; why have the blasts on the Berecynthian pipes fallen silent? Why are the pan-pipe and the lyre hanging up unused? I hate the hand that serves with restraint; scatter roses; let bad-tempered Lycus next door hear our mad uproar and also our female neighbor, who is not well-suited to the old man Lycus. [24] You, Telephus, who gleam with your thick glossy hair like the evening star in a clear sky—Rhode who's just the right age has her eye on you; as for me, I feel the heat of a slow-burning love for my own Glycera.

Like poem 1.27, this poem positions the speaker as a participant in the drinking, and it begins by highlighting his attempt to enforce sympotic decorum. This poem too supplies in full all the expected vocabulary and topoi that will establish—maybe even a bit too explicitly—its relation to the sympotic tradition. Poem 1.27 reveals its distance from that tradition by a subtle discursive wink; this poem instead makes the scenic context itself difficult to parse. Each section of this poem (lines 1–4, 5–8, 9–28) is easy to understand as a coherent instance of sympotic speech, but they seem to depict discontinuous moments or even different parties (a pedantic talk-fest at the beginning, gracious toasts and debates about drinking etiquette in the middle, and a mad ruckus at the end).

The scholarly reaction to the two poems is revealing: while most commentators note that at 1.27.18 readers must understand that the secret has passed from the tormented lover to his sympathetic adviser, few register this as any kind of disruption in the "mimetic" process of the poem;[46] commentators on poem 3.19, however, seem to feel that their primary duty is to explain how the speaker's words can be fitted into a continuous (or discontinuous) scene.[47] I recognize that the strategies of these poems differ substantially, but in both cases Horace is producing wrinkles that prevent "story" and discourse from being linked in the smooth way we expect for sympotic poems, and it is important that these wrinkles operate visibly enough to call attention to their own effects.

There is another significant difference between these poems that can help us frame the question of how such poems can be conceived as Horace's self-presentation in any meaningful sense. Poem 1.27 may offer a very vivid scene, but it is one that is untethered to any specific historical or cultural milieu (beyond the obvious fact that it is in Latin). Its rejection of "barbarian" practices (with Thracians and Persians as emblematic instances) and its deployment of mythology near the end would be at home in the shared Greco-Roman culture, at almost any moment from the seventh century through Horace's own time.[48] Poem 3.19 generally follows the same pattern,

---

46. Two examples of attempts to theorize the break are Lowrie (2009a, 113) and Martin (2002).

47. West (2002, 167–71) recounts earlier attempts to solve the conundrum and adds his own, which takes the present indicative verbs "narras" (3) and "taces" (8) as generalizing ("you are always going on about . . ."). This reading adds useful perspective, but I do not think it makes the poem's use of scenic context smooth and unproblematic.

48. The young man who whispers his secret is obliquely identified by his sister's (Greek) name Megylla (some editors argue for the spelling Megilla) and her geographical epithet "Opuntiae" (i.e.,

by drawing on the learned mythological debates common to both Greek and Roman intellectual life and by mixing transliterated Greek vocabulary for drinking ("cadum" in line 5, and "cyathis" in line 12 [cf. line 14]) and for music ("lyra" in line 20) with Latin terms, often placed in close proximity ("pocula" in line 12, "tibiae" in line 19,[49] and "fistula" in line 20).[50] But one element of this poem has no counterpart in poem 1.27: in the midst of calls for more wine, the speaker offers a toast to Murena on the occasion of entering the office of augur (lines 10–11).[51] This moment is a striking example of Horace's practice in the odes: he refers to contemporary people and events with bald specificity, which implies that he is not afraid to "break the spell" of a scene that otherwise might seem at home in an archaic Greek symposium, but such references can be (as in this poem) seemingly incidental to the scene the poem portrays. The effect of this practice can be traced in the commentaries, which frequently hunt deep into the poem for a name or reference that would imply a motive relevant to contemporary life and promote that to the overarching aim of the poem, subordinating everything else in the poem to that aim.[52] I am not dismissing the notion that honoring Murena is important to this poem, but I am registering this as a specific example of the broader habit of Horatian readers, namely, to resist the poem's structure and linear development by integrating across the poem whatever substantive point is deemed to be uppermost. While this habit can be seen in readings of all

---

from eastern or "Opuntian" Locris on the east coast of central Greece). But, besides the odd choice to identify a man by his female relative, this designation almost perfectly balances itself between Greek and Roman, since freedwomen and slaves (including prostitutes) in Italy were extremely likely to carry Greek names. Nisbet and Hubbard (1970, ad 1.27.10) suggest that "though natural in Hellenistic literature, the [geographical] specification here removes the characters from the real world of Roman society. Moreover, in the context of the symposium Megylla must be an *hetaera*, and an elegant young Roman would not care to know her brother." Further, there is a Locris in southern Italy, founded by Opuntian Locrians, so even the geographical designation could be less distinctly Greek than it appears. In sum, poem 1.27 certainly does not work very hard to establish itself as taking place in Horace's own Roman context or any other specific time and place.

49. Modified by the geographical epithet "Berecyntiae" (line 18), which points to the eastern Mediterranean.

50. The four names that appear in the last few stanzas all are Greek, but again this would not be unusual for inhabitants of Rome in the first century. It may be significant that all four names are not only *noms parlants* (as Greek personal names often are), but are particularly obvious in their semantic weight and thus characterize these figures: Lycus, the "wolfish" neighbor (perhaps also a nod to the iambic tradition), the "far-shining" Telephus whose beauty is compared to the evening star, "Rose," whose love blooms in season ("tempestiva"), and—appropriate through paradox (and through intratextual reference to poem 1.33)—"Sweetie" who is characterized as exciting a slow-burning love.

51. See Nisbet and Rudd (2004, 227) and other commentaries for speculation on the identity of this Murena.

52. E.g., the headnote on this poem by Nisbet and Rudd: "This ode celebrates the installation as augur of a certain Murena, though the situation does not emerge until vv. 10ff." (2004, 227).

kinds of poems, in the case of poems that make reference to contemporary civic life, there is the most danger of producing a kind of circularity, of making the poem say what we expect to it to say, by ignoring the specific way that Horace handles such references.

This question can be pursued further by examining a poem that many readers find to combine contemporary political content with sympotic topoi in a particularly unsettling way. Poem 2.7 seems to reverse the priorities we saw in poem 3.19: it unambiguously places first and foremost the painful problem of reintegrating the partisans of Brutus (including the poet himself) into civic life and only late in the poem wends its way into the heedless joys of sympotic revelry.

> O saepe mecum tempus in ultimum
> deducte Bruto militiae duce,
>   quis te redonavit Quiritem
>   dis patriis Italoque caelo,
>
> Pompei, meorum prime sodalium,   5
> cum quo morantem saepe diem mero
>   fregi coronatus nitentis
>   malobathro Syrio capillos?
>
> tecum Philippos et celerem fugam
> sensi relicta non bene parmula,   10
>   cum fracta virtus et minaces
>   turpe solum tetigere mento:
>
> sed me per hostis Mercurius celer
> denso paventem sustulit aere,
>   te rursus in bellum resorbens   15
>   unda fretis tulit aestuosis.
>
> ergo obligatam redde Iovi dapem
> longaque fessum militia latus
>   depone sub lauru mea nec
>   parce cadis tibi destinatis.   20
>
> oblivioso levia Massico
> ciboria exple, funde capacibus
>   unguenta de conchis. quis udo
>   deproperare apio coronas

curatve myrto? quem Venus arbitrum   25
dicet bibendi? non ego sanius
    bacchabor Edonis: recepto
        dulce mihi furere est amico.

O foremost among my companions, you who often together with me were brought to the brink of death while serving under Brutus's leadership, who restored you as citizen to your ancestral gods and to the Italian clime? Pompeius, with you often I broke up the lingering day with wine, wearing a garland on my hair anointed with eastern perfume. [8] With you I experienced the swift retreat at Philippi, when I shamefully abandoned my shield, at that time when heroism was shattered and soldiers in the midst of shouting threats struck the loathsome earth with their chins. But swift-winged Mercury lifted me up in a thick mist—frightened as I was—up and away from the enemy; you, on the other hand, the tide swallowed back into the war again, bearing you along through seething straits. [16] And so offer to Jupiter the banquet you owe him, and lay down your body, now worn out with long military service, under my laurel tree, and don't spare the wine jars that have been set aside for you. Fill the smooth cups with Massic wine that helps us to forget; pour out scents from the wide shells. Who will hurry up and finish the garlands with moist celery or myrtle? Whom will Venus[53] name the master of drinking? I will revel wildly, like a Thracian: it is a sweet pleasure to go mad, now that my friend has been recovered.

Significantly, while the poem as a whole does nothing to disrupt the impression of continuous speech (unlike poem 3.19), the sense of a sympotic setting is quite muted at the beginning. The first few stanzas concentrate on welcoming home Pompeius,[54] though the present joy of recovering this companion is made secondary to a surprisingly full rehearsal of their shared past experience. In these opening stanzas, the institution of symposium is very visible, but not (yet) as a setting for the present speech: like everything in the first four stanzas except for the key question "who restored you as a citizen?" ("quis te redonavit Quiritem" in line 3), the detailed image of sympotic pleasure in lines 5–8 is used to characterize the past, not the present. This fact is important not just

---

53. Like "snake eyes" in English, "Venus" can refer to a specific throw of the dice.
54. Not only is his identity difficult to pin down, but even the name in line 5 is an emendation on the basis of Porphyrio's note; most manuscripts have either "Pompi" or "Pompili."

for the particularly delicate rhetorical strategy of this poem, but also because
it gets at the heart of the difference between this poem's use of sympotic
topoi and that of the archaic Greek poets: rather than subtly melding together
symposium-as-setting and symposium-as-theme, this poem separates them,
placing symposium-as-theme in the earlier "political" part of the poem and
symposium-as-setting in the later "private" part of the poem.[55]

Reactions to this poem have justifiably seen it as an attempt to grapple
with the conundrum that is central to Horace's lyric career: What can/
should/must be the political meaning of his art? Luke Roman (2014, 212)
has interpreted poem 2.7 (along with a group of other sympotic poems) as
demonstrating "the delimited frame of Horatian lyric":

> yet in none of these cases is lyric hermetically sealed from the exter-
> nal elements: the definition of the sympotic *angulus* recalls to mind
> the very realms of activity (warfare, politics) from which it notionally
> affords shelter. . . . Lyric autonomy and the princeps' restoration of the
> Roman social fabric are, in fact, related ideas. Augustus' "refoundation"
> of Rome in the wake of the civil war is at once the subject of Horace's
> poetry, and its premise: the autonomization of the poetic calling relies
> at least in part on Augustus' creation of a stable social framework in
> which poetry can securely be pursued as a full-time occupation, and
> aesthetic absorption enjoys a moral justification. Turning away from
> the public realm to symposion, poetry, and aesthetic sophistication
> implies that the public realm is adequately cared for and regulated by
> an authoritative and reliable power.

Roman's formulation captures well the sense in which Horace's sympotic
poetry acknowledges the public world (and confirms Augustus's domination)
even while apparently retreating into a timeless realm of private pleasure.
I differ only in emphasizing (again, through readings that are as attentive
to the linear development of poems as to their overall "point") that Horace
never presents this as a finished process with a stable result; his poems repeatedly represent the defining moment in which this retreat occurs. Further, in

---

55. This is a good example of the limitations of Davis's (1991, 9) claim that scenic context acts as
"scaffolding": "Such fictionalized situations are aids to the construction of an ideational building. . . .
Implicit in my borrowed metaphor is the observation that parts of the cognitive 'scaffolding' may
be abandoned in the course of the poem once their rhetorical raison d'être had been fulfilled." In
other words, the scene is only an instrument that makes certain thematic statements possible. This
explanation covers some instances (even in those cases, I believe my overall argument shows why the
scene continues to have some relevance), but in this poem the scaffold gets constructed in the poem's
final stanzas, where it cannot function to set up anything.

keeping with my claim above that Horace shapes his poems to register the assumptions sympotic poetry makes about privacy and spontaneity, I would argue that in these poems that dramatize the turn toward private pleasure, the poetic design reveals that such a turn is not merely a natural or inevitable or personal state of affairs.

This claim can give us a productive lens through which to view an element of Horace's poetry that seems both utterly direct and confoundingly complex: his use of his own life as poetic material. In contrast to Catullus, who sees the power of poetry arising from the ways it blurs its difference from social speech, Horace grounds both the vatic authority and the emotional expressivity of his odes in a rigorously controlled poetic discourse. To put this in the terms of my introduction, Horace writes odes that make as few concessions as possible to notion of discourse in the service of "story." And yet it is equally clear that his strategy in the *Odes* is not to exclude "story" but to present scenes and characters and events and emotions in all their alluring specificity, while still requiring these features to announce their subordination to the discursive design of each poem.[56]

In the realm of public poetry, the long tradition of elevated poetic expression serving ritual or other authoritative goals (as summed up for Horace in the concept of the *vates*, the prophet-bard) is so well known that this practice is less striking; even in those instances, however, Horace takes the principle further than other poets, as I argued in the previous chapter for the case of hymns. In the sympotic poems we can see how Horace applies this principle to his own biography and even his own emotions, subjecting this most personal material to the clarifying filter of poetic discourse. It is this essential insight, by which he treats his own life with almost the same poetic toolkit as he applies to grand public events, that gives the *Odes* their distinctive quality in which the extremely personal and the extremely artful seem equally fundamental.

Poem 2.7 uses the norms and expectations that attach to sympotic poetry to explore precisely the question of how the topoi of "privacy" and "spontaneity" make visible their own political meanings. In contrast to McNeill (2001), who believes that this poem successfully establishes the speaking voice as

---

56. It is this distinctive approach to "story" and discourse that has encouraged readers to characterize Horace's *Odes* as purely or almost purely epideictic, or as merely using scenic elements as "scaffolding" that supports the real thematic work of the poem. What I hope my readings show is that when we pay attention to the detailed linear development of each poem, we can see that Horace uses "story," with its powerfully ambiguous status as internal or external to the poem's design, as a key component in his poetics. Although I disagree with Lowrie (1997) on the definitions of the narrative and lyric elements of these poems, I believe that this perception of the importance of representation finds an important parallel in her approach.

"private and spontaneous" (and therefore authentic, unconstrained),[57] I see poem 2.7 as pinpointing the way these notions are used as terms in a debate, the debate that the poem itself constructs.

Poem 2.7 presents biography, claims of political allegiance, and the poetic tradition as having equal power over shaping the poetic design. An analysis that leaves out any of these components or asserts that any is there simply as a foil for the others will be unsatisfying. Readers have long noted the effects of narrating personal history through (tongue-in-cheek) allusion to archaic Greek poetry (in lines 9–16).[58] Horace makes it impossible to miss the fact that he is representing his own life through the medium of the poetic tradition. In a poem that takes so many artistic and political risks, the ostentatious nature of these allusions may have the distancing or ironic effect that others have attributed to them, but they also have the effect of laying bare in an unusually explicit way Horace's approach to autobiography throughout this collection.

The impact of the symposium as a poetic and social institution is perhaps more subtle, but not less significant. Horace uses here the familiar sympotic theme of friendship to frame the political question of clemency as well as the communal grief felt over the losses suffered in the civil war. This sympotic frame highlights present pleasure as a good in itself and as an antidote to life's harder times, and thus friendship in this poem stands as an emblem of both the sorrow and the solace to be found in shared life. But just as Horace called attention to his poetic agency by retailing his own history through allusions to Archilochus and Homer, in its deployment of this sympotic material the poem does not seek to minimize or hide the rhetorical work required to reconceive civil war and its aftermath as episodes in a long friendship.[59] This, I think, is the primary effect of splitting the sympotic material into theme (early in the poem) and setting (in the last few

---

57. McNeill (2001, 118) introduces the section (titled "Free and Independent Support") in which he discusses poem 2.7 by highlighting Maecenas's hands-off style of patronage: "[Maecenas's] allowance of artistic autonomy enabled Horace to create his most effective technique for articulating and advancing Caesar's political inevitability in a non-threatening way: to wit, his presentation of himself as neither paid mouthpiece nor detached or subversive critic but as a free and independent Roman *spontaneously and privately* choosing the better option for his people's future" (emphasis added).

58. The detail about throwing away one's shield is a clear reference to a motif that appears in Archilochus fr. 5, and perhaps also in Alcaeus and Anacreon; the image in lines 11–12 of heroic death recalls multiple instances in the *Iliad*.

59. Davis (1991, 96–98) reads "sub lauru mea" (in line 19) as an emblem "for the lyric verse that is to provide solace and recreation for the war-weary soldier." I find this reading persuasive, but as with Roman's (2014) conception of this poem's political freight, I would just emphasize that the poem does not present this literary effect as simply a fait accompli but calls attention to it as a perpetual work in progress.

stanzas): this design exemplifies the ambiguous status of "story" in relation to discourse and demonstrates Horace's virtuoso control of the role "story" plays in his odes. And yet, at least judging from my own experience as a reader, this move does not rob the poem of its power both to evoke grief and to acknowledge the stability that has come with the Augustan regime. Thus this poem stands as another example of how Horace uses sympotic material: contrary to what we might have expected, he uses it not to naturalize individual poetic expression through canonical forms or the oddness of written song or his own impossible bind in relation to political speech, but to delineate exactly the limitations inherent in all these features of his own poetic practice.

In contrast to McNeill's claim that privacy and spontaneity are characteristics of this poem, then, I would say that these are topics it explores. Horace handles biographical material in a way that makes it central but points to the irresolvable issue of what "private" and "spontaneous" speech means in an artfully constructed ode destined for wide circulation, and especially an ode that is fully conscious of its tradition and of the fraught political climate within which it is produced and read. It will be useful to analyze in closing a few poems that highlight the "fact" about Horace that most obviously links his art and his life and his politics: his relationship with Maecenas. Much has been written investigating the historical aspects of this friendship,[60] and also the ways that Horace's poetry makes use of Maecenas as an element in its artistic design.[61] I seek here not to engage comprehensively with the question of what Maecenas means in Horace's poetry (not even just for *Odes* 1–3), but to draw attention specifically to how Maecenas (and "Maecenas") interacts with the logic of sympotic poetry I have been analyzing.

First, it is worth noting that Maecenas does not appear in sympotic poems as often as we might expect. Given the dominance of friendship as a theme in sympotic poetry and, as I have argued above, the role of the symposium in providing a way for Horace to comment on the stylized way that his poetry relates to public affairs and contemporary life, it might seem that a high proportion of Maecenas's appearances in the odes would come in sympotic poems. Further, the sympotic poems in which he appears do not develop the dramatic/mimetic potential of sympotic poetry very far. The most obvious instances of sympotic poems that involve Maecenas are closer to invitation

---

60. E.g., White (1993), Osgood (2006).
61. E.g., Zetzel (1982), Bowditch (2001), Gowers (2003).

poems than real-time renditions of sympotic song: poems 1.20, 3.8, and 3.29.[62] Of these, poem 3.29 is the most visible and most impressive, appearing as it does in a culminating position just before the final monumental close of the whole collection. It is also the poem in this group that tarries least with its sympotic content, making clear early on that "symposium" is invoked in this poem purely for its thematic content: contrasting public work with private pleasure and, later in the poem, the philosophical implications of life's short span. The fact that this poem seems uninterested in the scenic context of symposium does not make it irrelevant for my argument; rather this poem offers an excellent example of my main contention, that the sympotic genre for Horace is neither simply an empty gesture nor an attempt to recapture performative immediacy. The symposium is a rich source for a variety of poetic effects—sometimes Horace chooses to develop its power as a scenic context and sometimes as a carrier of themes, but most often as some mix of these two goals. In the case of 3.29, he ostentatiously shows how the thematic weight of the symposium allows him to blend an addressive opening (which implies the speaker's social aims) with a full-throated epideictic development.

Poem 1.20 has been well studied as an invitation poem, as a compliment to Maecenas (and expression of gratitude for his gift of the Sabine farm), and as a declaration of the poet's pride in repurposing a Greek "container" ("testa," line 2) with Roman contents.

> Vile potabis modicis Sabinum
> cantharis, Graeca quod ego ipse testa
> conditum levi, datus in theatro
>   cum tibi plausus,
>
> clare Maecenas eques, ut paterni   5
> fluminis ripae simul et iocosa
> redderet laudes tibi Vaticani
>   montis imago.
>
> Caecubum et prelo domitam Caleno
> tu bibes uvam: mea nec Falernae   10
> temperant vites neque Formiani
>   pocula colles.

---

62. See also poem 4.11, which is clearly in the mode of "preparations for a symposium" but oblique in its relation to Maecenas (cf. Murena in 3.19, though there Murena is imagined as being present, while in 4.11 Maecenas is made more central to the poem but not to the scene). Also significant for this pattern is *Epode* 9, addressed to Maecenas, which depicts the symposium more fully than either 1.20 or 3.8 do, but still situates it in the future, not the present.

You will drink cheap Sabine wine from ordinary cups, wine which I myself stored in a Greek cask, at that time when you were applauded in the theater, Maecenas, distinguished knight, such that the banks of your ancestral river and the cheerful echo of the Vatican hill repeated your praises. You will drink [i.e., at home] Caecuban wine and the grape crushed by a Campanian press; my cups never taste of Falernian vines and Formian hills.

While previous studies have made sense of the poem's content and diction, it has proven more difficult to explain the poem's almost perverse structure, in which a perfectly comprehensible, even graceful invitation to Maecenas in the first and third stanzas is split apart by the second stanza, which "spends too much time on blatant flattery of Maecenas's ovation," in the judgment of Nisbet and Hubbard (1970, 246). More specifically, the first and third stanzas are filled with the proper vocabulary for sympotic poetry (especially obvious in the focus on wine itself) and with the expected contrasts of Roman to Greek and humble to exalted. The second stanza departs from this pattern, offering instead a surprisingly detailed description of Rome's topography, enlivened with a variation on the pastoral pathetic fallacy, as the urban landscape of Rome joins in the applause. Once we focus on the operation of "story" and discourse in this poem, we can see that the most emphatic way the second stanza is different from the others is that it leaves behind the storyworld in which the speaker is inviting Maecenas for a drink and develops another, inner storyworld, a rich evocation of a specific moment in the life of the city and the life of the addressee.[63]

The strategy of the first and third stanzas is the one we expect in sympotic poems and invitation poems, as it links its apparent social utility with the aesthetic elaboration of its language and the thematic weight that language carries. The strategy of the second stanza relies instead on a different assumption about its verbal action, one closer in conception to praise poetry. This stanza accents the representational capacity of language, as it tells a story that "proves" the excellence of the honorand.[64] Each of these strategies

---

63. While it may seem intrusive in this poem, it turns out that such a veering away from the sympotic frame to an inner storyworld is a defining gesture of three of Horace's most famous sympotic poems, 1.7 ("Laudabunt alii"), 1.9 ("Vides ut alta"), and 1.37 ("Nunc est bibendum"). Significantly, in each of those cases, the poem never comes back to pick up the sympotic frame as it does here in the much shorter poem 1.20. See Lowrie (1997, 148) for discussion of this "open-ended" feature of 1.37 and 1.7.

64. Cf. Lowrie's (2009a, 69) astute observation that the poem at this point shifts away from its apparent goal of inviting and instead does what it describes the cityscape doing, namely, "redderet laudes."

demonstrates (even extols) a specific understanding of how poetic language relates to the world. In the first and third stanzas, the use of language seems more fully defined by the norms of language use in real social life, but these stanzas markedly press the thematic capacities of language as well, since the discussion of vintages develops into a richly evocative expression of identity, poetic ambition, and friendship.[65] On the other hand, in the second stanza, the language taps into the distinctively poetic powers of description and even personification, and so seems further removed from the give-and-take of language in ordinary life. And yet the effect of this second stanza is more direct, since it sheds the invitational/sympotic framework in favor of appearing to be what it really is, a poem praising Maecenas. I argued above that Horace designs other sympotic poems (especially 1.27 and 3.19) to call attention to the assumption that such poems will harmonize storyworld speech with poetic goals; in the short span of three stanzas, poem 1.20 manages to juxtapose two different versions of this assumption.

My final example in this set is poem 3.8, which, in contrast to 3.29 and 1.20, tips slightly toward the conversational mode. In its first phase it clearly establishes a scene of utterance: the physical setting in which the speaker is preparing for a ritual and the addressee is puzzled as to the ritual's purpose.

> Martiis caelebs quid agam kalendis,
> quid velint flores et acerra turis
> plena miraris positusque carbo in
>   caespite vivo,
>
> docte sermones utriusque linguae

What I, a bachelor, am doing on the calends of March,[66] what is the meaning of the flowers and incense and charcoal on fresh turf—this is what you are wondering, you who are well-versed in both Latin and Greek treatises.

The speaker's language seems aimed at answering his companion's query rather than at some kind of performance. In this opening, the speaker is quite precisely placed (literally and figuratively), and the addressee's presence in the scene is registered by the need to explain the ritual act being undertaken. But instead of naming Maecenas right away as a participant, Horace instead

---

65. The obvious metapoetic freight of Catullus 1, by which the concrete attributes of the book come to represent the aesthetic position the author is claiming for himself, offers an emblematic example of this technique.

66. The date of the Matronalia, a festival in honor of Juno in her function as a goddess of childbirth.

addresses him through a periphrasis, "docte sermones utriusque linguae" (line 5), a description that is certainly flattering (and probably accurate), but sits somewhat oddly in what is otherwise established here as a homely and intimate scene. The ritual itself is clearly marked as a private act of devotion (not a grand public occasion), and the reason given for the observance (in lines 6–8) is his escape from the deadly tree, as narrated in poem 2.13.

In these ways, the opening stanzas of 3.8 are more "story"-oriented than is typical for Horace's odes, but the "story" they contain points not exactly to his own personal history, but to the poetic uses he makes of that history in his lyric collection. The episode of the tree is emblematic for the nexus of personal history and poetic allusion in this collection. In poem 2.13 Horace had used this episode as a springboard for writing himself into the lyric tradition beside Sappho and Alcaeus. Poem 3.8 gestures back to that poem and its clever appropriation of autobiography for poetic purposes, but also introduces a different version of how the poet's life story comes to be poetically meaningful.

As the poem continues, its use of the symposium echoes patterns we have seen in poem 2.7 (where the symposium as scenic context develops *after* the use of the symposium as theme) and poem 3.19 (where the sympotic context is clear but we get conflicting clues about the storyworld scene). Poem 3.8 opens, as I have described above, by strongly establishing a scenic context, but the first three stanzas emphasize the preparations rather than pretending to take place during the drinking party. The fourth stanza then shifts to the moment of the party itself, with an encouragement to drink up. The remaining three stanzas maintain the structure of second-person address, but leave behind the real-time scene in favor of an almost epideictic treatment of sympotic themes.[67]

sume, Maecenas, cyathos amici
sospitis centum et vigiles lucernas
perfer in lucem: procul omnis esto   15
    clamor et ira.

mitte civilis super urbe curas:
occidit Daci Cotisonis agmen,
Medus infestus sibi luctuosis
    dissidet armis,   20

---

67. Davis (1991, 176) in a discussion of poem 3.29 ("Tyrrhena regum"), refers to poem 3.8 as a "sister ode" and contrasts its more forceful demands for putting away public cares to the strategy of 3.29, where "the starkly prescriptive aspect of the message is toned down."

servit Hispanae vetus hostis orae
Cantaber sera domitus catena,
iam Scythae laxo meditantur arcu
    cedere campis.

neglegens, ne qua populus laboret,   25
parce privatus nimium cavere et
dona praesentis cape laetus horae:
    linque severa.

(3.8.13–28)

In honor of your friend's escape, Maecenas, drink up a full hundred ladlefuls and make the wakeful lanterns serve until dawn. May all ruckus and anger be kept at bay. Put aside your political worries about the city: the troops of Dacian Cotiso have fallen; the threatening Parthians are at odds, their arms now bringing sorrow to themselves; [20] the Cantabrian, our ancient enemy on the Spanish coast, is now at last defeated and in fetters; now the Scythians give thought to retreating from the battlefields, with their bows unstrung. Not worrying whether the Roman people is struggling in some way, as a private person, stop your overcareful ways and happily receive the gifts of the present hour; leave behind weighty matters.

The linear progression of 3.8 raises two different questions. First, how should we interpret the scenic cues: Are they meant to add up to a real-time scene, an invitation, some combination?[68] The second question is how the use of "autobiography" in the earlier part of the poem relates to the thematic focus on public and private in its closing stanzas. Given my argument so far, it will be clear that I believe these two questions to be related: the treatment of the scene, which makes it both obvious and hard to pin down, chimes with the treatment of personal history, since the incident of the falling tree simultaneously thickens the texture of the storyworld context and—through intratextual allusion—reminds the reader that the collection is also a context for this poem. Thus the poem's overall development from an apparently casual scene to a fairly elaborate instance of epideixis attests

---

68. See Williams (1968, 103–7) for an ingenious, if tortured, reading that amply demonstrates his fundamental claim that Horace's poems make a "demand on the reader." It is significant that Williams thinks that the need for the extremely indirect strategy of this poem arises from the special status of Maecenas: "Horace naturally found it difficult to give Maecenas, the busy, important man of affairs, the conventional symposiastic advice to live only for the moment. He managed it in *Odes* iii.8 by giving the advice a setting which confined it to the present (and imaginary) moment in a private celebration" (107).

to the extraordinary subtlety with which Horace deploys various images of himself and his (social and poetic) agency.

Further, Maecenas's involvement in this poem adds yet another layer to this complex counterpoint of "story" and discourse. The early part of the poem introduces him as addressee by means of a flattering description (in line 5) but does not name him, thus producing the honorific gesture we expect, while subordinating his real historical existence to his function in the storyworld as a puzzled onlooker. Beginning in the third stanza, where he is named for the first time and treated like a proper sympotic addressee with lots of imperatives, his specific existence as a member of Augustus's inner circle becomes thematically central. Like the image of Horace himself in this poem, the image it offers of Maecenas blends together his identity as a real person and his function as an element in this poem's storyworld.

Horace's approach in these poems (and others that take up such issues) has sometimes been described defensively, as if Horace is just trying to escape with as much dignity as he can from the need to acknowledge Maecenas's patronage and Augustus's domination. We should remember, however, that although there was surely some expectation that he would reflect glory on his patron and the new regime, he could have done so merely by presenting images of peaceful private life that the Augustan regime makes possible. Instead, he creates poems that insistently ask readers to reflect on the relation between public and private in this new world and, further, on the function of poetry in constructing as well as commenting on the Augustan age. As Nisbet and Hubbard (1978, 109) say, after lamenting the choices Horace made in poem 2.7, "Yet after all, he could have said nothing." Rather than choosing this safer route,[69] Horace writes poems that call to readers' attention the question of how poetry relates to external/historical events and what "real" historical effects its statements might have.

More broadly, this whole set of sympotic poems shows us that Horace uses his biography as part of his poetic palette but that he also shapes his poems to mark the inclusion of that material as an act of aesthetic choice rather than the "natural" irruption of the poet's life into his works. This is different from the more familiar claim, that it is the fragmentary or contradictory nature of the information we get about Horace that prevents us

---

69. Murray offers an analysis of Horace's approach to the symposium that takes into account the different forms of social and political hierarchy in archaic Greece (the symposium as an institution of equals), Hellenistic Alexandria (invitation poems that honor patrons), and Augustan Rome. His verdict is that "the Hellenistic epigram belongs to a world divorced from public life," but that Horace recognized that "the symposium could give to the poet himself a role which would restore to him that social equality and that literary authority [of archaic Greece]" (1993, 96).

from having a clear view of the man.[70] I would argue that, no less than the fractured views we get of the poet's character, the well-rounded images that make him seem palpably real are part of this overall strategy. Parallel to the way that poem 1.27 generates a lively picture of sympotic life while also clearly marking the operation of poetic discourse in bringing that image into existence, even the poems that more centrally depict the poet's life and times continue to maintain a rigorous sense of that material as subject to the logic of poetic form.

---

70. One recent example, from the introduction of a volume titled *Perceptions of Horace* (Houghton and Wyke 2009, 2–3): "The sheer number and variety of 'Horaces' that have been extrapolated from this one poetic corpus . . . are the result—the paradoxical and yet natural result—of the profusion of apparently biographical material offered by the works which make up that corpus. . . . The multiple identities attributed to Horace not only prompt us to examine the ways in which 'Horace' as a text constructs its author, and how subsequent ages have constructed Horace from his texts; they also throw into particular relief wider questions about how we should approach the authorial voice in literature, and how we as readers are complicit in the construction of that authorial voice." As this last sentence shows, Houghton and Wyke are by no means pursuing a positivist or naïve analysis of Horace the poet/text, but it is striking that they situate their starting point in multiplicity and contradiction. McNeill (2001) acknowledges the intervention of poetic form but remains focused on the goal of reading through that image to a historical truth behind it; the difference between his approach and mine can be captured by his emphasis on the dichotomy truth/fiction as a grounding point: e.g., "When we encounter Horace in his works, we do not gaze directly on his actual face, nor are we looking at a wholly artificial mask whose features have been identified with his. Instead, we see the real Horace—obliquely, through the polished lens of his poetry, as one would see a reflection in a mirror" (8–9)

CHAPTER 4

Poetry as Writing

Haec Arethusa suo mittit mandata Lycotae,
    cum totiens absis, si potes esse meus.
si qua tamen tibi lecturo pars oblita derit,
    haec erit e lacrimis facta litura meis:
aut si qua incerto fallet te littera tractu,
    signa meae dextrae iam morientis erunt.

(Propertius 4.3.1–6)

Arethusa sends this message to her own Lycotas, if in fact you can still be mine, though you are away so often. If any part of this letter is erased or missing when you read it, that erasure will be caused by my tears; or if the shaky handwriting resists deciphering, that will be an indication that my hand's strength is reaching its end.

Propertius's fourth book famously rejects the dominance of the first-person form that had (in various guises) shaped the author's previous collections. Many of the poems in this book make clear that their speakers are distinct from the Ego (characterized as a poet and lover of Cynthia), and so could reasonably be called dramatic monologues, and several in addition to poem 4.3

185

make those speakers women (poems 4.4, 4.5, 4.7, 4.11).[1] Although some of Propertius's poems in earlier books (most notably 1.11) implicitly position themselves as letters—by assuming that the speaker and addressee are in different places and that the speaker wants to know what is happening in that far-off spot—nowhere else in his four books does he produce anything like this poem, which not only presents an epistolary frame but exploits all the implications of what it means to communicate by pen and paper at a great distance.[2]

Propertius orchestrates this opening to quickly establish the substance of the storyworld scene. Three elements of this scene are especially important: that the speaker is a woman; that she is trying to reach her husband across a great distance; and that writing is the means she chooses. Beyond establishing those aspects of the storyworld, these lines emphatically direct the reader to assume that Arethusa is a character who operates entirely within the storyworld, with no consciousness of what her words might mean for anyone other than Lycotas. Further, the content of Arethusa's mournful ruminations is almost exactly the same as what we are accustomed to read from the mouth of the Ego: complaints of being left behind by a lover who roams at will, and enumerations of her own heartfelt gestures of fidelity and loneliness. This poem is an oddity, but one that comments incisively on Propertius's poetics throughout all four books. It shows how close the Ego's usual effusions are to the status of a dramatic monologue, and that the main way such poems differ from dramatic monologues is by defining the first-person speaker as male and as a poet (though, as I have shown in chapter 1, not necessarily the author of these poems).

I would argue that the key dynamic that dominates Propertius's poetics (across all four books) is the tension between perceiving speech as enclosed within the storyworld and perceiving speech as poetry that circulates for readers. Catullus and Horace may find myriad ways to blur and combine these dimensions, but Propertius is more interested in what happens when they are defined as distinct but riveted together by the poem's formal structure. While this generalization obviously leaves out much of what is interesting in

---

1. Only in 4.3 and 4.11 does the female voice occupy the entire poem (in the manner of a dramatic monologue); poems 4.4, 4.5, and 4.7 are narratives spoken by the Ego in which a female voice is quoted at considerable length. Also, let me note that in this chapter most of the poems I will be discussing position the central figure as writing, not speaking; although that difference is central to my argument, I still feel that it will be clearer to maintain the term "speaker" for this position in the poetic structure, since that term reveals the parallel with the poems discussed in earlier chapters.

2. The model represented by this poem was certainly not lost on Ovid, whose letters of mythological heroines echo the feminine speaker and the emphasis on the actual process of writing, as well as on the tactile reality of the paper and the writing.

each poet (which I hope has come through in readings of individual poems), it can help us to see why the prospect of treating the storyworld act of communication as written rather than spoken is handled so differently by these three poets. Propertius, as my brief analysis of poem 4.3 suggests, uses written forms of communication to double down on the hermetic quality of his storyworld, sealing off even more decisively the characters' speech from the expressive capabilities of the poetry itself, which is clearly marked as operating at a level over the heads of the characters. Such a practice, pushed to its logical conclusion, would yield something like novelistic narrative, in which the novel's own discursive action is deemed to be of a different order from the words characters use to communicate.[3]

Catullus and Horace, on the other hand, more persistently explore what it would mean for the storyworld source of the first-person "voice" to be a letter. This practice could almost be seen as a return to the "organic" logic of archaic Greek performed poetry, since that older tradition depended on a kind of mirroring, as the image of song in its storyworld replicated the form in which the poem would be (re)performed. Thus, since Catullus and Horace are more interested in aligning the speaker's storyworld agency with the historical poet's artistic agency, they are more drawn to the possibility of composing poems that maintain the first-person structure but supplant storyworld speech with writing.

But there is a significant difference in the strategies Catullus and Horace devise. Although we have no way of knowing exactly what Catullus's original collection(s) would have looked like, we can safely rule out the possibility that he produced an entire collection of poetic letters, segregated from the poems that depict oral communication in the storyworld. Instead, he clearly thought of these epistolary poems as another way of pursuing the

---

3. I should note here another version of writing that is quite prominent in the work of Propertius and the other elegists: the habit of "quoting" inscriptions that are proposed or said already to exist in the storyworld. (See esp. Ramsby 2007 and some of the papers in Keith 2011.) Arethusa's poem ends with just such a gesture, a dedicatory inscription ("salvo grata puella viro," from a woman, grateful for her husband's safe return, 4.3.72) that will mark the end of Lycotas's danger and travels. This instance shows how, even though the practice of including inscriptions is different from designing the poem as a letter, it is supported by the same essential logic. First, and most obviously, it gives further body to the storyworld and the forms of communication native to it; when Arethusa reaches for an expression that will be long-lasting and public, what comes to her is not the circulation of a poetry book but a dedicatory inscription. Secondly, the characterological effect of the inscription operates in the same ironic way that Arethusa's whole speech does: it gives the reader access to her emotions while also encouraging the reader to see her perspective as limited; the poem is designed to elaborate on her longing, as well as her lack of knowledge and lack of control, and therefore refuses to authorize her optimism about Lycotas's chaste return to her bed.

aims we see throughout the polymetric collection.[4] Horace, on the other hand, not only segregated such poems from his songlike lyrics (as one would expect), but even seems to have conceived of them as separate from his other hexametric *sermones*.[5] As Ferri (2007, 122) has observed, "an entire book of poems purporting to be a collection of private letters was a novelty among ancient poetic genres, and one which Horace must have initiated with some determination." In other words, Horace seems to have wanted to mark these poems as both different from his other poems and as themselves forming a conceptual unit.[6]

Writing and Mediation in Catullus

Given the strong alignment in Catullus's poetry of the poetic speaker with the historical author, it is not surprising that the epistolary poems 35, 50, and 65 tend to focus on issues of poetic craft or, more accurately, to bring issues of poetic craft into contact with social and emotional issues. In these three poems, Catullus shines a spotlight on the double-edged capacity of writing: it can operate almost invisibly in aid of communication but it can also bulk large and call attention to itself as mediating the exchanges between people. This inherent duality is of interest both in itself and for the ways it expresses other tensions that structure Catullus's corpus, especially the tension between internal (that of the storyworld speaker) and external (that of the historical poet and his readers) perspectives that I analyzed in the previous chapter. In these poems, Catullus engages on multiple levels with the question of how poetry's communication with the reader relates to the speaker's communication with the addressee. These poems highlight images of texts, readers, translation, and, somewhat surprisingly, women as speakers and writers and readers.

---

4. The poems of Catullus that I will focus on here are 35, 50, and 65. Poem 68 is incredibly rich in many dimensions, not least its use of epistolary features, but given its complexity I don't feel I can do it justice within the current argument.

5. *Sermo* ("conversation") is the Latin word Horace chose as a title for the two books often referred to as his "Satires." There is significant debate as to how distinct the two types of hexameter poetry were for Horace. Horace used the term *sermo* to refer broadly to hexameter poetry of lower stylistic level than his lyric poems (as we see in *Sat.* 1.4.39–42 and *Epis.* 1.4.1), but I believe that within that broader class he conceived of the collection we now call the first book of the *Epistles* as having an identity distinct from his two books of satires. On this point, see the debate between Horsfall, Jocelyn, and Rudd (in *Liverpool Classical Monthly* 4 [1979]) and more recently de Pretis (2004, 19–22), who argues (with Jocelyn and Rudd) in favor of accepting the evidence of Porphyrio (ad *Sat.* 1.1.1), who says that Horace intended this collection to have the title *Epistulae*.

6. Throughout this chapter I will be discussing only the first book of *Epistles*. The second book obviously raises extremely important questions, but is so clearly built on different principles that it requires its own distinctive analysis.

In poem 35 the notion of mediation—of all that comes between two partners in a communicative exchange—is the dominant motif, though this theme is balanced by a powerful image that conflates reading with more immediate forms of contact.

Poetae tenero, meo sodali,
velim Caecilio, papyre, dicas
Veronam veniat, Noui relinquens
Comi moenia Lariumque litus:
nam quasdam volo cogitationes   5
amici accipiat sui meique.
quare, si sapiet, viam vorabit,
quamvis candida milies puella
euntem revocet, manusque collo
ambas iniciens roget morari.   10
quae nunc, si mihi vera nuntiantur,
illum deperit impotente amore:
nam quo tempore legit incohatam
Dindymi dominam, ex eo misellae
ignes interiorem edunt medullam.   15
ignosco tibi, Sapphica puella
musa doctior: est enim venuste
Magna Caecilio incohata Mater.

Dear papyrus, please tell my friend the tender poet Caecilius to come to Verona, leaving behind the walls of Novum Comum and the Larian shore; for I want him to hear certain thoughts of a mutual friend. And so, if he is wise, he will eat up the road, even though a beautiful girl calls him back a thousand times as he leaves, throwing her arms around his neck and asking him to linger. [10] If what I hear is true, she loves him desperately with an overpowering love; for from the very moment when she read the "Mistress of Dindymos" just begun, the poor girl has been devoured by the flames of passion, right down to her marrow. I forgive you, girl more learned than the Sapphic Muse, for the "Magna Mater" has been begun by Caecilius in a very lovely way.

The poem's main thrust is a request that Caecilius come to Verona to discuss his work in progress (a poem on the Magna Mater), and yet the poem first foregrounds the letter's status as mediator and then foregrounds the over-powering love felt by Caecilius's girlfriend as she calls him back. The poem declares its epistolary identity by making its address not to Caecilius himself but to the paper on which the letter is written ("papyre" in line 2). As most epistolary poems do, its content focuses on the distance between the speaker and the addressee, and the desire to close that distance, so the mention of the papyrus is not necessary to ground the epistolary conceit. Instead, I suggest that what is important about this opening gambit is that it places Caecilius in a third-person position, rather than in the second-person position where we would expect him to be.

There is no simple answer to the question of what this third-person position means. Some have read this poem as influenced by politeness strategies that require the speaker to use periphrases and compensatory praise to soften his basic message (that Caecilius's poem still needs a lot of work; see, e.g., Quinn 1970, ad 6). This is a valid reading, but if we follow this path we should notice, at a minimum, the degree to which we are assuming that the poems fulfill social functions in Catullus's historical life (in spite of or because of the fact that they are published as poems?). But what do we make of the fact that the publication of this poem, salted with "clues" that point to this very politeness strategy, flies in the face of the social tact that the poem, on this reading, embodies? While I think that the practice of indirection in this poem is important, I don't believe that it is generated by the pressures of politeness in real social life.

Beyond the instance of addressing the papyrus, indirection seems to be a fundamental principle of this poem: the majority of the poem (from line 8 on) is actually devoted to the description of the woman who is in love with Caecilius. She is depicted as intervening between the two men, or at least thwarting the speaker's desire that they should be able to speak face to face. But she is also a "middle term" in another way: in this figure Catullus introduces into the poem a powerful image that conflates the aesthetic pleasures of poetry with sexual desire.

Caecilius is described as *poeta tener* in the opening line, that is, as a love poet, even though the poem that he is composing is at least partially mythological, focusing on the Magna Mater. It is possible, as commentators have speculated, that Caecilius's poem would have turned the mythological material in the direction of the erotic, as we see Catullus doing in poem 63 or, differently, in poem 64. The question of whether such an eroticized mythological narrative qualifies for the adjective *tener* brings to our attention a much broader question that underlies much of Catullus's work: What relationship is assumed between the social relations depicted in the poetry and the social relations that the poem generates in its audience or between the audience and the poet? In this case, the poem envisions in very strong form an erotic effect on the audience. It does not directly correlate this effect with the *content* of the poetry, but rather with the skill of its execution; the closest we get to an explanation of why the woman falls in love with Caecilius after reading the inchoate poem is that she is "Sapphica . . . / musa doctior" (lines 16–17) and that the poem itself is "venuste / . . . incohata" (lines 17–18). *Doctus* and *venustus* are key terms in the vocabulary of Catullan aesthetic evaluation.

It is significant that Caecilius's voice / agency in this poem appears only through the mention of his poem. He is displaced from the usual second-person position of addressee by the papyrus, and even in this third-person position his actions are described but without attributing to him a voice or any detailed motivation (e.g., "si sapiet, viam vorabit" in line 7). The speaker, too, is partially displaced from the role of adviser in keeping with the fact that the papyrus is asked to use its voice for the speaker ("dicas" in line 2).[7] By contrast, the woman's voice ("revocet," "roget" in lines 9–10) makes her an estimable rival to the speaker, one whose influence must be countered head-on.

Of course, the very creation of her as a rival is a set-up: I am not claiming (nor is it particularly relevant, if true) that the woman's love is really the major obstacle to Caecilius's coming to Verona for literary advice. What is important is that the poem makes the woman central in a way that Caecilius himself is not and sets her up as the pivotal consciousness in this poem—the site of potentially authoritative social requests (lines 9–10), erotic passion (lines 12, 14–15), and aesthetic judgment (lines 16–18). This combination of attributes explains the potential for ambiguity in this poem—it is equally possible that the speaker is dismissive of her as a reader or genuinely sees her passion as evidence for the power of Caecilius's poem.

It is significant as well that this strategy emerges only in the poem's second half. In lines 1–7, the papyrus plays the role of a more positive middle term between the two men, holding out the hope of bringing them together, but still calling attention to the gap between them, the distance Caecilius must cover (in lines 3–4). It is as if the epistolary markers early in the poem (emphasis on the papyrus, on distance) and the woman's intervention later in the poem are two reflexes of the same impulse: to highlight the counterintuitive emotional and aesthetic power generated by intermediaries, that is, to parade rather than conceal all that comes between writers and readers. This poem pursues energetically many of the topics we associate with Catullus's description of his own poetic practice—the intertwining of erotic response and aesthetic response, the admiration for precise skill and learning (so-called "doctitude"), and the impression of a circle of like-minded poets

---

7. If we accept the interpretive consensus that reads "quasdam . . . cogitationes / amici . . . sui meique" in lines 5–6 as referring to his own thoughts by periphrasis.

fostering this new style—but it does so by sidelining the two male poets and developing instead images of agency in a papyrus and a female reader.

This poem has a light, playful tone, and perhaps that is why it has not often been read together with poems 50 and 65, two poems that advertise their literary ambitions unequivocally. But these three poems share a set of formal and thematic characteristics that can be enlightening when read as a group. In all three poems we get a representation of how poems operate in Catullus's storyworld, which in this respect models itself (as far as we can tell) on literary culture in contemporary Rome. Poetry appears in all three poems at the nexus between personal expression, a learned skill that testifies to elite cultural competence (e.g., mastery of meters and of mythological material, allusion to the tradition), and a socially valued luxury object that men circulate (and comment on) in the process of establishing and confirming friendships.[8] Poem 35 foregrounds the second and third (more sociological) items in this list, while poems 50 and 65 weave all three strands together more tightly. The role of the woman in poem 35, however, as an image of passion, makes clear that this poem too is generated by the same essential tensions. The playfully bizarre structure of address in poem 35 encourages us to take it as merely a variation that does not change the real underlying address, and thus the poem seems to maintain a view of poetry as a marker of masculine cultural competence and friendship; but highlighting the female reader also suggests that poetry communicates with readers along the tracks of unmediated social (and emotional and erotic) bonds. The fact that this second (partially disavowed) effect is accomplished through the image of a woman is not a coincidence, as readings of poems 50 and 65 will show. These latter two poems (unlike poem 35) make the speaker's emotions central, but also highlight questions about the technical skills and knowledge on which poetry like Catullus's depends.

Poem 50, probably the most famous of Catullus's epistolary poems, is also about the bond between two male poets, but here the speaker himself is the one who suffers the pangs of insatiable desire. Further, just as the speaker's own experience and expression are presented directly, so too is the addressee Licinius (Calvus) addressed directly in the second person without the intervention of personified paper. Poem 50 conforms more closely to the patterns we expect in Catullus (especially the sense of presence and immediacy that

---

8. For an extended analysis of poetry as "a gift of duty," see Stroup (2010). Krostenko (2001) on aesthetic evaluation as a social practice and Wray (2001) on Catullus's performance of manhood are also relevant for these notions of the social functions of poetry.

he builds around the act of address), but it too recognizes a tension between poetry seen as personal communication and other roles it might play.

Hesterno, Licini, die otiosi
multum lusimus in meis tabellis,
ut convenerat esse delicatos:
scribens versiculos uterque nostrum
ludebat numero modo hoc modo illoc,   5
reddens mutua per iocum atque vinum.
atque illinc abii tuo lepore
incensus, Licini, facetiisque,
ut nec me miserum cibus iuvaret
nec somnus tegeret quiete ocellos,   10
sed toto indomitus furore lecto
versarer, cupiens videre lucem,
ut tecum loquerer simulque ut essem.
at defessa labore membra postquam
semimortua lectulo iacebant,   15
hoc, iucunde, tibi poema feci,
ex quo perspiceres meum dolorem.
nunc audax cave sis, precesque nostras,
oramus, cave despuas, ocelle,
ne poenas Nemesis reposcat a te.   20
est vemens dea; laedere hanc caveto.

Yesterday, Licinius, being at leisure, we played a great deal on my tablets, since we had agreed to be a little precious;[9] each of us writing verses, playing now in one meter, now in another, we traded back and forth amidst our drink and laughter. [6] And in fact I left there set on fire by your charming wit, Licinius, to such an extent that, poor me, I could take no pleasure in food nor would sleep cover my eyes with rest. Instead, inflamed with passion, I tossed and turned over the whole bed, longing for dawn, so that I might speak with you and be with you. [13] But after my limbs, worn out with their struggle, lay half-dead on the bed, I made this poem, my love, for you, so that you could see from it the pain I'm in. Now, be careful about being overconfident, and, I beg you my sweet, don't scorn my earnest requests, lest Nemesis demand your punishment. She is a powerful goddess; beware of offending her.

---

9. I borrow here Fitzgerald's (1995, 36–37) translation for the untranslatable "delicatos"; see his discussion for fuller analysis of this word and its ramifications for Catullus.

The logic of this poem's content identifies it as epistolary (i.e., it is a request for face-to-face presence, so it must be a written request), but it avoids obviously calling attention to itself as a letter. Instead, this poem starts off focusing on another form of written communication: poetry. As others have noted,[10] the opening stage of this poem depicts a scene in which the two men communicated in writing even when they were together. Lines 1–6 offer an appealing image of the poetic life. The content of the *versiculi* is never mentioned and seems not to matter, so the poetry's function as expression is minimized; instead these lines embed the skilled production of written poetry within the pleasures and mutuality of real social experience.[11] This image shows learned written poetry functioning almost exactly like the famous sympotic "skolia," songs that wended their way through the party, with each guest adding a few verses. Like those Attic drinking songs, the poetry in this scene both creates and represents a sense of camaraderie.[12]

But in the next part of the poem (lines 7–15), all this changes, and the poem becomes a heated plea for Licinius's physical presence. This section makes no explicit mention of poetry, and instead the speaker recounts the many ways he suffers in body and mind by being separated from Licinius. These lines imply that while the content of yesterday's *versiculi* may not matter for their social effect, this very poem intends to function as a vehicle for expression, a way of communicating real needs to the addressee and producing real effects. And yet if we take account of the fact that this insatiable passion was generated exactly by that seemingly tame exchange of learned poetry on tablets, it seems less likely that poem 50 is drawing a hard-and-fast line between itself and those poems. I would argue that this poem is not segregating poetry into categories (technically skillful, written *versiculi* vs. emotionally powerful address), but blurring the lines between them.

Down through line 17, this poem takes the form of a retrospective narrative, even though its addressive structure (and use of second-person deictics, such as "*tuo* lepore" in line 7) makes clear that this narrative is aimed at some communicative goal.[13] The narrative ends with the declaration in lines 16–17

---

10. See especially Lowrie (2009a, 218–20).

11. Stroup (2010, 231) notes, "The exchanged poem becomes the physical object of the friends' affection, and the two are recast as bibliophiles who adore their poems not just for what they contain but also for the social meaning of their circulation." Lowrie (2009a, 218) in contrast argues that "the exchange of tablets displaces direct physical contact. At the heart of ostensible plenitude lies the mediation of the writing tablet." Lowrie's overall reading of the poem balances this claim against the ways that "writing can also bring people into contact from a distance."

12. Young (2015, 121) on the parallel with sympotic song.

13. But it avoids the most emphatic forms that addressive poems use to represent the desire for social effect (especially imperatives and questions); there are no second-person verbs in this section.

that the speaker has produced "this poem" ("hoc . . . poema"). In a remarkably bold move, the poem identifies itself as a poem and proclaims that its purpose is to communicate and transmit emotion as if it were a letter. The final lines are chock-full of imperatives and refer to the poem as transmitting "earnest requests" ("preces" in line 18). Thus, this poem that avoids the more expected ways of announcing its epistolary function and that opened with an image of poetry that is valued for everything except its communicative content, ends by asserting simultaneously its own specific status as an art object and its aim of having real social traction.[14]

But there are further ways that poem 50 demonstrates the entanglements of poetry, writing, and communication. I should admit that the simplicity I accorded to lines 16–17 above is a false simplicity, since it implies that the referent of "hoc . . . poema" is indisputably the text within which it appears. There is a good argument to be made that the poem that is referred to here is not poem 50, but the poem that follows it in the manuscript, Catullus's famous translation of Sappho 31.[15] My own inclination is to leave that question open. On the reading I gave above, these lines strongly assert the function of poetry in communicating the speaker's experience, though the poem as a whole moderates that claim. If we believe these lines to refer to poem 51, then the question of how a translation makes visible the speaker's pain is yet another instance of poetry's multivalent effects. Translation, especially as it is practiced by Catullus, is the most intense possible way to explore the question of what poetry is and what it does. Translation obviously functions as a credential of cultural competence and, when circulated, a valuable luxury object to be used in confirming literary friendships, but can it also encompass poetry's communicative and expressive aims?[16]

If we build into our reading of poem 50 the possibility that it is a preface or covering letter for poem 51, that connection strengthens in several ways the argument I made above. First, in storyworld terms, the notion that the speaker of poem 50 would make his suffering visible to the addressee by sending a translation of Sappho knits together even more closely the function of

---

14. Wray (2001, 98–99) suggests that the bilingual pun in "poema feci" accentuates the artful "making" the poet has achieved.

15. See especially Young (2015, 120–23) and Wray (2001, 98–99).

16. Young (2015) offers a large-scale analysis of the various ways that translation functions for Catullus. My claim here is inspired in part by Young's argument, which works out the political / sociological importance of translation (especially as it relates to Rome's imperial appropriation of Greek goods and the drive to mark them as ambiguously foreign / Roman), but also the "poetics of lyric appropriation" that confounds the divisions between translation and "original" poetry, between borrowing language and speaking for / as oneself, and enacts "a theory of poetic creation as a proudly derivative enterprise" (189).

poetry as learned and written (embodied in the *versiculi*) and the function of poetry as personal expression. Second, it shows the speaker of poem 50 to be a reader of Sappho (since translation always starts with reading) whose response to this foreign archaic poem, which he knows only through written transmission, mirrors that of Caecilius's girlfriend to his poem or the speaker's own response to Licinius's poetic *lepos*—it simply ravishes him.[17] Third, it brings the overall logic of poem 50 closer to what I argued for poem 35, where this eroticized response to reading is envisioned through the image of a woman's passionate longing: in poem 35 that feminine image substituted for the speaker; in poem 50 it complements and extends that of the speaker.

The role that translation has as a mediating term in poems 50 and 51 becomes sharper in poem 65, a more obvious instance of an epistolary preface.

> Etsi me assiduo defectum cura dolore
>   sevocat a doctis, Hortale, virginibus,
> nec potis est dulcis Musarum expromere fetus
>   mens animi, tantis fluctuat ipsa malis—
> namque mei nuper Lethaeo in gurgite fratris   5
>   pallidulum manans alluit unda pedem,
> Troia Rhoeteo quem subter litore tellus
>   ereptum nostris obterit ex oculis.
> * * * * * * * *
> numquam ego te, vita frater amabilior,   10
> aspiciam posthac? at certe semper amabo,
>   semper maesta tua carmina morte canam,
> qualia sub densis ramorum concinit umbris
>   Daulias, absumpti fata gemens Ityli. —
> sed tamen in tantis maeroribus, Hortale, mitto   15
>   haec expressa tibi carmina Battiadae,
> ne tua dicta vagis nequiquam credita ventis
>   effluxisse meo forte putes animo,
> ut missum sponsi furtivo munere malum
>   procurrit casto virginis e gremio,   20
> quod miserae oblitae molli sub veste locatum,
>   dum adventu matris prosilit, excutitur,

---

17. An effect made visible in the ways that the physical symptoms of erotic longing in poem 50 are closely modeled on the mesmerizing description central to poem 51 (and Sappho 31), as detailed and analyzed most recently in Young (2015, 123).

atque illud prono praeceps agitur decursu,
    huic manat tristi conscius ore rubor.

Even though I am weakened by constant grief, and care calls me away from the learned virgins, Hortalus, and my mind is not capable of producing the sweet offspring of the Muses, since it is tossed on such great seas of grief—for recently Lethean waters have washed over the deathly pale foot of my brother, whom the land of Troy stole from my sight and now crushes under the Rhoetean shore. [9] [lacuna of one line] Will I never again see you, brother dearer to me than life? And yet always I will love you, always I will sing songs made sad by your death, songs like those the daughter of Daulis sings, under the dense shade of branches, as she mourns the death of Itylus, lost to her. But nevertheless even in the midst of such great sorrows, Hortalus, I send to you this translated poem of Callimachus, [16] so that you should not think your words, entrusted in vain to the wandering winds, have chanced to drop out of my mind, like an apple sent as a secret gift by a lover, which rolls forth out of a maiden's chaste lap; she, poor girl, had hidden it under her soft clothing and it is shaken out when she jumps up at her mother's arrival, and it is driven forward in its downward flight, while a guilty blush spreads over her face.

Here, in contrast to poem 50, the function as a cover letter is made explicit: "mitto/haec expressa tibi carmina Battiadae" (lines 15–16).[18] Another contrast to poem 50 (if we read that as introducing poem 51) is that in poem 65 even though the translation is made more central to the poem as a whole (it is sent in lieu of the poem that the speaker cannot write, consumed by grief over his brother), nothing in this poem corresponds to "ex quo perspiceres meum dolorem" (50.17), that is, the suggestion that the content or tone of the translation itself communicates the speaker's state of mind. In fact, while poem 65 is very clear about its role as a cover letter, it says remarkably little about the translation, merely identifying it by its author.

On the basis of its overall impact—a letter to Hortalus in which the speaker explains why he is sending this translation and expresses his heartfelt commitment to honor his promises—we would characterize this poem as primarily focused on what I have called above the more social functions Catullus attributes to poetry. It clearly announces the speaker's intent to use

---

18. The translation offered here boils down the Catullan phrasing, bracketing the issues that attach to "carmina" (plural where we would have expected singular) and "expressa" (from "exprimo," used elsewhere [e.g. Terence *Ad.* 11] for translation, but also carrying a variety of other meanings).

the circulation of poetry to shore up his relationships with other educated elite men and (without comment, but no less clearly) displays the speaker's claim to cultural competence. And yet, as any reader will register, the poem seems to do everything in its power to disrupt these social operations: at every point, it derails or interrupts this otherwise unproblematic use of literature to authorize the speaker as a proper elite man.

In a sense, poem 65 combines the tendencies that we saw in poems 35 and 50. Like poem 35 it visibly takes the form of a letter that focuses on literary exchange between elite men; like poem 50 it eschews the more indirect form and expresses the speaker's own emotional state. It also introduces us to a new wrinkle in addressive structure. It superficially conforms to the expected practice by including a name in the vocative case in the first few lines; unlike in poem 50, however, in poem 65 we have to continue for many lines into the poem and wait for a second vocative address to Hortalus (at line 15) before the addressee's relation to the speaker or to the situation becomes clear.[19] What is more, in between the first mention of Hortalus and the lines that truly engage with him, there is a prominent development of a different second-person addressee: in lines 10–12 we get an apostrophic address to the speaker's dead brother.[20]

On the one hand, the address to Hortalus is marked as centrally important to the poem, and this implies that poetry is operating here as equivalent to the in-group talk (on literary and other subjects) that defines the bonds of these elite men. On the other hand, rather than produce a poem that fulfills that expectation, Catullus offers us instead a poem that indulges in (and comments on) deeply personal and emotional expression. The contrast between an ends-oriented letter and free-flowing lament is made clear not only by the apostrophe that substitutes the unnamed brother for Hortalus as addressee, but by the expansive language and imagery in which the death itself and the speaker's grief are recounted throughout the first fourteen lines. We could even read lines 3–14 (substituting "non" for "nec" at line 3) as a self-standing apostrophic poem, beginning with the speaker's expression of grief and culminating with the commitment to forever sing songs made sad by the brother's death, a claim that is then given poignant form with the image of the nightingale/Philomela. The thought experiment of reading these lines

---

19. Of recent readers, Woodman (2012) most strongly accentuates the way that a linear reading of this poem (as I advocated for Horace's odes) reveals that the "main point" is far from being evenly integrated over the course of the poem. I would just add that the elements that Woodman sees as being in tension are linked respectively to the addressive structure and to personal expression.

20. The hexameter line 9 is missing, so we don't know how the apostrophe might have been linked to the earlier sequence of thought that describes the brother in third-person terms.

separately underscores not only the abrupt shift that is necessary in line 15 to bring the poem back to Hortalus and back to its epistolary function, but also the enormous weight that rests on the poem's first word, "etsi" (although), and on the vocative address to Hortalus in the second line. "Etsi" establishes that everything down through line 14 is a subordinate clause of concession and, thus, introduces the enormous arc of suspense that this poem maintains between its first and second addresses to Hortalus. These two words, then, allow the poem to offer as its "main point" the polite grace note it provides to the speaker's gift, while almost everything else in the poem implies that the poem is attempting to satisfy an essentially insatiable need for lament.

In keeping with the pattern we have seen in poems 35 and 50, overpowering emotion is depicted here, at least in part, by feminine figures.[21] The first instance—in lines 2–3, the Muses have been abandoned by the grieving poet and therefore cannot bear their usual "fruit" / offspring—preserves something close to normative gender roles, by depicting the male poet as aided (or, in this case, unaided) by the female Muses and their fecundity. But this image is less decisively gendered than it seems at first, since the agency for producing poetry is not the poet himself but "mens animi," an archaizing expression for consciousness or mental capacity. The two later instances even more forcefully align the male poet with feminine emotions. In lines 13–14, just before the second address to Hortalus, the speaker follows up the prophecy of his sad songs with the simile of the nightingale, in which the bird is assimilated to Philomela, mourning for her son Itylus. And the poem closes with an elaborate and arresting simile, featuring a nubile girl who allows the love gift of an apple to roll from her lap and thus betray her secret. Although there is substantial debate as to the particulars of this simile and its implied tenor, it is clear that the speaker himself is represented by the blushing girl; just as the simile of the nightingale followed closely upon a statement about himself ("canam" in line 12),[22] so the final image also expands on the claim that the speaker did not want Hortalus to think he had forgotten his promise.

Wray (2001) and Young (2015) have each made thought-provoking and persuasive arguments as to how the feminizing language and imagery in this poem point to the translation that follows and, more broadly, to a relation that Catullus is seeking to construct with Callimachus. This seems absolutely right, given the unsubtle ways that the translation flaunts its ability to voice

---

21. The feminized elements of this poem have been generally recognized but are especially central to the arguments of Wray (2001, 197–203) and Young (2015, 131–32).

22. Even if we accept the much less likely "tegam" (V) here, it would still be a first-person verb.

a feminine perspective, both that of Berenice and that of the lock itself.[23] I would add to those, however, an argument that focuses more closely on the internal logic of poem 65 itself. As I have shown above, a key feature of this poem is that it sets up unambiguously in its first lines the fact that it needs to communicate something to Hortalus and then delays and sidelines that message until late in the poem, where it is given briefly and unequivocally, only to be followed by another vivid elaboration, just slightly more germane to the speaker's relationship with Hortalus. In other words, the moments in the poem where feminine figures are most visible are the moments where it departs most strongly from its instrumental function as an epistle and from poetry's function in the masculine literary culture. Thus, as in poem 35, the notion of poetry as bound up with communicating personal experience—the idea that poetry's content matters—is segregated to a feminine sphere, while the masculine sphere remains focused on its social functions. The over-all effect in poem 65 is not to discount the importance of poetry's power to give voice to emotional experience and to communicate that experience to readers—who could come away from this poem with that idea?—but the poem is structured almost as if its most powerful lamentations are uttered straight to the reader, in a dimension parallel to that in which the speaker presents his translation to Hortalus. And in this dimension, the speaker can speak and feel as a woman.

The other two epistolary poems (35, 50) also subtly foreground the experience of readers—one could almost say that they represent poetry from the reader's side as much as from the writer's side. In poem 35, in addition to the attention-grabbing focus on the girl and her impassioned reception of Caecilius's poetry, we should also remember that the speaker himself is articulating the position of a reader—of a very particular kind of reader (the critic or editor), but still of a reader. Poem 50 is a little more ambiguous, since what has kindled the speaker's imagination is Licinius's charm and wit ("tuo lepore / incensus, Licini, facetiisque" in lines 7–8), attributes that could apply either to his social persona or to his poetry. We should note, however, that this ambiguity is one that Catullus has carefully crafted in his poetry, since he constructs an aesthetic vocabulary that intentionally groups together these two forms of activity. Even with this central ambiguity, however, we can say that this poem focuses on the experience of reception, the point of view of the person who witnesses another's charming behavior or reads another's charming poem. Especially in light of the potential connections between this

---

23. On the gender of the "coma" and its significance, see Acosta-Hughes and Stephens (2012, 231–32).

poem and the translation of Sappho, we might consider the possibility that that poem's eloquent elaboration of the experience of looking on from the outside, of catching the heat of desire through the eyes, is reflected here in poem 50's description of what it feels like to have a reading experience that gets "under your skin."[24] In both poems 50 and 51, what is at stake is not just the experience of desire, but the combination of desire and distance, of the heat generated by the lover's immediate presence and the specific physical, emotional, imaginative, and aesthetic repercussions of the fact that the desire cannot be consummated. In both poems, there is a moving expression of loneliness as well as desire, of the separateness the speaker feels even while being almost completely consumed with thoughts of the beloved. These images take up exactly the experience of reading, the odd combination of intimacy and separateness, the reality of one's emotional reaction to the scenes and words even within the knowledge that this access is "unreal," mediated, virtual.

Horace's Publicly Private *Epistles*

I suggested above that our interpretations need to take account of the fact that Horace chose to construct a whole collection around the notion of poetic letters, rather than following the path of Catullus, who sprinkles his "letters" in among other poems. Equally important is the somewhat surprising fact that once Horace defined this collection as letters (therefore as story-world writing that also has the status of a poem), in these twenty poems he does not consistently encourage in the reader the impression of reading real letters. Few of the poems have the formulaic epistolary openings and sign-offs.[25] Several do highlight the distance between speaker and addressee or the need for information, but these topics we would expect in real letters do not appear consistently and when they do appear are quite obviously converted into thematic material rather than being used to give texture to the storyworld. Rarely do the poems allude to the facts of letter-writing itself—for example, to the act of writing/dictating or to the messenger who will carry the letters, all topics we see frequently in the letters of Cicero and, with very different effect, in Propertius's poem 4.3 quoted above, as well as in Ovid's *Heroides* (and in the exile poetry to be discussed in the epilogue).

---

24. In Young's (2011) memorable phrase for the image of bodily disintegration for the metapoetic drama in which translator confronts source text.

25. Besides the instances I will discuss below, 1.3.30 "debes hoc rescribere"; 1.6.67 "vive, vale"; 1.10.1–2 "urbis amatorem Fuscum saluere iubemus / ruris amatores" and line 49 "haec tibi dicta-bam"; 1.13.19 "vade, vale."

The overall effect, then, is to establish that Horace felt strongly about setting these poems apart in their own collection, but that he was not interested in deepening the reader's sensation of getting access to a real letter. Instead of a robust storyworld context, what Horace achieves in defining these poems as letters is a very pointed inquiry into the relation of readers to writers, especially as conditioned by the broad circulation of literate poetry. In his earlier lyric collection he had explored a public dimension through the traditions of performance, of ritual, and of historical reference (all these features of the *Odes* imply a broader audience), but the poems themselves—by design—do not acknowledge that Horace's own audience will receive these poems as written texts rather than as song or speech.[26] In the *Epistles*, on the other hand, the poems are defined as written texts in their storyworld "origin," and this fact opens a new range of possibilities for playing out the relation between for-us and not-for-us.

The first book of *Epistles* explores the relation between readers and writers with new intensity by reformulating the tension between public and private. It has been generally recognized that part of the appeal of poetic letters is the frisson they create by accentuating the private nature of the communication in the storyworld even while violating that privacy in allowing readers to peek inside. Oliensis has refined this principle in ways that make it more productive for my purposes. Drawing on Erving Goffman's notion of the "backstage" (Oliensis 1998, 168), she emphasizes that Horace allows readers a glimpse not only into his (purported) private life, but into moments or aspects of that life that even other storyworld inhabitants are not supposed to see. Nowhere is this revelation more striking than in the way this collection approaches the question of patronage or, more broadly, the pleasures and pains of friendships with the great men of the day. As Oliensis (155) says, "What makes Horace's epistolary exploration of these issues exciting, even nerve-racking at times, is that it is conducted in full view of his patron." While Oliensis analyzes Horace's counterintuitive strategy of displaying "backstage" behavior primarily in terms of how it shows the poet facing Maecenas and Augustus, I will focus instead on the implications of this practice for how Horace registers in this collection his consciousness of readers in other times and places.[27]

Horace has created in his epistles not only a level that is not-for-us (i.e., not for readers who have no access to the real historical poet), but a level that is

---

26. Books 1–3 of the *Odes* were (probably) published together in 23 BCE; the first book of *Epistles* in about 19 BCE.

27. See Oliensis (1998, 191) on the ways that acknowledging a broader community of readers conditions the effects of Maecenas and Augustus as overreaders.

not for Maecenas: even this most privileged addressee is treated in this collection as if he both is and isn't the intended recipient of these musings. Maecenas is the patron who must be handled with kid gloves (and whose demands can be implicitly critiqued in letters to other people) but is also a trusted confidant before whom Horace can display all his wavering and doubts and temper tantrums. It is almost as if Maecenas's special status as a real person with real power over Horace (and real claims to Horace's goodwill and gratitude) has been partially subsumed into his more general status as a reader. Horace has found a way to express through poetic structure (as well as thematically) the tangled questions about authenticity, personal expression, freedom, and self-determination that have long been recognized to shape this collection.

With this in mind, I would like to focus on a few letters that mesh the poetic conception of the collection most closely with the demands of "ordinary" letters. I noted above that many of the poems in this collection barely register the epistolary conceit and instead take the form of extended meditations that seem only minimally influenced by either the identity of the addressee or the implied "occasion" of the letter.[28] I do think there is more to explore in the question of how even these essay-like poems relate to the conception of epistolarity that Horace apparently wanted to foreground in this collection, but rather than pursuing that question here I will turn instead to analyzing what Horace does in the poems that more specifically refer to the nature of letters in social life. The poems I'll concentrate on here do not necessarily strive for the "realistic" impression of letters, but they use the function of letters in real life—personal communication that often blends practical goals with the pleasure of making contact—as part of their structure and themes. Poems 1.5 and 1.9 advertise their status as very specific types of letters with obvious real-world correlates: poem 1.5 is an invitation, and poem 1.9 is a letter of recommendation. Poem 1.8 does not fit so neatly any specific letter-type, but it stands out for its fanciful elaboration of the typical letter by using the Muse as messenger. All three of these poems pointedly develop the illogical amalgam of public and private on which

---

28. My own typology of the book (excluding poems 5, 8, 9, and 13, which will be discussed in detail) would go something like this: poems 1, 2, 6, 16, 17, 18, 19, and 20 have little to no impression of the epistolary form (though the last poem in the book is the only one that seems almost impossible to read as a letter; see Mayer 1994, 49); of the other poems, 3, 4, 7, 11, 14, and 15 make use of the theme of distance between the speaker and addressee and/or the fact that the speaker expresses curiosity about where the addressee is or what he is doing as a way of fleshing out the epistolary conceit. Poem 10 fits in this group as well, though it plays with the expectations governing it: most of the poem is emphatically about the difference between country and city and the differing preferences of the speaker and addressee, but only in the final lines does the poem actually place the speaker in the country. Poem 12 is similar, though with less emphasis on questions of place.

I have argued the collection as a whole rests and in fact is designed to explore. I will close with a briefer consideration of two other famous poems (1.13 and 1.20), which exhibit two different ways this collection makes the relation of author to reader a central issue.

Three of these five poems (1.8, 1.9, and 1.13) foreground the principle of mediation, but to different ends than we saw in Catullus. In Horace, the theme of mediation is closely related to his preference for representing the "backstage": by inverting the expected relation between backstage and the official performance, Horace is calling attention to the process by which the performance gets produced and thereby diminishing its claim to be natural, unpremeditated, etc. Similarly, he uses mediating figures in the poems to cut against the assumption of untrammeled social intercourse and instead focuses our attention on the elements of design and decision-making that generate these poems.

Poem 1.5 is perhaps the epistle closest in conception to the *Odes*, in that it uses the framework of an invitation to expand on the themes of friendship, wine, and the need for moderation in all things, including in exercising moderation.[29] But beyond the obvious differences (meter, diction, syntax, a more diffuse style) this poem also promotes its epistolary status by weaving together an image of what the addressee is imagined to be doing (lines 8–9 and 30–31) with images of the speaker's house and the delights that await. In other words, while this poem does pursue the typical themes associated with the symposium, it does so in a way that maintains more strongly the speaker's storyworld motivation (inviting Torquatus to a party).[30]

Si potes Archiacis conviva recumbere lectis
nec modica cenare times holus omne patella,
supremo te sole domi, Torquate, manebo.
vina bibes iterum Tauro diffusa palustris
inter Minturnas Sinuessanumque Petrinum.   5
si melius quid habes, arcesse, vel imperium fer.
iamdudum splendet focus et tibi munda supellex:

---

29. It recalls *Odes* 1.20 (especially in the confession that only unfancy food and drink will be on offer and the implication that the addressee has more important things to do as well as better wine to drink). But in its bid for letting go (here, specifically in spending and in speaking freely, lines 12–20) it also recalls "recepto / dulce furere est amico" (2.7.27–28) and "insanire iuvat" (3.19.18).

30. Another important feature of this poem is its ostentatiously casual reference to Caesar's birthday (lines 9–10) as the reason why Torquatus can carouse well into the night (cf. similar treatment of Murena's augurship in *Odes* 3.19). For an interpretation that makes this fact more central to the overall impact of the poem, see Oliensis (1998, 182–84). For my purposes, this reference is part of the overarching structure I am delineating, in which this poem's big thematic moves are all tightly worked into the fabric of the storyworld situation.

mitte levis spes et certamina divitiarum
et Moschi causam: cras nato Caesare festus
dat veniam somnumque dies; inpune licebit   10
aestivam sermone benigno tendere noctem.
quo mihi fortunam, si non conceditur uti?
parcus ob heredis curam nimiumque severus
adsidet insano: potare et spargere flores
incipiam patiarque vel inconsultus haberi.   15
quid non ebrietas dissignat? operta recludit,
spes iubet esse ratas, ad proelia trudit inertem,
sollicitis animis onus eximit, addocet artis.
fecundi calices quem non fecere disertum,
contracta quem non in paupertate solutum?   20
haec ego procurare et idoneus imperor et non
invitus, ne turpe toral, ne sordida mappa
corruget naris, ne non et cantharus et lanx
ostendat tibi te, ne fidos inter amicos
sit qui dicta foras eliminet, ut coeat par   25
iungaturque pari: Butram tibi Septiciumque
et nisi cena prior potiorque puella Sabinum
detinet adsumam; locus est et pluribus umbris;
sed nimis arta premunt olidae convivia caprae.
tu quotus esse velis rescribe et rebus omissis   30
atria servantem postico falle clientem.

If you can recline as a guest on couches made by Archias and you're not afraid of dining on a modest platter of nothing but vegetables, then I will look for you at my house, Torquatus, at sunset. You will be served wine bottled when Taurus was consul for the second time, in between the swamps of Minturnae and Petrinum in Campania. If you have something better, have it sent, or bear with my household rule. Already the hearth is bright and clean for you, and so too the furnishings. Put aside superficial hopes and the struggle for riches and Moschus's case: Caesar's birthday tomorrow offers an excuse for sleep. We can extend the summer night with friendly conversation with no fear of the consequences. [11] For what was fortune given to me if I am not allowed to make full use of it? The man who scrimps and saves too strictly out of concern for his heir is just about a madman: I will start drinking and scattering flowers and not even care if others think I am reckless. Is there anything that intoxication cannot bring about? It reveals secrets, it bids hopes come true, it pushes the spiritless man into battle, it removes burdens from the worried mind, it teaches us skills. Who has not been made eloquent by generous cups, whom have they not made free in the midst of grinding poverty? [20] I, properly and not unwillingly, am ordered to take care of the following: that no shabby coverlet or dirty napkin makes you wrinkle your nose, that the wine jug and platter reflect back your face, that there will be no one who blabs outside what has been said among trustworthy friends, that this is a party of equals. I will have Butra and Septicius here for you, and (unless a previous dinner and a more attractive girl claims him) Sabinus. There is room for more hangers-on, but it's oppressive to pack in too close guests of goat-ish odor. Write back to tell me how many you would like us to be, and setting aside your business affairs, slip out the back door to elude the client keeping watch in the atrium.

Unlike similar poems in the *Odes*, this poem explicitly takes up and develops the theme of privacy or, more accurately, the threat of publicity. Much of the poem (lines 12–29) turns on a tension between two competing notions of the freedom that (ideally) characterizes the symposium. First, in lines 12–20, the speaker enlarges on the original offer of festivity by giving voice to a desire for unbridled pleasure and a mini-panegyric on the power of wine to overcome all restrictions. In thought, this passage recalls the traditional powers associated with Bacchus—he who loosens tongues, lifts burdens, and makes the world look rosy—but instead of extolling divinely authored freedom, this poem frames such lack of restraint in distinctively human terms. Among the forms of restraint that are kicked over here are the expectations of an heir (13), the judgment of one's fellows ("patiarque vel inconsultus haberi" in line 15), pessimism ("spes iubet esse ratas" in line 17), fear ("ad proelia trudit inertem" in line 17), and worry ("sollicitis animis onus eximit" in line 18). Horace also gestures here toward a more skeptical or ironic estimation of wine's powers by claiming that it can teach skills ("addocet artes" in line 18), make everyone eloquent (line 19), and make even a poor man unconstrained (line 20).

But instead of extending this image of liberation and optimism, the poem's final section takes a sharp turn to detail various unpleasant realities that might burden the mood of the party (lines 21–29). Of course, the speaker enumerates these elements only to say that he will take care that they are absent, but still the insistent list of dirty surroundings, loose-lipped fellow guests, and smelly hangers-on cannot help but bring before us the negative image of a badly run party to compete with the pleasures and freedom described in the previous lines. The poem ends with a final negative image: in order to enjoy the ideal gathering proposed, Torquatus has to make his escape past a hovering client (line 31).

These negative images do not undercut the more obvious thematic energy in this poem that extols the pleasures of relaxation and good company. But the unexpected conjunction of elements here subtly reinforces a tension inherent in an invitation poem, namely, the public nature of an apparently private and practical communication. All the "letters" in this book are private in the sense that they are addressed to specific people and claim to have some message of relevance for the addressee, but the ones that define themselves as performing a specific social function are also more likely to contain an implicit recognition of the odd fact that such a document is also a poem for readers. In the case of this poem, that acknowledgment comes most strongly in the paradoxical insistence that the goings-on will not be publicized (lines 24–25), but it is also present more subtly in the contrast between the freedom and release described in lines 13–20 and the reminders (in lines 21–29) of the effort required to produce that impression of freedom. The negative images in the latter part of the poem betray the fact that all that talk of letting go and being free is an ideal that is far from guaranteed, even with the magical help of wine. Recall that several of the burdens that wine is said to relieve have to do with the surveillance and judgment of others and that the list of wine's remarkable powers ends with two examples that are surely meant to remind us not of liberatory pleasures but of the self-deception of drinkers: wine does not, in fact, make everyone eloquent or release a poor man from his debts. Although these last two items are more ironic in tone than the rest of the list (and thus subtly ease the transition to the next section), they also slightly color the earlier assertions that depict the speaker as being willing to have his private actions scrutinized by others without caring about the result ("patiarque vel inconsultus haberi" in line 15).

This poem is neither dour nor pessimistic, but its overall effect is to temper the naïvely rosy outlook of lines 13–20 with a recognition of the stubborn forces that oppose that outlook and especially to draw attention to the implications of publicity. Further, this poem (even apart from its reference to Caesar's birthday) participates in the exploration of *amicitia* that threads this collection together. Since the question of equality among the guests and their trustworthiness (lines 24–26, 28–29) is among the ideals that are hedged in the poem's latter section, the poem records its own act of breaking faith in making public what is private and in airing relationships that contain elements of both equality and hierarchy. Like the client whom Torquatus is to slip past, the ever-present realities of the social world are not defeated or removed, just temporarily avoided. Thus this invitation embodies the logic of the collection as a whole, which depends on both creating an image of privacy and violating it.

The invitation to Torquatus acknowledges thematically its unaccountable status as a publicly circulated poem; my next two examples deploy instead something like the mediating structure we saw in Catullus. In *Epistles* 1.8 and 1.9, Horace uses a triangulating structure in two different ways, though perhaps in both cases this feature reflects the pressures brought to bear on the epistolary situation by the exorbitant status of the imperial family. Poem 1.8 offers an instance of triangulation very similar to Catullus 35, in which the papyrus was bid to bring a message to Caecilius. In this case the Muse is introduced as the intervening agent, who will convey news of Horace's own melancholy mental state and politely ask how the addressee Celsus is getting along in the retinue of Tiberius. Although this poem is silent on Celsus's poetic ambitions, in *Epistle* 1.3 he is warned away from overreliance on the library in his own compositions. It seems significant, then, that in *Epistles* 1.8 Celsus is not identified as an author and there is no discussion of literary topics, but still the Muse is asked to play the part of the go-between.

> Celso gaudere et bene rem gerere Albinovano
> Musa rogata refer, comiti scribaeque Neronis.
> si quaeret quid agam, dic multa et pulcra minantem
> vivere nec recte nec suaviter, haud quia grando
> contuderit vitis oleamve momorderit aestus,   5
> nec quia longinquis armentum aegrotet in agris;
> sed quia mente minus validus quam corpore toto
> nil audire velim, nil discere, quod levet aegrum,
> fidis offendar medicis, irascar amicis,
> cur me funesto properent arcere veterno,   10
> quae nocuere sequar, fugiam quae profore credam,
> Romae Tibur amem, ventosus Tibure Romam.
> post haec, ut valeat, quo pacto rem gerat et se,
> ut placeat iuveni percontare utque cohorti.
> si dicet "recte," primum gaudere, subinde   15
> praeceptum auriculis hoc instillare memento:
> ut tu fortunam, sic nos te, Celse, feremus.

At my request, Muse, please bid Celsus Albinovanus (companion and scribe to Nero) joy and prosperity. If he asks how I'm doing, tell him that though I make many impressive statements, I am living neither as I should nor pleasantly—and it's not because the hail has beaten down the vines, or because the summer heat has nipped the olives, or because the herd is ailing in faraway fields, but because, being less strong in my mind than in my whole body, I am not willing to listen or learn anything that would improve my condition; I am vexed with my trusty doctors and angry with my friends, because they try to rouse me from my deathlike torpor; [10] I pursue what harms me and flee what I believe would do me good; at Rome I long for Tibur and at Tibur, changeable like the wind, I long for Rome. After this, ask how he is faring, how he's managing his business and himself, how well he has impressed the young commander and the cohort. If he says, "I'm fine," first remember to congratulate him then to slip this advice into his ear: as you bear your good fortune, Celsus, so we will bear with you.

The content of this short letter is superficially more ordinary than that of *Epistle* 1.3, though also clearly pointing toward philosophical precepts. Most of the letter is focused on Horace's description of his own inability to live according to the precepts he claims to believe in and his resistance to the very advice that would improve his situation. In Catullus's poem 35, the body of the letter was focused on Caecilius and his (literary / erotic) situation; the triangulating form in that case highlights the "conversation" between the first-person speaker (letter-writer) and the paper (i.e., the conversation in which the letter-writer entrusts his thoughts to the paper rather than the conversation in which the paper transmits those thoughts to the addressee). In this Horatian case, however, the poem presents for us the scene in which the Muse will deliver the speaker's message to Celsus: it first plays out how the Muse will describe the speaker's unhappy plight (lines 3–12) and then pictures the Muse asking Celsus about his own contentment and offering him a bit of advice. Unlike the Catullan poem, in which the triangulating structure puts the addressee in the third person, the intervention of the Muse in this poem's long central section transforms what could have been simple first-person indicative statements into indirect discourse. In other words, while the Catullan poem uses the intervention of the papyrus to displace the addressee, this poem uses the intervention of the Muse to make the speaker's relation to his own words (in fact, his own words about his own state of mind) more oblique, as if he is partially displaced from his own speaking position.

It is also significant that the messenger here is not an inert piece of paper brought to life by a clever act of personification, but the most authoritative poetic agent imaginable. In fact, surely part of the wit of this poem relies on the fact that the Muse is invoked to effect an exchange of (almost) utter banality ("Oh, I'm not great, kind of depressed—how are you?"). Especially in light of the fact that the other poem to mention Celsus and Tiberius's retinue (*Epistle* 1.3) focuses almost exclusively on their literary ambitions and self-consciously raises its style toward the epic instead of the epistolary,[31] the introduction of the Muse as messenger early in 1.8 excites the expectation of a poem very different from the one that follows. Thus the Muse's role as intervening messenger between speaker and addressee is highlighted even more, since her thematic function is so minimal.

Near the end, this poem echoes the structure of the Catullan poem by putting Celsus in the third person ("si dicet" in line 15), but with a twist: the final line of the poem offers to the Muse a direct quotation of what she should say to Celsus and thus manages to reassert the normal first-/second-person epistolary structure (if we bracket out our knowledge that this is introduced as a quotation).[32] Not only is this final line striking for the directness of the second-person form, but its content is much more unambiguously didactic (and authoritative) than the rest of the poem would have led us to expect. Most of the letter seems to be only tangentially connected with Celsus's service to Tiberius, but near the end we are reminded of the great stakes of being in the retinue for such an elevated figure. In the last line, when the letter speaks unambiguously in the second person and warns Celsus to not forget his friends, the poem comes close to voicing the idea that proximity to the imperial family is dangerous because of the difficulty of finding the right way to behave toward them (i.e., how easy it is to offend them, the many missteps possible) but also because of how this proximity will be perceived by others, who will be jealous or resentful or critical of perceived sycophancy. The first of these difficulties is not voiced, but the latter is. To throw off the cloak provided by the triangulating form at this final moment and speak directly in the second person seems to underscore the continuing presence of Celsus's friends from his previous life, who will be watching to see how he conducts himself in his new elevated circumstances. This twist is even more striking when we consider that the content of the central lines seemed to deprive the speaker of any authority he might have had as a moral adviser, since he admitted his own inability to live up to the precepts he endorses.

In sum, this poem reflects on privacy in two different ways. First, parallel to what I argued above for Catullus 35, the very use of an intervening figure brings into high relief the work and strategy involved in communication, rather than minimizing that dimension by focusing our view on the

---

31. Florus, the addressee of 1.3 is also the addressee of 2.2, a much more elaborate poem reflecting on literary practice.

32. The Catullus poem similarly ends with a reassertion of first-/second-person structure, addressed to the learned girl.

happenings in the storyworld. Catullus's choice of the paper itself as messenger maintains his general practice of situating the speaker in the storyworld, while Horace's choice of the Muse for this role maintains his general practice of calling attention to the poet's control of discourse. While both these figures of mediation implicitly comment on the fact that the poem makes public an apparently private letter, Horace's use of the Muse reminds us of his choice to present a whole collection of poetic letters by emphasizing its status as artistic design. The second way this poem foregrounds privacy is that when it finally does get to second-person address in its last line, it raises the social issue of how others will judge Celsus's behavior. This strengthens the impression of a real letter, since it sounds like friendly advice (the private nature of which is emphasized by telling the Muse to slip it into Celsus's ear), but this effect only makes the letter's public nature more jarring. The final line is saying *publicly* that Celsus needs to be careful about the impression others will form of him—another excellent example of the backstage logic that governs the collection as a whole.

The possibility of offending the imperial family may not be voiced in *Epistle* 1.8, but it lurks everywhere in *Epistle* 1.9. Perhaps it is this awareness of pitfalls that makes this poem so unusually short, or perhaps it is an embodiment of the advice not to ask too much of the high and mighty, including not too much of their time.

> Septimius, Claudi, nimirum intellegit unus,
> quanti me facias; nam cum rogat et prece cogit,
> scilicet ut tibi se laudare et tradere coner,
> dignum mente domoque legentis honesta Neronis,
> munere cum fungi propioris censet amici: 5
> quid possim videt ac novit me valdius ipso.
> multa quidem dixi, cur excusatus abirem,
> sed timui, mea ne finxisse minora putarer,
> dissimulator opis propriae, mihi commodus uni.
> sic ego maioris fugiens opprobria culpae   10
> frontis ad urbanae descendi praemia. quodsi
> depositum laudas ob amici iussa pudorem,
> scribe tui gregis hunc et fortem crede bonumque.

[Tiberius] Claudius, Septimius alone clearly sees how important I am to you; for when he asks me and entreats that I should try to praise him to you and induce you to take him in, as a man worthy of the mind and home of Nero who selects only what is honorable, thinking that I serve the role of a closer friend, he sees what I am capable of and knows it better than I do. [6] Obviously I spoke at length on the reasons why I should be let off from this demand, but I was afraid of seeming to pretend that my effectiveness is less than it is, to be concealing my resources and keeping the benefits for myself alone. And so, in avoiding hostile judgments for a greater fault, I sink to the privileges of town-bred assurance. But if you find it praiseworthy that I have given up my restraint at the bidding of a friend, then please enroll this man in your entourage and believe him to be a good brave man.[33]

Like the previous poem, this one combines the triangulating strategy with the logic of the backstage. The triangulating effect operates here not by inventing an agent between speaker and addressee, but instead makes the speaker himself the mediating agent, who introduces Septimius to Tiberius. In addition to placing great emphasis on the speaker's position as go-between, the poem plays up the fact that Septimius's judgment of the speaker's connections differs from that of the speaker himself and (it is implied) of Tiberius. The speaker here, in the position of the papyrus in Catullus 35 or the Muse in *Epistle* 1.8, comments ironically on the naïveté or misjudgment of the person who initiates the communication (Septimius in this case, the letter-writers in the cases of the other poems).

This irony points up one of the main advantages of the triangulating structure, that it can unify two different positions (the letter-writer and the papyrus, the letter-writer and the Muse, Septimius and the speaker), and thus avoid the pitfalls associated with any one position and maximize its potential for ingratiation. The other poems that use the triangulating structure do not highlight the possibility that the go-between will alter the message, or that the message will be delivered more effectively by this intervening agent than it would have been by the speaker himself, though that notion is present. This is only a short step from the related recognition that writing communicates without the supervision of the writer, that writing is sent out into the world as a messenger but not completely controlled by the intentions of the sender (a notion explored more fully in poems 1.13 and 1.20, which I discuss below).

In Catullus 35 and Horace's *Epistle* 1.8 the device can soften what might otherwise be unpleasantly direct advice: the core message will be received by the addressee, but the addressee will also perceive the politeness strategy employed and may give the speaker credit for trying to spare his feelings. How does this strategy operate for the reader? In storyworld terms, we too

---

33. The translation here borrows phrases from Mayer (1994), especially in lines 4 and 11.

give the speaker credit for this politeness strategy (perhaps even more credit than it deserves since its obviousness as a strategy only underlines both the didactic/corrective nature of the message itself and the speaker's self-satisfaction in coming up with this detour). But this strategy also closely tracks the aesthetic act of mediation, of indirection and, in a more complex way, poetry's "parasitic" relation to the discourse of real social life. The detours and elaborations through which social speech gets transmuted into poetry are echoed by the way these poems clothe the didactic message in a clever costume, though also make clear that this is not merely a change in appearance. It is not coincidental that in both cases the intervening messenger is an agent who plays a central and ambiguously independent role in poetic discourse: paper (the written materials on which poetry circulates) and the Muse (the divine agent who empowers the poet but never yields her unique authority). Of these two agents, obviously the Muse is pictured as having her own power, while the paper is pictured as being the servant of the writer, but the use of both as intervening agents reveals that they share a spectrum of independence.

When the more obvious triangulating structures of Catullus's poem 35 and *Epistle* 1.8 are compared to the variation we see in *Epistle* 1.9, the odd position of the speaker highlights the combination of power and dependency within the central node. A tone-deaf reading of this poem, a reading that misses the markers of irony ("nimirum" and "unus" in line 1; see also line 6), would see it as a straightforward statement of the speaker's influence with Tiberius. But the reading that picks up on these cues and applies them appropriately to limit the claims that the speaker makes for his own powers is literal-minded or naïve in a different way. In storyworld terms, if the speaker truly believed that Septimius's confidence in his influence was misguided, he wouldn't be writing this letter. Equally important, when we take the poem as discourse that assumes readers as its audience, we see that what is being demonstrated in this poem is neither the speaker's consciousness that his influence with Tiberius is limited nor even the speaker's self-deprecating wit, but the intertwining of social and aesthetic logic on which this poem's detours depend and especially the role of indirection in this hybrid logic.

This poem not only makes the bold decision to address a member of the imperial family (Horace could have easily written a poem addressed to Septimius in which he disavowed his influence with Tiberius but then said he was willing to try anyway because he owes it to Septimius as a friend), but invents a structure that raises the social stakes of this move even further, by foregrounding the confidence it implies in his powers (both social and poetic powers). The unusual structure of this poem applies the backstage strategy in a surprising way, since it lays before Tiberius the debate between Septimius and Horace about his influence (e.g., "multa quidem dixi, cur excusatus abirem" in line 7). In this instance, strikingly, the backstage revelation exposes not the speaker (who is shown denying his influence with the imperial family), but Septimius. The speaker ties himself (and his language) in knots trying to show that he is not taking anything for granted about his relationship to Tiberius; but at the same time he risks showing Septimius to be exactly the wrong kind of person (the kind who wheedles people into using their influence in his favor) and even showing himself to be diminishing Septimius in order to curry favor with Tiberius.

Of course, risk-taking is exactly the mechanism that drives the backstage strategy, and we see here as elsewhere that the audacity of this move is framed with a recognition that one is submitting to the judgments of one's peers (or, in this case, one's superiors). This poem also picks up on the surveillance motif that ended the previous poem: the reason the speaker gives for finally acceding to Septimius is that he didn't want others to think his modesty was false ("sed timui, mea ne finxisse minora putarer" in line 8). Like the previous poem, too, this one closes (after much of the letter has focused more on Septimius and Horace than on Tiberius) with a surprisingly direct second-person message, even using the imperative ("scribe," "crede" in line 13). The act of trust in revealing how underlings talk among themselves when strategizing about how to approach the powerful has merited this final confidence, when the speaker does what he has claimed throughout he cannot (and should not) do.

The poem's odd contortions construct Tiberius as the spectator (almost a visible version of an overreader though, by definition, that figure cannot appear in the text) of the scenes that take place out of his view but within the shadow of his power. *Epistle* 1.9 recognizes fully and almost effusively Tiberius's special position (by highlighting the speaker's sense of the magnitude of what he is asking in contrast to his own modest status), while it simultaneously takes the risk of showing how relationships are distorted within the zone of contact around the imperial family. The poem flatters Tiberius both by acknowledging his unusual position and by assuming that he will honor the truth-speaker who can show how such a position affects social relations. Central to the logic of this poem is the fact that the speaker is pleading for admission into Tiberius's "grex" not for himself, but for another; the triangulating strategy works by assigning to two distinct persons the desire to impose on the great man and the modesty that recognizes the distance between the petitioner and his target. The poem—especially because it gives us a full backstage view of Septimius's pressing request—shows Tiberius (and the reader) both Septimius's eagerness and the speaker's hesitation. In comparison to the other poems that use the triangulating motif, this poem not only loosely allows for the possibility that the intervening agent will change the message but *requires* that he alters it (though it shows the original "message" as well to make clear what alterations have been made).

The elements of revelation and tactful restraint, of self-confident request and self-mocking irony that shape *Epistle* 1.9 are paralleled in the two poems in this collection that dramatize the act of releasing the book to readers, poems 1.13 and 1.20. But perhaps the clearest link between the poem to Tiberius and these two poems is the varying degrees of independence with which the intervening agent is endowed in each case. Each of these latter poems focuses on the relation between the author, the reader, and the text, but with very different emphases: poem 1.13, contrary to any storyworld logic, purports to be a message sent en route to the messenger who is delivering a set of *carmina* to Augustus;[34] in poem 1.20, the readers are relegated to the background as we see the author-figure directly address the book. But both poems are built around the image of an author's futile attempts to control what happens when the text meets the reader.[35]

I find wholly convincing Oliensis's suggestion (1998, 190–91) that these two poems are parallel in their function, even though the envoi function of 1.13 is muted by its position in the middle of the collection. These two poems offer compelling, even affecting images of an author bumbling through gestures of authorial control that are destined to fail, as if specifying an ideal state of mind for the reader (1.13.3 "si validus, si laetus erit," etc.) or condemning the book's desire for admiration (1.20) will somehow avoid the pitfalls of making the work available to readers. Where these two poems differ, beyond the obvious fact that poem 1.20 employs a personified book and evades the epistolary frame completely, is that poem 1.13 is specifically about delivering Horace's poetic output to Augustus, while 1.20 is about publishing it in the modern sense, by which it will become available to any readers who wish to take it up. Thus reading these two poems as parallel underscores my claim that Augustus (and Maecenas in a different way) is treated in this collection as *both* a unique reader with a unique position and as a reader like any other, a function partially previewed by the treatment of

---

34. Its lack of dramatic logic is flagged in line 1 ("ut proficiscentem docui te saepe diuque"): Why would the speaker write a letter to reiterate the instructions he has just given in person and how are we supposed to imagine this letter delivered? This framing also calls attention implicitly and, in this case, almost parodically to the artifice of the epistolary structure.

35. Ferri (1993) and Oliensis (1998) have noted the parallel between the role of the messenger in poem 1.13 and that of the book in poem 1.20.

Tiberius in poem 1.9. Further, the close conjunction between these poems (both of which make full use of backstage expression) also bears out the way that this collection has constituted privacy as a powerful force in social life and in communicative practices, even as these poems are themselves based on the impulse to violate that privacy.

It is not an accident that poem 1.13, in which Augustus figures as reader, explores in detail the power that readers have over the reception of the text. The speaker's instructions to Vinnius imply that the book (and by extension the poet) must be modest in its demands, waiting for the reader to express an interest, and recognizing that it can only hope for a good reception if the reader takes it up in a good mood and at leisure.

> Ut proficiscentem docui te saepe diuque,
> Augusto reddes signata volumina, Vinni,
> si validus, si laetus erit, si denique poscet;
> ne studio nostri pecces odiumque libellis
> sedulus inportes opera vehemente minister.
>
> (*Epis.* 1.13.1–5)

As I explained to you repeatedly and at great length when you were leaving, Vinnius, hand over these sealed volumes to Augustus, if he is feeling well, if he is in a good mood—in short, if he asks for them, so that you don't go wrong in your zeal for me and bring my books into disfavor by being overly energetic in your office as servant.

Poem 1.20, on the other hand, invests very little energy in imagining the motivations, reactions, etc. of readers. It represents them as easily bored lovers (line 8), as provincials distant from the privileged cultural life of the capital (line 13), and as schoolchildren reading under compulsion (lines 17–18). While both poems are very interested in the dynamic by which the author only partially controls the book and the reader's experience, poem 1.13 focuses on the reader's reception as the element that will be decisive, and poem 1.20 focuses on the book's inherent independence of its author (and the nature of publicity itself) as the decisive element.

Reading these two poems in parallel reveals the implications of the two strands I have been tracing in this collection: the role of mediating figures, and the focus on privacy and its violation. These two poems can also help us to gauge the extent to which the power wielded by Augustus (and Maecenas and Tiberius) makes them a different kind of reader from the general reader of posterity. I would argue that poem 1.20 puts general readers in the position that Tiberius occupies in poem 1.9 and Augustus in 1.13. That is, in poem 1.20 the general reader is privy to the hopes and hesitations that precede the book's availability and is in a sense recognized obliquely as having power over the reception of the book. The major difference between general readers and Horace's powerful contemporaries, however, is also registered in these poems. It has long been noted that personal autonomy in relations of patronage is a central theme of this collection.[36] The prominence in this collection of both mediating figures and backstage expression is clearly in the service of this theme, since these structural principles reflect the ways that personal and political power distorts both knowledge and communication in social settings. Messenger figures of various types call attention to the ways that approach to the high and mighty requires strategy, even apart from managing the content of one's message. On the other hand, the use of backstage expression balances out this implication by demonstrating confidence, even recklessness, in approaching these men and thus presenting them (to themselves and also to other readers) as tolerant and capable of forgiving missteps. Thus even the collection's insistent interest in treating Augustus et al. as readers and accentuating their commonalities with other readers shows that it is commenting on the constraints produced by the new political order (while it is also operating under those same constraints).

------

36. Prominent examples are Johnson (1993) and Bowditch (2001).

Epilogue
Ovid in Exile

his, precor, atque aliis possint tua numina flecti,
　　o pater, o patriae cura salusque tuae!
non ut in Ausoniam redeam, nisi forsitan olim,
　　cum longo poenae tempore victus eris:
tutius exilium pauloque quietius oro,
　　ut par delicto sit mea poena suo.

(Ovid, Tristia 2.573–78)

By these and other arguments, I pray, may your divine will be swayed—
o father, o you who are the salvation of and object of devotion for
your country—not that I be allowed to return to Italy (unless perhaps
someday when you will be won over by the long duration of my punishment), but I beg for a safer and slightly tamer place of exile, so that
my punishment should fit the crime.

These lines bring to a close Ovid's second book of his poems from exile; in
this case, the whole book consists of one long plea for leniency directed at
Augustus. It is hard to imagine a poem that more unambiguously positions
itself as real, consequential speech: addressed to Augustus, these lines are the
poetic equivalent of a legal document that states the petitioner's case and

asks for a specific remedy.[1] Here, if anywhere, we might think that "story" and discourse meld into one: the poem does not represent but constitutes a speech to the emperor, and the speaker's goals line up with those of the historical poet. Further, these lines integrate their poetic character with their expressive purpose: even though the content of these couplets is a real request for real relief, they make use of distinctively poetic effects (see especially the elaborated vocative in line 574) in the manner of performed poetry, which uses its formal features to heighten its ritual authority.

The opening of this same poem, however, gives a very different impression of its aims:

> Quid mihi vobiscum est, infelix cura, libelli,
> ingenio perii qui miser ipse meo?
>
> (2.1–2)

What business do I have with you, books, my ill-fated obsession, I who have been pitifully ruined by my own talent?

The poem opens with an apostrophic address to the books themselves and continues for many couplets with bitter reflections on the mixed blessings poetry has brought this speaker before, in line 27, addressing Augustus directly.[2] The effect recapitulates in miniature the opening of the first book of the *Tristia*, in which a poem addressing the personified book as it begins its journey back to Rome is followed by a poem placing its speaker in the midst of a storm at sea on the outward journey to Tomis, praying to the sea gods.[3] The inaugural moment in each book uses a form of unreal address to identify the speaker with the historical poet Ovid and to foreground (through the image of the book) his attempt to communicate with readers; this strong orientation toward

---

1. Cf. Lowrie (2009a, 363–74), who considers this poem a meditation on the performative power of poetry (and its limits) in comparison to the performative power of legal discourse. See Ingleheart (2010) on its relation to forensic oratory.

2. The second-person plural address to the books is not sustained, and instead we get mostly unaddressed rumination (though at line 9 there is a generalizing second-person singular). In lines 7–8 and 23–26 Caesar's actions are described in the third person, the latter section coming just before the turn toward addressing him directly. *Tr.* 3.1.76 repeats this pattern of discussing Augustus in the third person just before addressing him directly.

3. The third poem in this sequence again shifts the orientation of "story" and discourse: like Propertius's poem 1.3, it is an unaddressed retrospective narration (in this case of the exile's last night in Rome).

readers is then followed in each case by a reassertion of the speaker's place in the storyworld, and his speech is reoriented to storyworld goals.[4]

This recognition of the general reader as an audience does not rob these poems of their consequential engagement with Augustus (and with specific contemporary readers), but it implies that this communicative aim alone cannot account for Ovid's poetic practice here.[5] Ovid's exile poetry offers us the opportunity to explore how the "story"/discourse structures I have analyzed in the work of Catullus, Propertius, and Horace might play out not only with the passage of time (Ovid was a younger contemporary of the latter two poets, as we learn in *Tristia* 4.10.45–50), but in a corpus that unambiguously applies the communicative aims of poetry to real-world circumstances. I will not attempt here anything close to a full analysis, but instead restrict myself to sketching out the implications of my approach in just two central respects: the relationship to the emperor and the impact of acknowledging the written medium. In fact, these two aspects are conceptually linked, since it is in part by highlighting their written medium that these poems develop a two-track notion of their own impact: as attempts to win the poet's recall and as poems that offer a variety of effects for later and more distant readers. In what follows I will seek to explain and (briefly) demonstrate that claim with examples from the *Tristia*.[6]

No aspect of this poetry has been more debated in recent decades than the approach it takes toward Augustus, who had been sole ruler of Rome for over three decades by the time of Ovid's exile and, according to these poems, required nothing more than his own fiat to relegate or recall a citizen. Although there are widely varying viewpoints, that discussion has focused on the question of how sincere are the speaker's repeated claims that he accepts Augustus's power and only asks humbly for forgiveness. Most readers acknowledge that in these poems expressions of repentance share the page with self-justification and even thinly veiled rage against the emperor's authoritarian decree, but is this the self-contradiction we might expect in a harried speaker pleading for his life or is it the wily design of a poet seeking to frame his humble petition with effects that draw into question the justice of his punishment? In recent decades, the scholarly consensus has moved

---

4. Here it is especially relevant to recall that the term "story" does not imply that the events narrated are made up—even nonfictional narratives have a "story" component.

5. Such a practice has been recognized, but the discussion of it has been based on an amorphous conception of "posterity" as simply the undifferentiated counterpart to contemporary readers. I will take up further below the other major way scholars have formulated the engagement with readers, that is, as a kind of asynchronous blackmail threat against Augustus's reputation.

6. Focusing on the *Epistulae ex Ponto* would yield slightly different results, since my analysis below depends in part on the coexistence of letter-poems with other poem types, but the large-scale principles can still usefully be applied to the later collection.

decisively toward various degrees of suspicion in assuming that the text communicates to Augustus and, separately, to the reader.[7] Various approaches have situated the communication to the reader in intertextual allusions (to a large range of other authors and especially to Ovid's earlier works), the treatment of mythological exempla, double entendres (such as Casali's reading of *Tristia* 1.1.21), and other sources of coded meanings.[8] I believe that recognizing how Ovid orients "story" to discourse—in patterns that both repeat and depart from those we saw in Catullus, Propertius, and Horace—can offer another way to grasp the dual communicative channels in these poems and their implications.

My brief examples above from the first two books of the *Tristia* show what it would mean to see the earnest speech addressed to Augustus as enclosed within the storyworld; in other words, contrary to a first impression of this corpus, we can see these poems as representing such pleas, not just enacting them. Key to this framing is the act of identifying these poems as part of a book that circulates to a wide readership.[9] While the opening programmatic poems of books 1 and 3 (featuring the personified book) have been thoroughly studied,[10] I believe my approach can offer insights into other poems of the collection, especially the question of how communication with readers operates and what it means for the agenda of the collection.

Horace's first book of *Epistles*, discussed in the previous chapter, provides a useful comparison. Horace's collection ends with a poem in which the author-figure addresses a personified book as he sends it out the door, and it is in this gesture that he makes clear the public nature of these "letters." Ovid's collection, however, begins with such a poem, thus establishing from the start that the poems are designed for readers in addition to (or perhaps even in place of) their named addressees.[11] Further, as this opening poem proceeds, it is remarkably explicit in announcing the strategy of the

---

7. For a key statement of this principle, see Casali (1997, 81), who begins by retranslating *Tr.* 1.1.21 "quaerenti plura legendum" as "he who requires must read more" (in contrast to the more natural translation "the one who asks for more details must read") and then continues: "If one wishes to look for more (than what is written), the only option is to read more. To read more than what is written."

8. In a view that takes into account the structure of address, Barchiesi (2001, 86) sets up the terms that would justify extreme interpretive suspicion, among which is the case when "the text is intended for a peculiar addressee, Augustus, who can hardly be considered part of the 'normal' audience to which the publication of the work appeals; the more this audience is distanced from the addressee, the more a road opens up for a subversive reading."

9. Roman (2014, 239) argues that "the literary implications of world-wide empire and imperial circulation of books" is central to Ovid's poetics even in his early works.

10. Two influential examples are Hinds (2006) and Newlands (1997).

11. This effect is underscored by allusion to Catullus 1 in the concrete physical details of the book, lines 5–12.

collection: to make known the poet's dire predicament (and to tell his side of the story) to general readers.

> invenies aliquem, qui me suspiret ademptum,
>   carmina nec siccis perlegat ista genis,
> et tacitus secum, ne quis malus audiat, optet,
>   sit mea lenito Caesare poena levis.
>
> (1.1.27–30)

You will find someone who sighs over my relegation, and who weeps as he reads those poems you carry, and who wishes silently (lest any ill-wisher overhear) that Caesar would relent and my punishment be lightened.

Although this sympathetic reader is pictured as a man in the Roman street, his reaction is described in affective terms that do not differentiate it from the reaction of any reader at any time who learns of Ovid's tribulations through the poems. The two collections written in exile (especially the latter) are dominated by poems addressed to specific individuals on the model of Horace's epistles, and yet that image of intimate communication is conditioned by moments like this, which point persistently to a readership for whom the poems are *representations* of letters and yet still wholly persuasive and affecting.[12]

I noted above that the openings of books 1 and 2 of the *Tristia* envision and personify poetry books (i.e., collections on papyrus rolls) as the format in which these poems will circulate. Such a collection implies that the individual poems (even if they were originally composed on the occasions they depict, according to the model of archaic Greek lyric) now acquire in addition to that occasional function a new function as elements of the composite artwork that is the book. I have, throughout the present study, pursued the implications of this fact, especially as it implies a form of artistic agency (and desire to communicate) at the level of the collection as a whole that coexists with the more visible agency wielded by the speaker in individual poems.[13] In the *Tristia*, the speaker within individual poems so closely approximates

---

12. This perspective is central to Hinds (2006), though most of this article is focused on how the *Tristia*'s strategy is based in reference to the poet's earlier works. "The poems of *Tristia* 1 are in a *practical* sense epistles in that they have to be sent, in real life, over a distance to Rome. . . . But in terms of internal *literary* format, the typical elegy in *Tristia* 1 (or *Tristia* 3 or 4) is no more (or less) an epistle than any personal poem whatsoever with a named or implied addressee" (421; emphasis in original).

13. As discussed in the introduction, Krevans (1984) has been central to my thinking on this topic.

the poet himself (in motivation as well as in situation and attributes), that we might think the productive tension between these two positions has evaporated, but I believe that in the design of the collection we can see Ovid still deploying this powerful duality.

There is, of course, an extremely strong coherence in theme, topic, and form throughout the five books of the *Tristia*, with the partial exception of book 2, which stands out both for its unique addressee and its uniquely extended form. And yet the collection exhibits a surprising degree of variation in the orientation of "story" to discourse, partially masked by the narrow spectrum of topics and themes. Although most of the poems take the form of letters to specific (unnamed) individuals back in Rome, this particular form of poem exists within a more varied pattern than is usually discussed. Some poems, for example, emphatically show the poetic speaker responding to his immediate surroundings and thus feature storyworld speech (not writing), in the format I have discussed above, especially for Propertius's first book and for Catullus. It is significant that these poems cluster in the first book and take their dramatic setting as the journey outward from Rome (1.2, 1.4, 1.10, 1.11).[14] These poems that seemingly eavesdrop on the timorous prayers of the exile share the book with other poems that present themselves as written attempts to communicate his situation to those who are not present with him: apart from the obvious case of 1.1, poem 1.3 offers an unaddressed retrospective narrative (similar to Propertius 1.3). In contrast to a coarse-grained view of this first book (which sees it as headed by a programmatic poem that acknowledges its status as a book for readers, but mostly consisting of poems that mimic private letters), in fact the range of forms in the book is varied and complex.

The third book adds a new possibility: poems that provide no alibi for themselves as storyworld communication and instead offer a combination of description and complaint implicitly taking the reader as addressee.[15] Poems 3.8, 3.9, and 3.12 contain no address, but they make use of apostrophe and one instance of self-address (3.8.11).[16] These poems are among the

---

14. Poem 5.5, which offers a variation on the type of ritual-preparation poem we saw in Horace's odes, is also (roughly) of this type. Hinds (2006) argues that over the course of the five books of the *Tristia* there is "a belated assimilation of the internal literary format of the exile poetry to the external, real-life fact of its always being written for posting" (421).

15. In communicating directly to readers without developing a not-for-us scene of storyworld communication, these poems come close to the form that Culler labels "epideictic," but they do not quite fit that pattern since they depend in significant ways on the speaker's storyworld situation.

16. The apostrophes are to Corinth (3.8.4), to Perseus and Daedalus (3.8.6), to Germania (3.12.47), to Pontus (3.12.52). Poem 3.12 also ends with a brief prayer to the gods. Given the importance of apostrophe to the structure of these poems, one might also include in this group the wholly

most ruminative in the whole collection, as they detail the exile's fantasies of escape and/or reunion along with memories of life back in Italy, though they also continue to explain and describe his condition, rather than taking it for granted as a wholly inward-focused poem might do.[17] This pattern reappears in later books as well, specifically in the famous poem 4.2, which generates the image of a triumph in Rome strictly from the poet's own invention, as well as the more personal 4.6 and 4.8.[18]

My point is that, unlike Horace's first book of epistles, which consistently maintained the pattern that each poem was addressed to a single individual and did not openly contradict its epistolary premise,[19] Ovid constructs a collection that makes the epistolary nature of the poems more emphatic than Horace had, and yet that also includes many poems that do not use the basic epistolary structure of address. In addition to the subtle formal differences I have described above, the poems that most visibly depart from the epistolary structure are the ones that baldly present images of the papyrus collection (especially 1.1 and 3.1) or that address readers explicitly (such as 4.1 and 5.1), and it is not surprising that these poems appear at the beginning of each book (as noted above, the beginning of *Tristia* 2 conforms to this pattern). The closing poems of each book (again, a place where such a perspective is fully at home) also tend to be explicit about wider circulation.[20] Because such

---

apostrophic 3.13, addressed to the *genius natalis* and (like the other poems of this group) including a vividly imagined scene (in this case, of birthday rituals back in Italy). Poem 3.10 is an interesting borderline case: it is almost completely on the unaddressed model, but presumes with its use of deictics (see especially "istic" in its first line) that its reader is in Rome.

17. Poem 3.8 also includes one of the most striking images of the exile's struggle to understand his "self" in his extreme circumstances. Although visions of his (sometimes hoped-for) death are prominent throughout the collection, this poem introduces that dark thought with the image of the speaker standing face to face with the "forma" of his own destiny: "haerens ante oculos veluti spectabile corpus / adstat fortunae forma tegenda meae" (3.8.35–36; Stubbornly before my very eyes, as if a visible body, there stands the shape of my own fate, soon to be buried). I am tempted to read this odd combination of inwardness and outwardness in light of the nonepistolary form of this poem.

18. Each of these poems includes moments of address, though the overall structure seems conceived as less anchored to the logic of address: an apostrophic address to Caesar at 4.2.47–56; "credite" at 4.6.39 picked up by "sodales" in line 45; and 4.8 closes with second-person plural address to unnamed persons to take the speaker's trials as a warning. The use of second-person plural in the latter two poems seems close to an address to readers.

19. The only exception is poem 1.20, the one that Ovid most ostentatiously imitates. As I have discussed in the previous chapter, Horace does not adorn those poems with many epistolary formulations, nor does he often remind the reader of their concrete material form as letters, but the form of address in each case except for 1.20 assumes private communication (often in spite of physical distance) with a single person.

20. Poem 1.11 "explains" that the poems of the book were written aboard ship and even addresses the reader directly ("candide lector," 1.11.35). Poem 3.14 addresses someone who will function as a literary executor. Poem 4.10 is the famous "autobiography," which is aimed at exactly those readers who know the poet only by reading: "Ille ego qui fuerim, tenerorum lusor amorum, / quem legis, ut noris, accipe posteritas" (4.10.1–2; "Who was this I you read, this trifler in tender

poems appear at the beginnings and ends of the books, it is easy to see them as paratexts bracketing and accounting for the letter-poems, and therefore to see the strategy of the collection as something like a corpus of letters with an editor's preface. Just as we would not take the editor's account of how these letters were preserved as part of the letters themselves, readers are tempted to segregate the perspective of these poems—a perspective implying that communicating directly, not incidentally, with later readers is a key goal—from our analysis of the insistently addressive poems that make up most of these books. But if we pay attention to other less obvious ways that this collection acknowledges its communication with readers as a major aim, we will see that it takes into account not just the existence of future readers, but the fact that communication with those readers through poetry has its own logic and its own shape. This poetry is, at a fundamental level, for-us, even though it is also so pressingly fixated on producing effects in the poet's own world.

Of course, the most obvious way that these poems are for-us has long been recognized: later readers are instrumental to the threat that these poems constitute against Augustus's good name as a benign ruler. The examples I tallied above are consistent with the assertions made explicitly at several points (e.g. poem 4.9, on which see especially Oliensis 2004) that convincing this readership of Augustus's tyranny will be the poet's final revenge. I absolutely agree with the consensus interpretation of such moments. Even here, though, I would argue that paying attention to the relation between "story" and discourse can give us further insight into this strategy. Here, too, the comparison with Horace's first book of epistles shows the way.

The influence of Horace's poetic epistles for Ovid's two collections from exile has long been recognized and explored, notably by Alessandro Barchiesi, who has investigated the parallel instances of "educating" Augustus in Horace *Epistles* 2.1 and in Ovid.[21] I would like to demonstrate briefly, however, another way that Horace's epistolary collection provides a model for Ovid, focusing not on the letter explicitly addressed to Augustus but on

---

passions? / You want to know, posterity? Then attend" [translation from Green 2005]); see also the closing address to the "candide lector" (line 132), with incisive comment in Oliensis (2004, 304–6). Poem 5.14 emphatically alludes to Horace's ode 3.30 as a capstone for a collection, though Ovid's version (in keeping with the design of the collection as a whole) hybridizes this public gesture with an address to his wife and transforms the projected future of Horace's songlike poems ("dicar," 3.30.10) into a recognition of the written form of his own poems ("dum legar," 5.14.5).

21. See also Ingleheart (2009), who brings out well the fact that Horace stands as a contrastive model in substance, not just in form. The earlier poet's career can be seen both as an example of a poet firmly in Augustus's camp and as someone who, as a veteran from the wrong side at Philippi, benefited from the much-bruited imperial *clementia*. See further Roman (2014, 253–54), who uses this pairing as a way to talk about a decisive late-Augustan shift in the "gentleman's agreement" that governed assumptions of poetic autonomy.

the overall strategies I analyzed in his first book of letters. Specifically, we can see Ovid in the exile poetry using Horace's backstage strategy as a contrastive backdrop for his own attempt to communicate with the implacable emperor. I argued in the last chapter that this backstage strategy risks offending powerful men, but the potential payoff is that it allows Horace to explore the very dynamics of communication in unequal friendships and even to flatter his addressee, by implying that the addressee is interested in recognizing the ways that power distorts relationships and seeking to minimize those distortions. Ovid quite obviously and emphatically takes the opposite tack, by filling the poems with fulsome praise of the emperor and repeatedly declaring his own unworthiness. Further, in poems addressed to peers and family members, rather than to the princeps himself, the speaker generally maintains the same position,[22] again in contrast to Horace's practice in his first book of epistles, where he indirectly spoke frank truths to his elevated overreaders in poems addressed to others.[23] The very consistency displayed implies that the speaker says nothing out of Augustus's earshot that he would not say to him directly, but when we measure it against Horace's radical strategy, Ovid's practice conjures before us a regime of surveillance that applies strict standards of imperial orthodoxy even to private communications, an implication already present in the choice not to name the addressees.[24] Such an ostentatious show of abiding by the party line might cause suspicions of insincerity in any case, but I would argue that the implied critique here is mobilized specifically by the contrast with Horace's practice in his epistolary collection and by the ways that Ovid has called readers' attention to the wide circulation of his poems and thus signaled that the poems are to be taken as representations of storyworld speech, not as his own attempt to communicate with the emperor.

If the goal really were just to enlist later readers in this after-the-fact condemnation of Augustus, why make the address to contemporaries so

---

22. Just to point to one example, *Tristia* 3.6 comes close in spirit to letters in Horace's collection, but the differences are revealing. Like many of Horace's epistles, this one foregrounds the theme of friendship particularly as it relates to the tension between public demonstration and privacy / secrecy. It further singles out its unnamed addressee as being unusually endowed with candor toward his friends, a characteristic that even Augustus recognized in this man (lines 7–8). Within this setting of intimacy and openness, the letter then proceeds to make clear that the speaker never shared with this friend the secret of the mistake that caused his banishment—in other words, in this most intimate letter to a most trusted friend, the speaker maintains on this point the same reticence he enacts and describes in *Tristia* 2.207–10, addressed to the emperor.

23. Oliensis (1998, 154–91).

24. Cf. Casali (1997, 84): "Ovid's reticence not only creates a certain climate of interpretation; it creates a certain political climate, a climate of anguish, oppression and fear. . . . These lines (4.5.15–17) evoke an atmosphere of 'Big Brother' dictatorship, and are hardly complimentary to Augustus."

prominent? This practice turns Augustus into an overreader who is forced to witness not rebellion but clenched-teeth submission, an image that lays bare an ugly element of the Augustan peace. The shadow of Augustus as overreader means that even Ovid's friends and family members who receive poems addressed specifically to them and who can perceive them, at least in part, as functional letters, also play a role not too different from that played by the distant readers of the future.[25] Although it was possible for these people to try to intervene (and no doubt some probably did), it was perhaps never likely that prompting such intervention was the main goal, as opposed to presenting Augustus (and other readers, contemporary and later) with the image of such a network of sympathizers. Even if no one chose to approach Augustus on Ovid's behalf, these poems effectively depict a world in which members of the elite accede to Augustus's domination out of fear or hopelessness (and, in the many letters addressed to faithless friends, out of self-interest), not because they genuinely support the *pater patriae* and his regime. Certainly these poems could potentially apply pressure for Ovid's recall; I am arguing, however, that that goal depends at least in part on effects that take the pleas and complaints and justifications of this corpus as representations of such speech acts, not as the speech acts themselves. In other words, this strategy applies to Augustus assumptions about the meaning of the poems that apply to all readers of all periods.[26]

What I find most affecting about the exile poems (and many other first-person poems in Latin) is that their engagement with readers is not based on fantasy—either the fantasy that these poets inhabit a song culture, in which live performance *was* poetry, or the fantasy that books can re-create the experience of face-to-face communication. Instead, these poets take writing and book circulation for exactly what it is and invent ways of communicating with contemporaries and with unknowable future readers in light of these realities. One obvious implication of long-lasting and widespread circulation for Ovid's poems is that he can shape (and has shaped) later generations' conception of the man from whom the key period of Roman history takes its name. No mean feat. But I also think that, beyond revenge against the

---

25. Roman (2014, 260) suggests that the *Tristia* contains evidence of two conflicting impulses: conciliating the emperor and "speak[ing] *ipso facto* as a marginalized, un-Augustan voice, and . . . mak[ing] the most of his adversarial position." My claim is that these impulses are not distributed across different passages in the collection but coextensive as the very foundation of this corpus.

26. I suggest this effect coexists with the specific effect Barchiesi detects in *Tristia* 2, that of segregating Augustus from other readers on the basis of his lack of skill / experience in reading elegy and thus showing the emperor as "a didactic addressee exposed to the ironic superiority of an audience possessing better interpretive abilities" (2001, 100).

tyrant, the *Tristia* have in view other aims with respect to those later readers. Although scholarship has moved beyond a reductive notion of the "merely" literary or aesthetic, we have not yet fully described the exact properties of an engagement that takes place through texts and through specifically poetic discourse, an engagement that recognizes its limits (I know that my response to these poems can neither comfort Ovid nor pain Augustus), that recognizes the genuine weight of not-for-us alongside the ways that poems speak to readers like me, and yet that also counts this contact as human communication in the most important respects. I have tried in the readings and arguments offered in this book to get closer to a precise conception of this engagement.

🍂 Works Cited

Acosta-Hughes, B., and S. Stephens (2012). *Callimachus in Context: From Plato to the Augustan Poets* (Cambridge University Press)

Albert, W. (1988). *Das mimetische Gedicht in der Antike: Geschichte und Typologie von den Anfängen bis in die augusteische Zeit* (Athenäum)

Athanassaki, L. (2004). "Deixis, Performance, and Poetics in Pindar's First Olympian Ode," in Felson (2004b), pp. 317–41

Athanassaki, L. (2014). "Creative Impact of the Occasion: Pindar's Songs for the Emmenids and Horace's Odes 1.12 and 4.2," in *Defining Greek Narrative*, edited by D. Cairns and R. Scodel, Edinburgh Leventis Studies 7 (Edinburgh University Press), pp. 197–225

Austin, J. L. (1975). *How to Do Things with Words*, 2nd ed., edited by J. O. Urmson and Marina Sbisà (Harvard University Press)

Barber, D. (2010). "Speaker and Addressee in Horace's *Odes*," PhD dissertation, University of Virginia

Barchiesi, A. (2001). "Teaching Augustus Through Allusion," in *Speaking Volumes: Narrative and Intertext in Ovid and Other Latin Poets*, edited and translated by Matthew Fox and Simone Marchesi (Duckworth), pp. 79–103

Barchiesi, A. (2002). "The Uniqueness of the *Carmen Saeculare* and Its Tradition," in *Traditions and Contexts in the Poetry of Horace*, edited by Tony Woodman and Denis Feeney (Cambridge University Press), pp. 107–29

Barchiesi, A. (2007). "*Carmina: Odes and Carmen Saeculare*," in *Cambridge Companion to Horace*, edited by S. J. Harrison (Cambridge University Press), pp. 144–61

Barchiesi, A. (2009). "Rituals in Ink: Horace on the Greek Lyric Tradition," in Lowrie (2009b), pp. 418–40; originally published in *Matrices of Genre: Authors, Canons and Society*, edited by M. Depew and D. Obbink (Harvard University Press, 2000), pp. 167–82

Bartsch, S. (1994). *Actors in the Audience: Theatricality and Doublespeak from Nero to Hadrian* (Harvard University Press)

Batstone, W. (2011). "Catullus and the Programmatic Poem: The Origins, Scope and Utility of a Concept," in *A Companion to Catullus*, edited by M. B. Skinner (Wiley-Blackwell), pp. 235–53

Bell, C. (1992). *Ritual Theory, Ritual Practice* (Oxford University Press)

Bell, C. (1997). *Ritual: Perspectives and Dimensions* (Oxford University Press)

Bing, P. (1988). *The Well-Read Muse: Present and Past in Callimachus and the Hellenistic Poets* (Göttingen)

Bing, P. (2009). *The Scroll and the Marble: Studies in Reading and Reception in Hellenistic Poetry* (University of Michigan Press)

Bowditch, P. L. (2001). *Horace and the Gift Economy of Patronage* (University of California Press)

Breed (2003). "Portrait of a Lady: Propertius 1.3 and Ecphrasis," *Classical Journal* 99.1:35–56.

Breed, B. (2006). *Pastoral Inscriptions: Reading and Writing in Virgil's Eclogues* (Duckworth)

Butler, J. (1990). *Gender Trouble: Feminism and the Subversion of Identity* (Routledge)

Butler, J. (1993). *Bodies That Matter: On the Discursive Limits of "Sex"* (Routledge)

Cairns, F. (2012). *Roman Lyric: Collected Papers on Catullus and Horace* (de Gruyter)

Calame, C. (2004). "Deictic Ambiguity and Auto-Referentiality: Some Examples from Greek Poetics," in Felson (2004b), pp. 415–43

Casali, S. (1997). "*Quaerenti plura legendum*: On the Necessity of 'Reading More' in Ovid's Exile Poetry," *Ramus* 26.1:80–112

Chatman, S. (1978). *Story and Discourse: Narrative Structure in Fiction and Film* (Cornell University Press)

Chatman, S. (1990). *Coming to Terms: The Rhetoric of Narrative in Fiction and Film* (Cornell University Press)

Citroni, M. (1983). "Occasione e piani di destinazione nella lirica di Orazio," *Materiali e discussioni* 10–11:133–214

Citroni, M. (1995). *Poesia e Lettori in Roma Antica* (Laterza)

Citroni, M. (2009). "Occasion and Levels of Address in Horatian Lyric," in Lowrie (2009b), pp. 72–105

Coleman, K. (1990). "Fatal Charades: Roman Executions Staged as Mythological Enactments," *Journal of Roman Studies* 80:44–73

Conte, G. B. (1994). "Genre between Empiricism and Theory," from *Genres and Readers: Lucretius, Love Elegy, Pliny's Encyclopedia*, translated by Glenn Most (Johns Hopkins University Press), pp. 35–66

Culler, J. (2001). *The Pursuit of Signs: Semiotics, Literature, Deconstruction.* 2nd ed. (Routledge)

Culler, J. (2015). *Theory of the Lyric* (Harvard University Press)

Currie, B. (2004). "Reperformance Scenarios for Pindar's *Odes*," in *Oral Performance and its Context*, edited by C. J. Mackie, Mnemosyne Suppl. 248 (Brill), pp. 49–70

D'Alessio, G. B. (2004). "Past Future and Present Past: Temporal Deixis in Greek Archaic Lyric," in Felson (2004b), pp. 267–94

Davis, G. (1991). *Polyhymnia: The Rhetoric of Horatian Lyric Discourse* (University of California Press)

Depew, M. (2000). "Enacted and Represented Dedications: Genre and Greek Hymn," in *Matrices of Genre: Authors, Canons and Society*, edited by M. Depew and D. Obbink (Harvard University Press), pp. 59–79

de Pretis, A. (2004). *"Epistolarity" in the First Book of Horace's Epistles* (Gorgias Press)

Dupont, F. (1985). *L'acteur-roi, ou, le théâtre dans la Rome antique* (Belles Lettres)

Dupont, F. (1999). *The Invention of Literature: From Greek Intoxication to the Latin Book*, translated by Janet Lloyd (Johns Hopkins University Press); original French edition *L'invention de la literature: De l'ivresse grecque au livre latin* (La Découverte, 1994)

Edmunds, L. (2001). *Intertextuality and the Reading of Roman Poetry* (Johns Hopkins University Press)

Fain, G. L. (2008). *Writing Epigrams: The Art of Composition in Catullus, Callimachus, and Martial* (Éditions Latomus)

Farrell, J. (2009). "The Impermanent Text in Catullus and Other Roman Poets," in *Ancient Literacies: The Culture of Reading in Greece and Rome*, edited by W. A. Johnson and H. Parker (Oxford University Press), pp. 164–85

Feeney, D. (1998). *Literature and Religion at Rome* (Cambridge University Press)

Feeney, D. (2005). "The Beginnings of a Literature in Latin," *Journal of Roman Studies* 95:226–40

Feeney, D. (2012). "Representation and the Materiality of the Book in the Polymetrics," in *Catullus: Poems, Books, Readers*, edited by I. Du Quesnay and T. Woodman (Cambridge University Press), pp. 29–47

Feeney, D. (2016). *Beyond Greek: The Beginnings of Latin Literature* (Harvard University Press)

Felson, N. (2004a). "The Poetic Effects of Deixis in Pindar's Ninth Pythian Ode," in Felson (2004b), pp. 365–89

Felson, N., ed. (2004b). "The Poetics of Deixis in Alcman, Pindar, and Other Lyric," special issue, *Arethusa* 37.3

Ferri, R. (1993). *I dispiaceri di un epicureo*. Vol. 11 (Ist. Editoriali e Poligrafici)

Ferri, R. (2007). "The *Epistles*," in *Cambridge Companion to Horace*, edited by S. J. Harrison (Cambridge University Press), pp. 121–31

Fitzgerald, W. (1995). *Catullan Provocations: Lyric Poetry and the Drama of Position* (University of California Press)

Fitzgerald, W. (2000). *Slavery and the Roman Literary Imagination* (Cambridge University Press)

Flower, H. (1996). *Ancestor Masks and Aristocratic Power in Roman Culture* (Clarendon Press)

Fordyce, C. J. (1961). *Catullus: A Commentary* (Oxford University Press)

Fowler, D. (1995). "Martial and the Book," *Ramus* 24.1:31–58

Fowler, D. (2000). *Roman Constructions: Readings in Postmodern Latin* (Oxford University Press)

Fraenkel, E. (1961). "Two Poems of Catullus," *Journal of Roman Studies* 51:46–53

Furley, W. (2014). Review of J. W. Day *Archaic Greek Epigram and Dedication*, *Classical Philology* 109.1:83–85

Gleason, M. (1995). *Making Men: Sophists and Self-Presentation in Ancient Rome* (Princeton University Press)

Green, P., trans. (2005). *Ovid: The Poems of Exile* (University of California Press)

Goold, G. (1999). *Propertius. Elegies*, rev. ed. (Harvard University Press)

Gowers, E. (2003). "Fragments of Autobiography in Horace, *Satires* 1," *Classical Antiquity* 22:55–92

Gunderson, E. (2000). *Staging Masculinity: The Rhetoric of Performance in the Roman World* (University of Michigan Press)

Gutzwiller, K. (1998). *Poetic Garlands: Hellenistic Epigrams in Context* (University of California Press)

Gutzwiller, K., ed. (2005). *The New Posidippus* (Oxford University Press)

Habinek, T. (1998). *The Politics of Latin Literature: Writing, Identity, and Empire in Ancient Rome* (Princeton University Press)

Habinek, T. (2005). *The World of Roman Song: From Ritualized Speech to Social Order* (Johns Hopkins University Press)

Hall, J. B. (1995). *Ovidius. Tristia* (Teubner)

Hardie, P. (2002). *Ovid's Poetics of Illusion* (Cambridge University Press)

Henderson, J. (1999). *Writing Down Rome: Satire, Comedy and Other Offences in Latin Poetry* (Clarendon Press)

Henrichs, A. (1994–95). "'Why Should I Dance?' Choral Self-Referentiality in Greek Tragedy," *Arion*, 3rd series, 3.1:56–111

Heyworth, S. J. (2001). "Catullian Iambics, Catullian *Iambi*," in *Iambic Ideas: Essays on a Poetic Tradition from Archaic Greece to the Late Roman Empire*, edited by A. Cavazere, A. Aloni, and A. Barchiesi (Rowman & Littlefield), pp. 117–40

Heyworth, S. J. (2007a). *Sexti Properti Elegos* (Oxford University Press)

Heyworth, S. J. (2007b). *Cynthia: A Companion to the Text of Propertius* (Oxford University Press)

Hinds, S. (1996). "Books, poetic," in *Oxford Classical Dictionary*, 3rd ed. (Oxford University Press)

Hinds, S. (2006). "Booking the Return Trip: Ovid and *Tristia* 1," in *Oxford Readings in Ovid*, edited by Peter Knox (Oxford University Press), pp. 415–40; originally published in *Proceedings of the Cambridge Philological Society* 31 (1985): 13–32

Horsfall, N. (1979). "Horace: *Sermones* 3?," *Liverpool Classical Monthly* 4:117–19

Hošek, C., and P. Parker, eds. (1985). *Lyric Poetry: Beyond New Criticism* (Cornell University Press)

Houghton, L. B. T., and M. Wyke, eds. (2009). *Perceptions of Horace* (Cambridge University Press)

Hunter, R. (1993). *The Argonautica of Apollonius: Literary Studies* (Cambridge University Press)

Hutchinson, G. O. (2008). *Talking Books: Readings in Hellenistic and Roman Books of Poetry* (Oxford University Press)

Hutchinson, G. O. (2010). "Deflected Addresses: Apostrophe and Space," *Classical Quarterly* 60.1:96–109

Ingleheart, J. (2009). "Writing to the Emperor: Horace's Presence in Ovid's *Tristia* 2," in Houghton and Wyke (2009), pp. 123–39

Ingleheart, J. (2010). *A Commentary on Ovid, Tristia* (Oxford University Press)

Jackson, V., and Y. Prins, eds. (2014). *The Lyric Theory Reader: A Critical Anthology* (Johns Hopkins University Press)

James, S. (2003). *Learned Girls and Male Persuasion: Gender and Reading in Roman Love Elegy* (University of California Press)

Jocelyn, H. D. (1979). "Horace Epistles I," *Liverpool Classical Monthly* 4:145–46

Johnson, W. A. (2010). *Readers and Reading Culture in the High Empire* (Oxford University Press)

Johnson, W. R. (1982). *The Idea of Lyric* (University of California Press)

Johnson, W. R. (1993). *Horace and the Dialectic of Freedom: Readings in Epistles I* (Cornell University Press)

Kaufhold, S. (1997). "Propertius 1.3: Cynthia Rescripted," *Illinois Classical Studies* 22:87–98

Kennedy, D. (1993). *The Arts of Love: Five Studies in the Discourse of Roman Love Elegy* (Cambridge University Press)

Kennedy, D. (2014). "Crossing the Threshold: Genette, Catullus, and the Pyschodynamics of Paratextuality," in *The Roman Paratext*, edited by L. Jansen (Cambridge University Press), pp. 19–32

Keith, A., ed. (2011). *Latin Elegy and Hellenistic Epigram: A Tale of Two Genres at Rome* (Cambridge Scholars Publishing)

Klingner, F. (2008). *Horatius. Opera.* (de Gruyter)

Konstan, D. (2011). "The Contemporary Political Context," in *A Companion to Catullus*, edited by M. B. Skinner (Wiley-Blackwell), pp. 72–91

Kowalzig, B. (2007). *Singing for the Gods: Performances of Myth and Ritual in Archaic and Classical Greece* (Oxford University Press)

Krevans, N. (1984). "The Poet as Editor: Callimachus, Virgil, Horace, Propertius and the Development of the Poetic Book," PhD dissertation, Princeton University

Krevans, N. (2007). "The Arrangement of Epigrams in Collections," in *Brill's Companion to Hellenistic Epigram*, edited by P. Bing and J. S. Bruss (Brill), pp. 131–46

Kroll, W. (1968). *C. Valerius Catullus*, 5th ed. (Teubner)

Krostenko, B. (2001). *Cicero, Catullus, and the Language of Social Performance* (University of Chicago Press)

Kurke, L. (2005). "Choral Lyric as 'Ritualization': Poetic Sacrifice and Poetic *Ego* in Pindar's Sixth Paian," *Classical Antiquity* 24:81–130

Kurke, L. (2012). "The Value of Chorality in Ancient Greece," in *The Construction of Value in the Ancient World*, edited by J. K. Papadopoulos and G. Urton (Cotsen Institute of Archaeology Press), pp. 218–35

La Bua, G. (1999). *L'Inno nella letteratura poetica latina* (Gerni)

Levin, S. R. (1976). "Concerning What Kind of Speech Act a Poem Is," in *Pragmatics of Language and Literature*, edited by T. A. van Dijk (North-Holland), pp. 141–60

Liveley, G., and P. Salzman-Mitchell, eds. (2008). *Latin Elegy and Narratology: Fragments of Story* (Ohio State University Press)

Lowrie, M. (1997). *Horace's Narrative Odes* (Oxford University Press)

Lowrie, M. (2009a). *Writing, Performance, and Authority in Augustan Rome* (Oxford University Press)

Lowrie, M. ed. (2009b). *Oxford Readings in Horace: Odes and Epodes* (Oxford University Press)

Lowrie, M. (2010). "Performance," in *The Oxford Handbook of Roman Studies*, edited by A. Barchiesi and W. Scheidel (Oxford University Press), pp. 281–94

Luck, G. (1964). *Properz und Tibull, Liebeselegien* (Artemis)

Lyne, R. O. A. M. (1995). *Horace: Behind the Public Poetry* (Yale University Press)

Mankin, D. (1995). *Horace: Epodes* (Cambridge University Press)

Marchesi, I. (2008). *The Art of Pliny's Letters: A Poetics of Allusion in the Private Correspondence* (Cambridge University Press)

Martin, R. (2002). "Horace in Real Time: *Odes* 1.27 and Its Congeners," in *Horace and Greek Lyric Poetry*, edited by M. Paschalis, Rethymnon Classical Studies 1 (University of Crete, Department of Philology), pp. 103–18

Mayer, R. (1994). *Horace: Epistles, Book 1* (Cambridge University Press)

McCarthy, K. (2010). "Lost and Found Voices: Propertius 3.6," *Helios* 37.2:153–86

McCarthy, K. (2013). "Secrets and Lies: Horace *Carm*. 1.27 and Catullus 10," *Materiali e discussioni* 71:45–74

McElduff, S. (2013). *Roman Theories of Translation: Surpassing the Source* (Routledge)

McElduff, S., and E. Sciarrino, eds. (2011). *Complicating the History of Western Translation: The Ancient Mediterranean in Perspective* (St. Jerome Publishing)

McNeill, R. L. B. (2001). *Horace: Image, Identity, Audience* (Johns Hopkins University Press)

Meyer, E. (2004). *Legitimacy and Law in the Roman World: Tabulae in Roman Belief and Practice* (Cambridge University Press)

Miller, J. F. (2009). *Apollo, Augustus and the Poets* (Cambridge University Press)

Miller, P. A. (1994). *Lyric Texts and Lyric Consciousness* (Routledge)

Morgan, K. (1993). "Pindar the Professional and the Rhetoric of the Kōmos," *Classical Philology* 88.1:1–15

Morgan, L. (2010). *Musa Pedestris: Metre and Meaning in Roman Verse* (Oxford University Press)

Morrison, A. D. (2007). *The Narrator in Archaic Greek and Hellenistic Poetry* (Cambridge University Press)

Murray, O. (1993). "Symposium and Genre in the Poetry of Horace," in *Horace 2000: A Celebration*, edited by N. Rudd (University of Michigan Press), pp. 89–105

Mynors, R. A. B. (1958). *C. Valerii Catulli Carmina* (Oxford University Press)

Nagy, G. (1994). "Genre and Occasion," *Mētis* 9–10:11–25

Nagy, G. (2004). "The Transmission of Archaic Greek Sympotic Songs: From Lesbos to Alexandria," *Critical Inquiry* 31.1:26–48

Nappa, C. (2001). *Aspects of Catullus' Social Fiction* (Peter Lang)

Newlands, C. (1997). "The Role of the Book in *Tristia* 3," *Ramus* 26.1:57–79

Nicholson, N. (1999). "Bodies without Names, Names without Bodies: Propertius 1.21–22," *Classical Journal* 94:143–61

Nietzsche, F. (1889). *Götzen-Dämmerung* (C. G. Naumann)

Nisbet, R. G. M. (1995). *Collected Papers on Latin Literature* (Oxford University Press)

Nisbet, R. G. M., and M. Hubbard (1970). *A Commentary on Horace: Odes, Book I* (Clarendon Press)

Nisbet, R. G. M., and M. Hubbard (1978). *A Commentary on Horace: Odes, Book II* (Clarendon Press)

Nisbet, R. G. M., and N. Rudd (2004). *A Commentary on Horace: Odes, Book III* (Oxford University Press)

Oliensis, E. (1998). *Horace and the Rhetoric of Authority* (Cambridge University Press)

Oliensis, E. (2004). "The Power of Image-Makers: Representation and Revenge in Ovid *Metamorphoses* 6 and *Tristia* 4," *Classical Antiquity* 23:285–321

Olson, E. (1969). "The Lyric" *Bulletin of the Midwest Modern Language Association* 2:59–66

Osgood, J. (2006). *Caesar's Legacy: Civil War and the Emergence of the Roman Empire* (Cambridge University Press)

Parker, H. (2009). "Books and Reading Latin Poetry," in *Ancient Literacies: The Culture of Reading in Greece and Rome*, edited by W. A. Johnson and H. Parker (Oxford University Press), pp. 186–229

Petrey, S. (1990). *Speech Acts and Literary Theory* (Routledge)

Phelan, J. (2005). *Living to Tell About it: A Rhetoric and Ethics of Character Narration* (Cornell University Press)

Phillips, T. (2011). "Propertius and the Poetics of the Book: 1.18 and 3.15–17," *Cambridge Classical Journal* 57:105–35

Pincus, M. (2004). "Propertius's Gallus and the Erotics of Influence," *Arethusa* 37.2:165–96

Power, T. (2011). "Cyberchorus: Pindar's Keledones and the Aura of the Artificial," in *Archaic and Classical Choral Song*, edited by L. Athanassaki and E. Bowie, Trends in Classics 10 (de Gruyter), pp. 67–114

Pratt. M. L. (1977). *Toward a Speech Act Theory of Literary Discourse* (Indiana University Press)

Price, M. (1983). *Forms of Life: Character and Moral Imagination in the Novel* (Yale University Press)

Prince, G. (2003). *Dictionary of Narratology*, rev. ed. (University of Nebraska Press)

Prins, Y. (2004). "Voice Inverse," *Victorian Poetry* 42.1:43–59

Pulleyn, S. (1997). *Prayer in Greek Religion* (Clarendon Press)

Purves, A. (2014). "Who, Sappho?," in *Defining Greek Narrative*, edited by D. Cairns and R. Scodel, Edinburgh Leventis Studies 7 (Edinburgh University Press), pp. 175–96

Putnam, M. C. J. (2000). *Horace's Carmen Saeculare: Ritual Magic and the Poet's Art* (Yale University Press)

Quinn, K. (1970). *Catullus: The Poems*, 2nd ed. (St. Martin's Press)

Quinn, K. (1982). "The Poet and His Audience in the Augustan Age," *Aufstieg und Niedergang der römischen Welt* II, 30.1:75–180

Ramsby, T. R. (2007). *Textual Permanence: Roman Elegists and the Epigraphic Tradition* (Duckworth)

Richardson, L., Jr. (1977). *Propertius: Elegies I–IV* (University of Oklahoma Press)

Richlin, A. (1992). *The Garden of Priapus: Sexuality and Aggression in Roman Humor*, rev. ed. (Oxford University Press)

Robinson, M. (2013). "Propertius 1.3: Sleep, Surprise, and Catullus 64," *Bulletin of the Institute for Classical Studies* 56.1:89–115

Roller, M. (1998). "Pliny's Catullus: The Politics of Literary Appropriation," *Transactions of the American Philological Association* 128:265–304

Roman, L. (2001). "The Representation of Literary Materiality in Martial's *Epigrams*," *Journal of Roman Studies* 91:113–45

Roman, L. (2006). "A History of Lost Tablets," *Classical Antiquity* 25:351–88

Roman, L. (2014). *Poetic Autonomy in Ancient Rome* (Oxford University Press)

Ross, D. O. (1969). *Style and Tradition in Catullus* (Harvard University Press)

Rudd, N. (1979). "*Epistles* and *Sermones*," *Liverpool Classical Monthly* 4:147

Ruffell, I. A. (2003). "Beyond Satire: Horace, Popular Invective and the Segregation of Literature," *Journal of Roman Studies* 93:35–65

Santirocco, M. (1986). *Unity and Design in Horace's Odes* (University of North Carolina Press)

Saylor, C. (1967). "*Querelae*: Propertius' Distinctive, Technical Name for his Elegy," *Agon* 1:142–49

Selden, D. (2007). "*Ceveat lector*: Catullus and the Rhetoric of Performance," in *Oxford Readings in Catullus*, edited by J. H. Gaisser (Oxford University Press), pp. 490–559; originally published in *Innovations of Antiquity*, edited by R. Hexter and D. Selden (Routledge, 1992), pp. 461–512

Sharrock, A. (1990). "*Alternae voces*—Again," *Classical Quarterly* 40.2:570–71

Sharrock, A. (2000). "Constructing Characters in Propertius," *Arethusa* 33.2:263–84

Skinner, M. B. (1993). "Catullus in Performance," *Classical Journal* 89:61–68

Skinner, M. B. (2011). "Authorial Arrangement of the Collection: Debate Past and Present," in *A Companion to Catullus*, edited by M. B. Skinner (Wiley-Blackwell), pp. 35–53

Smith, B. H. (1968). *Poetic Closure: A Study of How Poems End* (University of Chicago Press)

Smith, B. H. (1979). *On the Margins of Discourse* (University of Chicago Press)

Stehle, E. (1997). *Performance and Gender in Ancient Greece* (Princeton University Press)

Stroh, W. (1971). *Die Römische Liebeselegie als Werbende Dichtung* (Hakkert)

Stroup, S. C. (2010). *Catullus, Cicero, and a Society of Patrons* (Cambridge University Press)

Syndikus, H. P. (2001). *Die Lyrik des Horaz*, ex. ed. (Wissenschaftliche Buchgesellschaft Darmstadt)

Thomson, D. F. S. (1997). *Catullus* (University of Toronto Press)

Tucker, H. (2014). "Dramatic Monologue and the Overhearing of Lyric," in Jackson and Prins (2014), pp. 144–56

Usener, H. (1901). "Italische Volksjustiz," *Rheinisches Museum für Philologie* 56:1–28

Veyne, P. (1988). *Roman Erotic Elegy: Love, Poetry and the West*, translated by D. Pellauer (University of Chicago Press); originally *L'Elégie érotique romaine: L'amour, la poésie et l'Occident* (Editions de Seuil, 1983)

Waters, W. (2012). "Apostrophe," in *Princeton Encyclopedia of Poetry and Poetics*, 4th ed., Roland Green editor in chief (Princeton University Press), pp. 61–62

West, D. (2002). *Horace Odes III: Dulce Periculum* (Oxford University Press)

White, P. (1993). *Promised Verse: Poets in the Society of Augustan Rome* (Harvard University Press)

Williams, G. (1968). *Tradition and Originality in Roman Poetry* (Clarendon Press)

Woodman, T. (2012). "A Covering Letter: Poem 65," in *Catullus: Poems, Books, Readers*, edited by I. Du Quesnay and T. Woodman (Cambridge University Press), pp. 130–52

Wray, D. (2001). *Catullus and the Poetics of Roman Manhood* (Cambridge University Press)

Wyke, M. (2002). *The Roman Mistress: Ancient and Modern Representations* (Oxford University Press)

Young, E. M. (2011). "Sappho under My Skin: Catullus and the Translation of Erotic Lyric at Rome," in McElduff and Sciarrino (2011), pp. 37–47

Young, E. M. (2015). *Translation as Muse: Poetic Translation in Catullus' Rome* (University of Chicago Press)

Zetzel, J. E. G. (1982). "The Poetics of Patronage in the Late First Century," in *Literary and Artistic Patronage in Ancient Rome*, edited by B. K. Gold (University of Texas Press), pp. 87–102

Zetzel, J. E. G. (1996). "Poetic Baldness and Its Cure" *Materiali e discussioni* 36:73–100

🦋 GENERAL INDEX

address
  to contemporaries, 5–6, 89n17, 226–27
  See also addressive poetry; apostrophe
addressee
  in Catullus, 77–80
  description of, 46, 79–80, 139n8
  readers as implicit. *See under* readers
  speaker and. *See* storyworld: communication within
  See also apostrophe
addressive poetry, 11–15, 19, 23, 31–32, 39
  in Catullus, 77–78, 83, 127–33, 151, 158–63, 188–99
  dramatic monologue and, 21–23
  in Horace, 99n34, 101n41, 178–83, 201–4, 207–15, 226
  in Ovid, 218–28
  in Propertius, 50–51, 55–56, 66–68, 74–75, 138–49, 142–44
  performed Greek poetry and, 24–26, 31
agency, poet's vs. speaker's, 13–20, 31–33, 36–37, 87–88, 140, 187, 222–23
  in Catullus, 54, 87–88, 153, 191–92
  in Horace, 54, 112, 165, 176, 182–83
  in Ovid, 222–24
  in Propertius, 66, 75–76, 137, 140–43, 150–51
Alcaeus, 5, 7n11, 181
allusion
  in Catullus, 125, 192
  in Horace, 176, 181
  intratextual, 124, 160, 181–82
  in Ovid, 221
  in Propertius, 65n60, 140
Anacreon, 39n3, 176n58
apostrophe, 59–60, 62–68, 74, 131–32, 138–39, 142–43, 198, 219, 223–24
Archilochus, 4–5, 176
audience
  contemporary with poet, 10, 28–29, 125, 135, 142, 151, 202–3, 218–28

internal to storyworld. *See* storyworld: communication within
  performer and, 26–29, 42, 47, 82–89
Augustus
  in Horace, 28n64, 96–98, 100, 202, 204n30, 215–17
  Horace's political relation to, 111–13, 165–66, 174–77, 183
  in Ovid, 218–222, 225–28
  in Propertius, 139, 144, 146
Austin, J. L., 14n30, 84

Barchiesi, A., 14, 225–27
book
  personified, 215–17, 219, 221–22
  as physical object, 152–55, 159–60, 180n65
  See also collections, poetic
Butler, J., 84–85

Caesar, Julius, 128–30, 132
Callimachus, 39n3, 94n29, 144–45, 165n44, 199
carmen/carmina, 86, 116, 120, 124–25
Catullus
  compared to Propertius, 76–80, 151
  cultural competence in, 192, 195, 197–98
  erotic effect of poetry in, 162, 190–92, 196, 200–01
  "everyday" and poetic in, 1–2, 15, 77, 113, 116–18, 120–22, 155–56, 159–60
  friendship in, 157, 192–95
  internal and external perspectives in, 151–56, 159–62, 188
  masculine status in, 124, 126–27, 161–63, 192, 200
  persona of, 126–27, 155
  translation in, 188, 195–96, 199–201
  urbanity in, 119, 158–59
  women and femininity in, 117, 127–28, 130, 188–92, 196, 199–200
  See also Index Locorum

❧ Index Locorum

CPSIA information can be obtained
at www.ICGtesting.com
Printed in the USA
BVHW031111310819
557206BV00001B/8/P

9 781501 739552